Indigenous Cosmopolitans

PETER LANG
New York • Washington, D.C./Baltimore • Bern
Frankfurt • Berlin • Brussels • Vienna • Oxford

Maximilian C. Forte

Indigenous Cosmopolitans

*Transnational and Transcultural Indigeneity
in the Twenty-First Century*

PETER LANG
New York • Washington, D.C./Baltimore • Bern
Frankfurt • Berlin • Brussels • Vienna • Oxford

Library of Congress Cataloging-in-Publication Data

Indigenous cosmopolitans: transnational and transcultural indigeneity
in the twenty-first century / [edited by] Maximilian C. Forte.
p. cm.
Includes bibliographical references and index.
1. Indigenous peoples. 2. Cultural fusion. 3. Cosmopolitanism.
4. Transnationalism. I. Forte, Maximilian C.
GN380.I5185   306—dc22   2009014920
ISBN 978-1-4331-0102-1

Bibliographic information published by **Die Deutsche Nationalbibliothek**.
Die Deutsche Nationalbibliothek lists this publication in the "Deutsche
Nationalbibliografie"; detailed bibliographic data is available
on the Internet at http://dnb.d-nb.de/.

Cover painting by David Neel, *The Young Chief*, 2002.

© 2010 Peter Lang Publishing, Inc., New York
29 Broadway, 18th floor, New York, NY 10006
www.peterlang.com

All rights reserved.
Reprint or reproduction, even partially, in all forms such as microfilm,
xerography, microfiche, microcard, and offset strictly prohibited.

Contents

List of Figures vii
Preface ix

Chapter One. Introduction: Indigeneities and Cosmopolitanisms 1
    Maximilian C. Forte

Chapter Two. A Carib Canoe, Circling in the Culture of the Open Sea:
    Submarine Currents Connecting Multiple Indigenous Shores 17
    Maximilian C. Forte

Chapter Three. Aboriginal Hip Hoppers: Representin' Aboriginality in
    Cosmopolitan Worlds 39
    Craig Proulx

Chapter Four. David Neel's *The Young Chief–Waxwaxam*: A Cosmopolitan
    Treatise 63
    Carolyn Butler-Palmer

Chapter Five. Whither the Historicities of Alutiiq Heritage Work Are
    Drifting 77
    Arthur Mason

Chapter Six. The Alto Balsas Nahuas: Transnational Indigeneity and
    Interactions in the World of Arts and Crafts, the Politics of Resistance,
    and the Global Labor Market 97
    Frans J. Schryer

Chapter Seven. Transnational Migration and Indigeneity in Canada:
    A Case Study of Urban Inuit 127
    Julie-Ann Tomiak and Donna Patrick

Chapter Eight. "Same Cat, Different Stripes": Hemispheric Migrations, New Urban Indian Identities, and the Consolidation of a Cosmopolitan Cosmovision.. 145
  Robin Maria DeLugan

Chapter Nine. Indigeneity in Tourism: Transnational Spaces, Pan-Indian Identity, and Cosmopolitanism.. 163
  Linda Scarangella

Chapter Ten. Conclusion: From Wandering Jew to Ironic Cosmopolite: A Semi-Utopian Postnationalism... 189
  Nigel Rapport

Contributors..211
Index..215

Figures

2.1 Members of Trinidad's Carib Community with Delegates to a Hemispheric Assembly of Indigenous Peoples Hosted by the Assembly of First Nations, Ottawa, Canada, 1991 28

4.1 David Neel, The Young Chief—Waxwaxam (2002) 73

4.2 David Neel, Portrait of Lily-Bee and Mertel Holloway (1985) 74

4.3 David Neel, Self-Portrait with Chief Charlie James Swanson (c.1990) 75

6.1 Office of the Consejo de Pueblos Nahuas del Alto Balsas, Mexico 107

6.2 An Example of an Amate (Bark Painting), Mexico 110

9.1 Entrance to Euro Disney's Buffalo Bill's Wild West Show, 2004 165

9.2 Ferlyn Brass 168

9.3 Some Native Performers and Author at Euro Disney 169

9.4 The Sheridan Inn, 2005 177

9.5 Lane's Fancy Dance 181

9.6 Brian's Hoop Dance 182

Preface

The project contained in this volume was developed over several months of correspondence between the contributors, starting in 2006 and leading up to its first incarnation as a symposium titled "Transnational Indigeneity: Contemporary Routes of Indigenous Signification and Interaction beyond Stereotypes of the Local or the Hype of the Global," hosted under the auspices of the joint meetings of the Canadian Anthropology Society (CASCA) and the American Ethnological Society (AES) held at the University of Toronto, May 8-12, 2007. The organizing theme for those joint meetings was "Indigeneities and Cosmopolitanisms," and a number of us felt both stimulated and provoked by it. We were aware that any attempt to forge an opposition between these two phenomena was largely contrived without basis in the historical, social, and cultural realities at the root of indigenous ways of seeing and being in the world. However, we also recognized that the debate we were engaging in was not so much one that stems from indigenous actors themselves, as much as a debate internal to anthropology, with consequences for how we seek to represent the worlds about which we claim to possess special, comparative knowledge.

In short, our attempt has been to bring forth non-Eurocentric perspectives in contrast to much of what undergirds the received thinking on cosmopolitanism, agreeing with those who observe that "analyses of cosmopolitanism are themselves rarely cosmopolitan" (Pollock, 2002, p. 19). Indeed the term "cosmopolitan" is that "presupposes a great deal, while at the same time it ironically undercuts its own logic: it assumes the universal intelligibility and applicability of a very particular and privileged mode of political identity, citizenship in the polis or Greek city-state" (Pollock, 2002, p. 20). Whatever the cosmopolis may be, Europe is one of its most recent newcomers. We argue that indigenous forms of cosmopolitanism not only unfold in the present, but also predate European conceptualizations of the cosmopolitan. In the process, we seek to share a different understanding in anthropology, of indigenous peoples as both rooted, and yet working out their ways of living and ways of thinking through various routes of transnational and transcultural experience.

◆ CHAPTER ONE ◆

Introduction: Indigeneities and Cosmopolitanisms

Maximilian C. Forte

Immersed as we are in both contemporary popular media, long traditions in anthropology, and an international indigenous rights discourse that furnishes depictions of indigenous peoples as rooted in place, who are cut off yet simultaneously suffering from a modernity that is only now supposedly encroaching their territories and ways of life, then we might understandably gain an ambient sense of indigenous peoples as culturally stuck to themselves, existing for themselves and unto themselves. Heightening this misperception is the long-standing figure of the "real Indian." In North America and the Caribbean, where the concept of "real Indians" is popular and prominent, the dominant notion of real indigeneity is that it must be racially unmixed, culturally undiluted, geographically remote, and materially impoverished. Now consider instead these mundane snapshots of contemporary indigenous life: indigenous arts and crafts in an urban souvenir shop sold to European tourists; indigenous migrant laborers moving between Mexico and California; indigenous philosophies of universal humanism; indigenous peoples in the mainstream media; indigenous performers in Paris; indigenous-led development programs; international indigenous organizations; pan-Indianism; and, the powwow, coming to a city near you—already there in fact, since urban Indian centers in the United States have spearheaded the resurgence and diffusion of the powwow (Nagel, 1995, p. 954). All of these snapshots of spheres of indigenous life in the twenty-first century show us some of the new landmarks in the territory referred to as "indigenous." But why are they significant, and in what terms?

While attachments to local places, the centrality of images of a native homeland, and struggles to protect territory or regain lost lands remain central features of contemporary indigenous politics and identifications, we are told from commentators in numerous quarters that the world in which indigenous peoples live and interact has changed considerably, enough to supposedly cast ways of being and becoming indigenous in a new light. However, the world indigenous peoples have known, from the time they became classed as "indigenous" due to the very fact of invasion and colonization by Europeans, has been a world that presumably has always been changing. Reinterpretations of the allegedly "new" ways of being and becoming indigenous have pushed some of us to understand the fact that indigenous peoples were never locked away in bounded places: Nicholas Thomas argued:

> ... while postmodernists have suddenly decided that we need to talk about cosmopolitanism and globalization, even in the eighteenth century many [Pacific] islanders had stepped outside their own societies and obtained vantage points upon their customary practices: their discourses if not their cultures were translocal and transposed. (1992, p. 218)

Thus, on top of the contemporary snapshots above, we could have added much older ones from centuries ago: indigenous peoples without a conception of "race" who deliberately adopted and assimilated others, long-distance exchanges by canoe, the development of regional lingua francas, marriage outside the group, and so forth. Still, one can certainly argue that while indigenous peoples frequently raided, traded, married, and migrated across considerable distances in the centuries before European colonization, the ruptures wrought by colonial conquests added a far broader dimension to the supra-local activities of indigenous peoples. Indigenous peoples are, as we must remember, the "legatees ... of the world's longest and most fraught engagement with globalization in its harshest forms, colonialism" (Pollock, 2002, p. 46). In addition, the changes that are often loosely referred to as "globalization" have rapidly multiplied and expanded in recent decades—so not everything is either so new, or so old, that debates about indigenous representation in anthropology can be quickly quelled.

We enter the dispute between the stereotyped images of the rooted indigene versus the transcendent globe-trotting cosmopolitan by posing the following four questions: What happens to indigenous culture and identity when being in the "original place" is no longer possible or even necessary? Does displacement, moving beyond one's original place, mean that indigeneity (being indigenous) vanishes or is diminished? How is being and becoming indigenous, experienced and practiced along translocal pathways? How are new philosophies and politics of indigenous identification (indigenism) constructed in new, translocal settings?

In addressing these questions the contributors to this volume seek to develop our understandings of cosmopolitanism, transnationalism, transculturation, and related processes and experiences of what others refer to as social and cultural globalization, as not spelling an end to ways of being and becoming indigenous. Instead, indigeneity is reengaged with wider fields, finding newer ways of being established and projected, and acquiring new representational facets. In this collection the authors bring several ethnographic case studies to bear on issues of indigenous rootedness and displacement, raising questions about indigenous traditions of being transposed and translocal, of local roots articulated through transnational routes, and the ways that transnational cultural and material resources are sometimes used to bolster the foundations of indigenous identity and community. The focus of this collection is on contemporary indigenous experiences and case studies situated in Canada, the United States, Mexico, Central America, and the Caribbean, but crossing many other borders as well. One of our aims is to debate any perceived antimony between indigeneity and cosmopolitanism, while highlighting the differences between the concepts, their overlaps, their mutually determining/eroding boundaries, and the prospects for new ways of conceptualizing these in relation to one another. The second aim involves the question of how cosmopolitanism relates to transnationalism in our understandings of indigenous cosmopolitans, while building on a small but significant corpus of contemporary research of varying relevance (i.e., Clifford, 1997; Coates, 2004; de la Cadena & Starn, 2007; Deloria, 2006; Sissons, 2005). The more theoretical and philosophical treatments are left for the next section.

Cosmopolitans and Cosmopolitanisms: Pluralizing the Field

Cosmopolitanism, conventionally speaking, is the travel partner of a number of concepts that limit the centrality of nationalism and other forms of particularism (see Cheah, 2006). As a conceptual travel partner, however, cosmopolitanism is understood as distinct from "globalization," which more often than not is equated with the spread of free market economics, free trade, free capital movement, and deregulation (Beck, 2004). While anthropologists struggled for years to gain ground for understandings of globalization as a bundle of cultural phenomena, it is evident that some feel that the battle has been lost, that globalization will always be more likely to be understood across disciplines and in the public arena as a euphemism for the spread of neo-liberal capitalism. Cosmopolitanism, on the other hand, provides safer and less contested ground for highlighting the cultural dynamics of what might otherwise have been understood as globalization. "Cosmopolitanization," as distinct from neo-liberal globalization, can be understood as:

> ... a multidimensional process that has irrevocably changed the historical "nature" of social worlds and the status of individual countries within those worlds. It involves the formation of multiple loyalties, the spread of various transnational lifestyles, the rise of nonstate political actors (from Amnesty International to the World Trade Organization), and the development of global protest movements against (neo-liberal)

globalism and for a different (cosmopolitan) globalization involving the worldwide recognition of human rights, workers' rights, global protection of the environment, an end to poverty, and so on. (Beck, 2004, p. 136)

The classic philosophical usage of the term "cosmopolitanism" was premised on the idea of a "citizen of the universe," which is not the same as utter rootlessness—a realization that will then become very important for anthropological studies of multiple, local cosmopolitans. Instead, what is imagined in the classic usage is "a universal circle of belonging that involves the transcendence of the particularistic and blindly given ties of kinship and country," a universalism of reason, rather than rootless nomadism (Cheah, 2006, p. 487). Yet "universal reason" is now too much of an abstraction that is more familiar in its Eurocentric groundings, or in the pretensions to universal representability and omniscience associated with monotheistic religions that emerged from the so-called high civilizations.

Not surprisingly, what Cheah calls proponents of a "new cosmopolitanism" attempt to dissociate cosmopolitanism from abstract, even theological notions of "universal reason," instead preferring to look for cosmopolitanism in "a variety of actually existing practical stances that are provisional and can lead to strategic alliances and networks that cross territorial and political borders" (2006, p. 491). The new cosmopolitanism consists of a synthesis of three theses: 1) that cultural and political solidarity and agency are no longer restricted to the national arena; 2) the globalization of political networks; and, 3) the formation of a "cosmopolitan consciousness" involving an "expansive form of solidarity" beyond territorial borders (Cheah, 2006, p. 491). The problem that this synthesis presents is that it tends to privilege the political over the cultural, whereas contributions to this volume tend to keep those two in balance.

Already the field of cosmopolitanism in anthropology has become one of plural and diverse cosmopolitanisms, with multiple definitions of what is cosmopolitan, and going well beyond classic Greek and Kantian origins even while doing little to indicate how cosmopolitanism in anthropology differs from related concepts of transnationalism and transculturation. There is a problem right here in fact, in getting past "the macronarrative of Western civilization," where "everything imaginable began in Greece" (Mignolo, 2002, p. 162). As a group in this volume we write against hegemonic stories of modernity that suppress coloniality and its production of differences on a planetary scale. Indeed, modern cosmopolitanism owes little to ancient Greeks. It is rooted in a different beginning: "the emergence of the Atlantic commercial circuit in the sixteenth century that linked the Spanish Crown with capitalist entrepreneurs from Genoa, with Christian missionaries, with Amerindian elites, and with African slaves" (Mignolo, 2002, p. 162). If we get past Greece, we also need to get past Immanuel Kant. Tributes to Kantian cosmopolitanism often leave out Kant's unvarnished racism, his classification of peoples according to skin color, moral character, and presumed industriousness (or lack thereof), usually reserving the best attributes for Europeans, the worst for Amerindians and Africans, as seen in full force in the second part of his Anthropology from a Pragmatic Point of View (Mignolo, 2002, p. 171).

What about anthropology today? As observed from his own initial survey, Alex Hall noted that, "Cosmopolitanism can be applied to so many phenomena that the clarity of the term can be lost" (2006, p. 25). Hall observes that cosmopolitanism can imply the political, moral, or aesthetic transcendence of local boundaries, as well as openness to difference while acknowledging what all humans have in common. However, he cautions, cosmopolitan ideals can be vulnerable to the critique that the elite articulation of such ideals is "a guise for the detrimental effects of neo-liberalism and the perpetuation of elite Western dominance" (Hall, 2006, p. 25). Indeed, some would argue that it is best not to define the term cosmopolitanism by some arbitrary moral qualities (such as openness to the world, empathy, etc.), which could lead us to dividing up the world into the good and the pure (the cosmopolitans) versus the bad, the recalcitrant, and the hostile (the noncosmopolitans, ignorant locals), which would be problematic for anthropology, according to de l'Estoile (2006), and most contributors to this volume agree. Instead, a better route might be to define cosmopolitanism by how people create and use transnational networks, that is, finding cosmopolitanism in "an impulse to knowledge that is shared with others, a striving to transcend partiality that is itself partial" (Robbins, 1992, p. 181). What anthropological work can also do to counter elite appropriations of cosmopolitanism is to highlight "emerging cosmopolitan empathies, attitudes, and encounters in unexpected places and among marginal people" (Hall, 2006, p. 25).

Aiding in the anthropological exploration of diverse and different cosmopolitans is the fact that whatever cosmopolitanism was thought to be, it has become fragmented into multiple contending conceptualizations. There is the spatial definition where the cosmopolitan is someone who moves across global space; the social definition of the stranger who never really belongs to any community; the political definition of a "citizen of the world" whose rights are liberal democratic and individualist ones supported by international institutions;[1] the structural definition of the class position of the cosmopolitan; the moral definition, featuring someone who shows solidarity with strangers; and, the essentialist definition: "We are all cosmopolitan because every individual human being is naturally endowed with certain capabilities and rights that take precedence over any system of symbolic classification" (Rapport & Stade, 2007, pp. 232-233). Having surveyed a wide body of literature on cosmopolitanism, Rapport and Stade note that with the plural definitions also comes an understanding that cosmopolitans are to be found everywhere in the world and in the literature, where we can encounter phrases such as: "'cosmopolitans and locals' ..., 'pre-modern and modern cosmopolitans' ..., 'working-class cosmopolitans' ..., 'Caribbean cosmopolitans' ..., 'Chinese cosmopolitans' ..., 'cosmopolitan patriots' ..., 'plural discrepant cosmopolitanisms' ..., and 'cosmopolitan cityscapes'" (2007, p. 223). Indigenous cosmopolitans must now be added to the list.

Vernacular and Everyday Cosmopolitanization

Indeed, indigenous cosmopolitans had better be included, for as Sichone (2006) argues, cosmopolitanism can no longer be understood simply as a Western discourse. We will find more evidence of cosmopolitan attitudes and practices in remote African villages and congested urban slums than among European elites, Sichone argues, pointing to examples of impoverished women in South Africa who take in and care for migrants and refugees from neighboring countries, while xenophobia runs rampant in Europe. These women, Sichone explains, "live their cosmopolitanism by welcoming the world." In contrast, European capitalist elites, far from demonstrating any devotion to the interests of humanity as a whole, appear to be far from cosmopolitan: particularistic, self-absorbed, introverted, and greedy. Of course, that argument can be made only if we disagree with de l'Estoile, and move into moral notions of cosmopolitanism, which also involves a narrowing of the field of possible definitions on which Sichone's argument implicitly and intuitively relies.

Understanding that there are multiple cosmopolitanisms and cosmopolitanizations is a crucial point for anthropology (Werbner, 2006, p. 497). The idea of "discrepant" cosmopolitanisms (Clifford, 1992, p. 108) indicating that there are many, different, cosmopolitan practices, histories, and worldviews, leads us to explore the so-called marginal cosmopolitanisms, or "vernacular cosmopolitanism" (Bhabha, 1996, pp. 195-196). This opens us to the realization that indigenous cosmopolitans can be both rooted and routed, nonelite yet nonparochial, provincial without being isolated, internationalized without being de-localized. One could make a broader point here too, that "the vernacular localizes the cosmopolitan as part of its own self-constitution ... often unwittingly relocalizing what the cosmopolitan borrowed from it in the first place" (Pollock, 2002, p. 39).

The point is that the idea of "indigenous cosmopolitans" is part of a growing understanding of vernacular cosmopolitanism, that is, real-life, actually lived, everyday practice rooted in specific cultural formations. Vernacular cosmopolitanism, even more than what is called "new cosmopolitanism," is an attempt "to come to terms with the conjunctural elements of postcolonial and precolonial forms of cosmopolitanism and travel, while probing the conceptual boundaries of cosmopolitanism and its usefulness as an analytic concept" (Werbner, 2006, pp. 496-497). Similarly, Beck's conceptualization of "everyday or banal cosmopolitanism" and "actually existing cosmopolitanization" is very useful for framing the analytical-empirical cosmopolitanism at the heart of most of the studies comprising this volume, as distinct from entirely normative and philosophical approaches (Beck, 2004, pp. 131-133; see also Gidwani, 2006, on the related idea of "subaltern cosmopolitanism").

In this analytical and descriptive frame the focus is on the "growing interdependence and interconnection of social actors across national boundaries, more often than not as a side effect of actions that are not meant to be 'cosmopolitan' in the normative sense" (Beck, 2004, p. 131). Action across borders, a heightened sense of the relativity of one's own social position and culture in a global setting, and interconnections between actors in diverse locations, lead us to an awareness of "cosmopolitanization"—meaning "latent cosmopolitanisms, unconscious cosmopolitanisms, passive cosmopolitanisms, which shape reality as a side effect of world trade or global dangers" (Beck, 2004, pp. 131, 134).

Cosmopolitanism and Otherness

If there is a plea embodied by this volume, it is that we need to bring the cosmos back into cosmopolitanism, to paraphrase Latour (2004, p. 456). Cosmopolitanism is not about a "universal culture" of sameness, as Beck argues, but is instead about "recognition of the otherness of the other, beyond the false understanding associated with territoriality and homogenization" (2004, p. 143). What I consider to be an eloquent articulation of cosmopolitanism as respect for otherness comes from Ronald Stade who invites us to reconcile the "project of a cosmopolitan anthropology with an ontology that is mindful of the social nature of the self," by turning "the universal figure of Everyone into a someone, in particular into someone else, that is, into an other" (Rapport & Stade, 2007, p. 228). Stade's argument, following Emmanuel Lévinas, is that we recognize that "otherness is a primordial human experience" (Rapport & Stade, 2007, p. 229). Stade reflects on the tension between anthropos (all humans) and ethnos (specific "peoples"), between cosmos (global commonality) and polis (everyday, localized diversity)—but he notes that clearly polis is a foundational element of the cosmopolitan and without it cosmopolitanism is simply "cosmic," without roots, divorced, and disembedded from actual human practice. Most of the authors in this volume focus on how the cosmos is arrived at or explored through the indigenous polis, by taking empirical and analytical approaches to the particularities and contexts of practice. This is what we sought to offer, that if there is anything meaningful, practical, and concrete about cosmopolitanism, then indigenous peoples would know a thing or two about it. We thus contribute to satisfying demands that some urge upon us: "The scholarly project of accumulating instances of cosmopolitanism from around the globe could help us make the point that the concept is neither a Western invention nor a Western privilege" (Robbins, 1992, p. 182), and thus far it is the indigenous cosmopolitan that is absent from the literature on cosmopolitanism (which is itself a rather curious statement about cosmopolitanist writings). Yet, this book is not driven by a need to "include" the indigenous, for reasons we share with Mignolo (2002, p. 174): "inclusion doesn't seem to be the solution to cosmopolitanism any longer, insofar as it presupposes that the agency that establishes the inclusion is itself beyond inclusion: 'he' being already within the frame from which it is possible to think 'inclusion.'"

One of the philosophers whose work has spearheaded the cosmopolitan project is Kwame Anthony Appiah (2005, 2006). In a 1997 article deliberately titled in paradoxical terms, "Cosmopolitan Patriots," one that is cherished by a number of the contributors to this volume, Appiah argues that while humanism is consistent with the desire for "global homogeneity," that is not what cosmopolitanism is about. Instead, "The cosmopolitan also celebrates the fact that there are different local human ways of being" (Appiah, 1997, p. 621). Appiah makes the case for the figure of the "cosmopolitan patriot," arguing that there is no point in roots if you cannot take them with you, and here he asks (and answers) questions that are especially pertinent to our collective study:

> Where, in other words, would all the diversity we cosmopolitans celebrate come from in a world where there were only cosmopolitans? The answer is straightforward: the cosmopolitan patriot can entertain the possibility of a world in which everyone is a rooted cosmopolitan, attached to a home of one's own, with its own cultural particularities, but taking pleasure from the presence of other, different places that are home to other, different people. (Appiah, 1997, p. 618)

At the same time, in line with what some have called the "new cosmopolitans" (in Vertovec & Cohen, 2002), we do not see adherence to traditions, localities, ancestry, and so forth, as expressions of either hatred or petty self-interest. The broader point of the volume is that today "silenced and marginalized voices are bringing themselves into the conversation of cosmopolitan projects, rather than waiting to be included" (Mignolo, 2002, p. 174).

Indigenous Cosmopolitans

The authors contributing to this volume investigate cosmopolitanism as both rooted in and routed through particular settings. In the case of my chapter on the Caribbean, the "people of the sea" is more than just metaphor—it is a context of local and regional cosmopolitan practice that extends centuries back in time and circulates around an actual sea. Within that setting, that historical and contemporary social and cultural context, I speak of the cases of five specific actors ranging from a Trinidadian, self-identified as Carib, with indigenous ancestry on both sides of her parentage, who resides abroad and blogs as both a nationalist and universal aboriginalist; a shaman, traveler, musician, and eco-tour guide all bundled together in one person; a Carib chief who learns the discourse of international indigenism through personal networks of exchange and travel; to the crew of a canoe, sailing to reunite disparate Carib communities across the region, but filming the event for eventual broadcast on the BBC and PBS. Perhaps the figure that caused the most controversy with reviewers is that of the blogger, Guanaguanare, with her dedication to promoting the idea of a universal aboriginality that is decoupled from territory/property, someone who, as Appiah stated above, values her roots as something that she can take with her in moving abroad.

Craig Proulx's chapter on Aboriginal hip hop in Canada, with comparisons drawn from Aboriginal Australia, moves between rural and urban, between reservation and city and back again, in a loop of relocation and translation. Like myself and other contributors, Proulx examines the changing forms of expressing and living aboriginality, disputing notions of authenticity that fix into place the aboriginal and that take place-centered orientations of indigenous affiliation as "the sine qua non of indigeneity," because these circumscribe our understandings of indigeneity on the move. His chapter thus presents a challenge to researchers: to move away from a reserve-centric focus just as many Aboriginals in Canada have had to move, and in moving this does not necessarily mean "leaving behind." As Proulx explains, these Aboriginal Canadian hip hoppers are "rooted cosmopolitans," and indigeneity is not premised on either immobility or remoteness. In the process he introduces us to the culturally and politically charged ways that hip hop facilitates and accompanies the translation of aboriginal cultures in urban arenas: "Hip hop's sense of style helps update the performance of tradition. Hip hop is the means through which traditions can be understood, reworked, re-presented, and thereby made relevant to youth accustomed to non-Aboriginal informational delivery systems." He explains how hip hop can enable a pan-Aboriginal reconstitution and re-presentation of de-territorialized traditions, and shows us how the characters in his story are "cosmopolitan in their knowledge of their worlds, the outer worlds that impinge upon them, how they are changed by them, and how they can change them."

Carolyn Butler-Palmer's focus is on the work of Canadian photojournalist, painter, and hereditary Kwagiutl carver David Neel, who shows us how "cosmopolitan" evokes a sense of both cultural connectedness and mobility. One of his creations is simultaneously a depiction of a Kwagiutl tale and a reference to the four sacred directions of Thai Buddhism. He himself relocated to Thailand. In some ways David Neel puts into practice what Guanaguanare calls for in the first chapter of the volume. In contrast with James Clifford's sense of cosmopolitanism, which seems to be the consequence of any sort of human migration, Butler-Palmer reserves the term "to map movement that also manifests an ethic of cross-cultural engagement." Her approach to cosmopolitanism is one that consists of three components: mobility, morality, and multiplicity. Neel's work evinces a moral humanism, very similar to Guanaguanare's, and from an indigenous standpoint, using motifs of indigenous provenance that are outwardly embracing of all humanity, disclosing "an ethic of human relations based on the recognition of differences, the movement toward others, and a resulting sense of balance." Butler-Palmer's description of the role of color in Neel's work is meant to show the complementarity of the local and cosmopolitan, much like Guanaguanare's metaphor of the Catáhua tree.

Arthur Mason's chapter is one of a subgroup in the volume that deals with tourism, a powerful processual context for the exchange of culture, focusing specifically on "heritage work" on Kodiak Island, Alaska, an exchange that occurs through a complex interplay of history, migration, politics, and economics. Such heritage work, he argues, "assists in the wider reorganization of spatial and temporal rhythms necessary for legitimizing new social orders, identities, and communal action at the local level." Following Clifford, Mason notes that heritage work responds to demands that originate both inside and outside indigenous communities. Heritage work brings to bear an entire infrastructure laden with cosmopolitan possibilities: "The very technologies and forms of identity and heritage making in Alaska are shifting, and are now linked to the larger American political landscape, capitalism, scientific authority, and state intervention, as well as to local sentimentality, and in the case of the Alutiiq, preservation of ancestral authority." Alaska appears as a crossroads of cultures, with Inuit, Anglo-Americans, and Russian-Native Creoles, a situation that makes it similar to the Caribbean. We see how school museums perform a function of integrating the mindsets of Kodiak children into larger imaginings of an outside world, specifically the United States, distant yet present, creating and participating in a new symbolic order, with attendant changes in language, and in conceptualizations of time and space. Paradoxically, and this is the other side of the cosmopolitan process, the Kodiak experience with "modernity" both inspired and provided the material resources for "reindigenization." When U.S. government negotiations with Alaska Natives over land claims began, the following transformation occurred: "Aware of the potential economic gain, social honor, and modernizing role from participating in the process, Kodiak's leaders who previously had defined themselves through their Russian American ancestry began to identify themselves through their Native ancestry." Indeed, it is a very significant reality of indigenous cosmopolitanism that some of the symbolic and material resources for indigeneity can be derived from the wider world outside of the immediate setting, reworked locally, and indigenized. Mason points us in the direction of what might be a fundamental realization: that there really can be no indigeneity without cosmopolitanism, and vice versa (see Stade and Appiah as discussed in the preceding sections).

Frans Schryer, like Mason, follows arts and crafts, development schemes, and complex political economic transformations in his discussion of Mexican Nahua indigeneity, again a confluence of forces that is highly productive of cosmopolitanism. Schryer devotes substantial attention to the work of indigenous leaders in building a movement of opposition to the building of a dam. He shows us how the local promotion of indigenous leaders occurs via transnational networking, leaders who may outlast the organizations they initially represented, and who promote emblematic, standardizing symbols of indigeneity even if they themselves may have little grounding in the culture that they represent, in ways reminiscent of Brysk (1996), in parallel to the first chapter's discussion of a Carib leader's engagement in transnational indigenous networks. In addition to political activism, Schryer shows how arts and crafts markets plug the Nahuas into regional and world economies, and specifically that of tourism. Nahua self-representation is now painted across a global canvas, and through broadened fields of interaction, especially when marked by conflict; what Schryer shows is that representations of indigenous as Other can be sharpened, rather than diminishing the content of indigenous alterity. Schryer also explains what he calls the process of "inverse cosmopolitanism," whereby Nahua migrants to the U.S. reproduce "a strong local identity and village endogamy," thus rerooting themselves through foreign routes. In the U.S. some Nahuas even become "Aztec."

In their chapter, Julie-Ann Tomiak and Donna Patrick focus on urban Inuit in Canada. This is an interesting case study which, although it parallels some of the material on migrations in the chapters by Mason and Schryer, points to something different: a domestic indigenous transnationalism, internal cosmopolitanism, where "urban Inuit space is created and used as sites where Inuit from a wide range of historical-geographical trajectories come together." Here the cosmopolitan process comes into play in relations between both longer-term urban Inuit and relatives back home, up north, and new Inuit arrivals to the city, specifically Ottawa, the Canadian capital. In this case, urban Inuit community centers become the arena for a dynamic interaction that still privileges Inuit place, even if seemingly out of place.

Robin Maria DeLugan also examines migration showing us how "by exchanging homelands in Mexico, Central, and South America for distant destinations, native people challenge stereotypes that their identity is inextricably rooted to place of origin." DeLugan describes and analyzes how mutual recognition is formed among native people from across the continent, gathered in U.S. urban centers such as San Francisco, a recognition that they share common and related historical conditions and cultural affinities—a cosmopolitanism across and among indigenes that in some ways echoes one of the messages in the Tomiak and Patrick chapter, as well as the first chapter. Here we are dealing with the creation of a hemispheric indigenous identity, "a collective identity that is based on an inclusive and cosmopolitan view of human being and belonging in the world." In some respects, DeLugan takes previous work on "urban supratribalism" (cf. Cornell, 1988) a big step forward by considering this migratory and hemispheric context. The analytic scope of the chapter is ambitious, for DeLugan proclaims that what we are witnessing is a transnational indigenous parallel of the "Black Atlantic," referencing but not restrained by locality. Clearly, DeLugan is pushing forward the theme of "vernacular cosmopolitanism," as discussed in preceding sections, a cosmopolitanism that emerges not from the privileged centers of world power, but in spite of them, from the margins. Similarly, she endorses Appiah's concept of "rooted cosmopolitans," where indigenous communities do not just have a past, they also have a future. Contrary to liberal neo-Kantianism, DeLugan argues that "Indigenous cosmopolitanism with its simultaneous emphasis on rootedness and universality ... understands that differences can co-exist in a framework of universal relatedness."

Linda Scarangella's fascinating chapter, focusing on traveling Indian shows in places such as Euro Disney in Paris, brings back in the tourism theme that is prevalent in this volume (especially in the chapters by Mason and Schryer), except that in this case the travelers are indigenous, and they perform indigeneity both for foreign audiences and for themselves. While noting that there is considerable disagreement among anthropologists as to what cosmopolitanism refers to, Scarangella observes that it is commonly "presumed that indigenous people are the Others linked to locality that cosmopolitans engage with, not cosmopolitan themselves." Rapport will later back up Scarangella for rightly understanding what is not just commonly presumed, but formally defined. For Scarangella, "cosmopolitan" is to be used in its broadest sense as consisting of mobility, recognition of interconnectedness, openness toward cultural difference, and engagement with Others, a formulation that is similar to Butler-Palmer's. Scarangella disagrees with the view that indigenous persons performing in places of spectacle, putting on cultural displays for foreign gazers, are simply part of an "exploitative commercial enterprise." Such a story "does not completely explain Native performers' experiences of identity or why they participate in these spectacular spaces." In such performative spaces, Native performers have an occasion to reflect on the meanings of their cultural identity. Moreover, Native performers "connect to both tribal and broader indigenous or pan-Indian identities in this transnational space," with the performers coming from different First Nations and maintaining their local identities through both performances and personal acts. The act of traveling itself signifies breaking a barrier, "moving beyond local and tribal identity to a broader sense of being indigenous." In her analysis, Scarangella subscribes to Ulrich Beck's idea of the dialogic imagination in cosmopolitanism, showing us that the performers are reflexive in comparing, reflecting, articulating, and reworking their ideas of indigeneity. Like Proulx in this volume, Scarangella finds value in the simultaneous combination of the rooted and the routed: "Local roots are articulated in transnational spaces, and transnational spaces generate occasions for the expression of a broader indigenous identity that includes while it transcends local and tribal expressions." Like DeLugan, her chapter also speaks of the formation of a transnational, supratribal pan-Indianism. As noted previously, Scarangella, like Mason, points us to a significant realization of the connection between indigeneity and cosmopolitanism: "Being and becoming indigenous today may very well mean engaging in cosmopolitanism, or at least transnational and translocal lifestyles." The performance of a pan-Indian indigeneity in a transcultural and translocal space facilitates cosmopolitanism, Scarangella argues, "where performers and the public engage with cultural difference, and where performers seek to increase cultural understanding."

The concluding chapter by Nigel Rapport, one of the most prominent anthropologists to carry forward the cosmopolitan agenda in anthropology (see Rapport, 2006, 2007), from a methodological individualist and Kantian perspective, is somewhat of an "odd man out" in the collection, and following a cosmopolitan ethic was included for that reason as well. As a prominent cosmopolitanist writer, Rapport was asked to read and comment on all of the chapters, while delivering his own inputs. He comments on the experience of travel, central to most of the chapters, and argues that moving away from or between homes and "experiencing change" is something "practiced by many and possessing consequences for all; with the result that it becomes neither easy nor wise to attempt to demarcate or differentiate, in any absolute way, between 'hosts' and 'guests.'" Who is "at home" is, for Rapport, more of a matter of the nature and purpose of particular exchanges, rather than "absolute identities." Rapport is well aware that the most common definitions of cosmopolitanism, represented by our dictionaries, often contrast the cosmopolite with the native, local, or indigene. Instead, Rapport invites us to consider cosmopolitanism more as a "habit of mind," one that is post-national in particular. Rapport's provocation is to use the figure of "the Jew," given how "the Jew" has been "typified by arch nationalists as something of an anti-indigene, an anti-local, an anti-patriot, the perennial pariah, the floating outsider, lacking loyalty to place, untrustworthy and thus potentially a criminal," a provocation because this history can be "a terribly sober reminder of what can happen with studies of indigeneity that read ideologies of fear of the world into indigenous lifeworlds." From "the Jew" as historic metaphor, Rapport takes us to meet actual, living Jews, in a bar in Newfoundland, Canada. In the process of presenting his very intriguing, engaging, and challenging analysis of persons and conversations in the bar, Rapport shares some critical insights about indigeneity and cosmopolitanism: "Actually existing cosmopolitanism was varied, plural and polythetic [following Robbins]: actually existing indigeneity could be expected to be likewise." Rapport is prescribing cosmopolitanism with a specific angle here, the post-nationalist one, which is not necessarily post-indigenous (Guanaguanare in the first chapter possesses a complexity that transcends even this, however: she is indigenous, nationalist, and universalist, seen as a continuum rather than a snake's pit of contradictions.) In prescribing post-nationalism Rapport argues, "One need not imagine the absolute overcoming of localism or even chauvinism so much as their ironization. Absolute notions of identity are made contingent by their being contextualized alongside others: one of a number of identities that contest for space in the same place; one of a number of identities to which the same individuals contract a belonging."

If there could possibly be one single lesson (there are in fact many) that this volume wishes to impress upon readers, it is this: that the indigene and the cosmopolite should not only no longer be seen as incongruous and contradictory, in reality they are one and the same. However, one lesson not to be taken away from this collection is that by proclaiming that the indigene is cosmopolitan, we have thus added a dignity and respectability that the indigene might not have possessed otherwise.

Notes

1   Ironically, while the individual and notions of individual human rights are privileged in liberal neo-Kantian discourse of cosmopolitanism, this does not transcend either nationalism or the nation-state. As Turner (2002, p. 50) explained very lucidly: "Nation-state citizenship and nationalist ideology have been, in the modern world, powerful agencies for creating individual identities. Modern notions of social rights have defined citizenship as primarily a political and juridical category relating to liberal individualism. This juridical identity of citizens has evolved according to the larger political context, because citizenship has necessarily been constructed within a definite political community, namely the nation-state … citizenship-building was also, and necessarily, nation-building. The creation of the institutions of citizenship in legal, political, and social terms was also the construction of a national framework of membership within the administrative structures of the state."

References

Appiah, K.A. (1997). Cosmopolitan Patriots. *Critical Inquiry*, 23(3), 617-639.

———. (2005). *The Ethics of Identity*. Princeton, NJ: Princeton University Press.

———. (2006). *Cosmopolitanism: Ethics in a World of Strangers*. New York: W.W. Norton.

Beck, U. (2004). Cosmopolitical Realism: On the Distinction between Cosmopolitanism in Philosophy and the Social Sciences. *Global Networks*, 4(2), 131-156.

Bhabha, H. (1996). Unsatisfied: Notes on Vernacular Cosmopolitanism. In Laura García-Moreno & Peter Pfeifer (Eds.), *Text and Nation* (pp. 191-207). London: Camden House.

Breckenridge, C. A., Pollock, S., Bhabha, H. K., & Chakrabarty, D. (Eds.). (2002). *Cosmopolitanism*. Durham, NC: Duke University Press.

Brysk, A. (1996). Turning Weakness into Strength: The Internationalization of Indian Rights. *Latin American Perspectives*, 23(2), 38-57.

Cheah, P. (2006). Cosmopolitanism. *Theory, Culture & Society*, 23(2-3), 486-496.

Clifford, J. (1992). Traveling Cultures. In Lawrence Grossberg, Cary Nelson, & Paula Treichler (Eds.), *Cultural Studies* (pp. 96-116). London: Routledge.

Clifford, J. (1997). *Routes: Travel and Translation in the Late Twentieth Century*. Cambridge, MA: Harvard University Press.

Coates, K. (2004). *A Global History of Indigenous Peoples: Struggle and Survival*. Basingstoke, UK: Palgrave Macmillan.

Cornell, S. (1988). *The Return of the Native: American Indian Political Resurgence*. New York: Oxford University Press.

de la Cadena, M., & O. Starn. (Eds.). 2007. *Indigenous Experience Today*. Oxford: Berg.

de L'Estoile, B. (2006). Making Friends in Different Worlds: The Anthropologist as a Professional Cosmopolitan. Paper presented at the 2006 conference of the Association of Social Anthropologists of the UK and Commonwealth, University of Keele, 10-13 April.

Deloria, P. J. (2006). *Indians in Unexpected Places*. Lawrence: University Press of Kansas.

Gidwani, K. I. (2006). Subaltern Cosmopolitanism as Politics. *Antipode*, 38(1), 7-21.

Hall, A. (2006). Cosmopolitanism and Anthropology. *Anthropology Today*, 22(4), 25-26.

Latour, B. (2004). Whose Cosmos, Which Cosmopolitics? *Common Knowledge*, 10(3), 450-462.

Mignolo, W. D. (2002). The Many Faces of Cosmo-polis: Border Thinking and Critical Cosomopolitanism. In Carol A. Brenckenridge et al. (Eds.), *Cosmopolitanism* (pp. 157-187). Durham, NC: Duke University Press.

Nagel, J. (1995). American Indian Ethnic Renewal: Politics and the Resurgence of Identity. *American Sociological Review*, 60 (6), 947-965.

Pollock, S. (2002). Cosmopolitan and Vernacular in History. In Carol A. Brenckenridge et al. (Eds.), *Cosmopolitanism* (pp. 15-53). Durham, NC: Duke University Press.

Rapport, N. (2006). Anthropology as Cosmopolitan Study. *Anthropology Today*, 22(1), 23-24.

———. (2007). An Outline for Cosmopolitan Study: Reclaiming the Human Through Introspection. *Current Anthropology*, 48 (2), 257-283.

Rapport, N., & R. Stade. (2007). A Cosmopolitan Turn-or Return? *Social Anthropology*, 15(2), 223-235.

Robbins, B. (1992). Comparative Cosmopolitanism. *Social Text* (31/32), 169-186.

Sichone, O. (2006). Xenophobia and Xenophilia in South Africa. Paper presented at the 2006 conference of the Association of Social Anthropologists of the UK and Commonwealth,

University of Keele, 10-13 April.

Sissons, J. (2005). *First Peoples: Indigenous Cultures and Their Futures*. London: Reaktion Books.

Thomas, N. (1992). The Inversion of Tradition. *American Ethnologist*, 19(2), 213-232.

Turner, B. S. (2002). Cosmopolitan Virtue, Globalization and Patriotism. *Theory, Culture & Society*, 19(1-2), 45-63.

Vertovec, S., & Cohen, R. (Eds.). (2002). *Conceiving Cosmopolitanism: Theory, Context, and Practice*. New York: Oxford University Press.

Werbner, P. (2006). Vernacular Cosmopolitanism. *Theory, Culture & Society*, 23(2-3), 496-498.

◆ CHAPTER TWO ◆

A Carib Canoe, Circling in the Culture of the Open Sea: Submarine Currents Connecting Multiple Indigenous Shores

Maximilian C. Forte

It is still the case that no one lives in the world in general. Everybody, even the exiled, the drifting, the diasporic, or the perceptually moving, lives in some confined and limited stretch of it—"the world around here." (Geertz, 1996, p. 262)

PLACE. It cannot be circumvented. But if you wish to benefit from this place, which has been given to you, consider that henceforth all the places of the world are converging ... the place widens out from its irreducible center, as much as from its incalculable outer frontiers. (Glissant quoted in Dash, 2006, p. 64)

A Fragmented Caribbean Story

"*Peoples of the sea.*" The Caribbean Sea looms large in the works of modern Caribbean poets and philosophers (such as Derek Walcott and Edouard Glissant) who search for the root qualities of Caribbean cultures, past and present, and envision the region in terms of cultural currents and historical tides, of arrivals from beyond and movements within a sea that is like a glue that binds together an archipelago of fragments broken off from the mainland (Walcott, 1992). "*Peoples of the sea*" contains a couple of paradoxes that feature prominently in the historical and cultural commentary on the Caribbean. The first paradox is that the *insular* Caribbean, that is, the island Caribbean, has been open since the inception of human habitation, with regular inter-island trade, migration, and warfare being the norm of indigenous life on the islands prior to European colonization. The second paradox is that the Caribbean began to experience a greater degree of inter-island isolation only with the advent of colonialism and the imposition of the nation-state form, a global current that came from outside the region, that resulted in greater provincialization and insularity within the region, insularity in the normal senses in which it is apprehended. The search for forms of greater inter-state integration in the Caribbean, taking various shapes from the time of the West Indies Federation (1958-1962), to the Caribbean Free Trade Area (CARIFTA, 1965-1973), then the Caribbean Community and Common Market (CARICOM, 1973 to the present) and the Association of Caribbean States (ACS, 1994 to the present), all serve to attest to some level of "official" recognition of the fragmentation of the Caribbean by separated states.

"*Peoples of the sea*" is how Cuban writer Antonio Benítez-Rojo (1996, p. 26) characterized the inhabitants of the region. "The culture of the Caribbean," Benítez-Rojo wrote, "is not terrestrial but aquatic, a sinuous culture where time unfolds irregularly and resists being captured by the cycles of clock and calendar" (1996, p. 11). This is a sea that unites as much as it divides, and as Edward Baugh (2006) explained, this sea defines a semiclosed, half-open region. Ranging across the literary works of Derek Walcott, Edward Kamau Brathwaite, and Wilson Harris, Baugh (2006, pp. 58-59) summarizes their vision of the Caribbean: a curved space, circle of sorts, closed but open; receptacle of migrations, the sea that speaks of "all of the voyages," rippling back outward with new and reverse migrations; the beach that receives the seed and driftwood from across the seas; a womb of possibility, spawning the islands.

When people live in "the world around here," as the anthropologist Clifford Geertz said when attempting to relocalize our perspectives in a context of overly hyped "globalization," it is the world that has also inhabited the place "around here" that makes the Caribbean, as Glissant suggests in the opening quote. The world itself is *around in here*. Historian Eric Williams (1970, p. 69) famously characterized the region as "the cockpit of Europe," the islands serving as pawns in European plays for power staged in the Caribbean Sea. Indigenous peoples in the Caribbean archipelago were deeply placed with the wider Caribbean cultural experience—they did not have the luxury, and sometimes not even the desire, to remain outside of that experience. They have helped to shape that experience, often not visibly or prominently, and have been shaped by it, often visibly and acutely. Today indigenous peoples of the Caribbean live largely on the margins of national consciousness in their respective states, widely viewed as small and impoverished minorities of remaining communities, organizations, and individuals who actively self-identify as either Taíno (in the Greater Antilles and especially in communities of immigrants from Puerto Rico and the Dominican Republic in the United States),

Garifuna (along the Caribbean coast of Central America and in Los Angeles), or Kalinago and Carib (in Dominica, St. Vincent, St. Lucia, and Trinidad) (Forte, 2006).

This chapter is a story that might be about cosmopolitans who are Caribs, or vice versa, told through elements of local biographies, translocal movements, and transcultural experiences. I say that it might be such a story because we are not yet certain that the idea of cosmopolitanism offers anything new, anything more, or anything better than the intersections and overlaps of a number of already existing concepts used to describe and understand life beyond the local.[1] Among such concepts, we have classical religious and secular notions of "universalism" (the local, the other, are ephemera at best, as we are all one); "metropolitanism," the domination of the underdeveloped (post) colonial world by Europe and North America (Rodney, 1973; Williams, 1970), with the critique of metropolitan domination and local outward orientation to be found in the works of Caribbean scholars who formed part of the New World Movement; again in the Caribbean, in the work of Cuban scholar Fernando Ortiz, the idea of "transculturation" involving the process of transition from one culture to another, acquiring a new culture, uprooting a previous culture, and the creation of new cultural phenomena (Ortiz, 1995); "creolization," a concept with especially strong resonance in the Caribbean and a long history of usage as a means of describing the creation of new cultural forms from the mixture of previous cultural forms, both local and metropolitan (see Glissant, 1989; Hannerz, 1992, p. 266; Khan, 2001; Priam, 2005); the "plural society thesis" also has a long history not just in the history of social science in the Caribbean, especially in the work of Jamaican anthropologist M. G. Smith (1965) but also in everyday parlance in places such as Trinidad and Tobago, the center of this chapter. Echoes of the plural society thesis are to be found in local ideas of what is a cosmopolitan society (Munasinghe, 2002, 2006), usually emphasizing the local presence of peoples of diverse ancestries, with limited exchange and mixture among (some of) them. In contrast to the thesis of creole society as one of fusion and mixture, the cosmopolitan society is one of cohabitation and segregation. In local Trinidadian parlance, and unlike what some of the scholars above suggest, terms such as "creole" can be racialized (East Indians referring to African descendants as "creoles"), while the cosmopolitan "tossed salad" can sometimes be used synonymously in everyday speech with what among scholars is considered its opposite: the creolized "callaloo" (stew) society.

The point I wish to make here is that "cosmopolitanism" in current scholarly treatments comes after a long line of similar and related concepts have already been deployed—there are in fact too many of these concepts to allow for a manageable treatment of all of them, in relation to one another, in a chapter such as this one. Suffice it to say that cosmopolitanism comes after many other conceptualizations of the universal and the particular, the global and the local, self and other, here and there. What the current cosmopolitanism might allow, coming as it does at this time, is the opportunity to bring in newer discussions of transnationalism and transculturation that fuse or extend older discussions. The central thrust of this chapter is to underscore that there is a false dichotomy dividing indigeneity and cosmopolitanism by demonstrating that this binary construct does not adequately describe the realities of indigenous peoples in the Caribbean.

The Characters and the Settings

This is a story with five actors, operating within or across six distinct discursive and social fields. One of the actors is an Internet blogger, a Trinidadian woman resident in Canada, who chooses personal anonymity while she identifies herself as a Carib Indian descendant—she is what I will call the universalist aboriginal.[2] The second is a shaman, Cristo Adonis, an active member of the Carib Community of Arima, Trinidad, prominent in the media—Cristo, the traveler, self-described "child of the world," whom I nonetheless describe as Carib cosmopolitan rather than a cosmopolitan Carib. The third occupies the position of "president" of the Carib Community of Trinidad, a modern corporate title—Ricardo, who has traveled to multiple high-level indigenous gatherings across the hemisphere and has learned the language of international indigenous activism, and discovered a transnational indigenous narrative that stresses the commonalities of "cultural loss" among most indigenous populations in the hemisphere. The fourth actor is also a Carib descendant, stout, proud, and loud, the self-described Trinidad and Tobago Carib Queen of Miami, at home in Trinidad as much as she is at home in the American powwow circuit—her name Catherine Ramirez. The fifth actor is a canoe, actually the crew of the canoe, known as the Gli-Gli Carib Canoe, and the people met along its journey.

I chose to discuss each of these actors for a number of reasons: because I have known them personally; because I have collaborated with them in different ways and to different extents at different times; because they are fairly distinctive when compared to one another; because they either bridge multiple settings of action (see below), or, because they instead magnify one particular setting; and finally, because I am most comfortable writing about them as much they are comfortable with my writing.[3] This is not to suggest that otherwise these central characters are wholly unrepresentative, presented as a result of personal idiosyncrasy. Instead, they represent a cross-section of locations (at home and abroad), class positions (mostly working-class, but with some exceptions such as Catherine Ramirez), with some diverse political allegiances (most identifying with the ruling People's National Movement, a primarily urban and Afro-Trinidadian party, but not all, such as the Trinidadian blogger), and their narratives stand out as the ones that are most likely to be repeated and reproduced by others within their community, or by the commentary in the national media. Nonetheless, it would be problematic to assert that these characters are the most representative ones. Their presence in this story is still largely due to the fact that they were the most accessible persons.

From what I can discern, this story transpires in the following settings, and each setting is not limited to one actor, nor is the reverse the case: (1) the universalist aboriginal, at one with the world; (2) the transnational, inter-indigenous world of pan-indigenism; (3) the traveling worlds of eco-tourism and shamanic conferences; (4) the regional, the translocal network of contacts and exchanges among nearby Carib communities in the Caribbean archipelago; and, (5) the local cosmopolitan, demonstrating an openness to difference without becoming fused with it, being familiar with something without becoming married to it, or making use of elements of other local cultures and reworking them as indigenous, in a process that seemingly bridges Trinidadian meanings of "cosmopolitan" with social scientific conceptualizations of creolization. As I say, these are settings, indicating venues and placements within which certain thinking is done, rather than either a mere "typology" or an undifferentiated sense of undefined zones of mixing between indigeneity and cosmopolitanism.

The Plot

My aim is to show that being indigenous is *not* a matter of introversion and seclusion, of being remote and isolated, scorning and shunning outside influences, avoiding exchange, or not looking for new ways of becoming indigenous. Nor are cultural and politico-economic forms of globalization inexorable forces, like mythical juggernauts running rampant over unprepared, hapless locals, despite the pronounced degree of Caribbean integration into the capitalist world-system.[4] Whatever globalization may be, it is neither unmediated nor entirely uninitiated by local actors. The problem at hand, in this volume, in this chapter, and within anthropology more broadly, stems from conceptualizations of indigeneity and cosmopolitanism as essentially opposed or strikingly different in cultural content, space, and scale.[5]

Cosmopolitanism can take on the air in some writings of a universal, world-transcending entity that is "out there" in the wider ambient. In other words, in practical terms, cosmopolitanism strikes me as occupying a non-time and non-place, based on the kind of analysis of the world put forth by Appadurai (1997, 1999), that is, a post-local world of global flows where intimacy has come to an end. Indigeneity, on the other hand, might be cast in opposition, as narrow, singular, provincial, and small-scale in its practical manifestations, characterizations recognized by Hannerz (2004) and Friedman (2004). I argue that such a portrait would be misguided, that any actually existing cosmopolitanisms are plural and placed, and that indigeneity is one way of being cosmopolitan in the world, while the social processes attached to cosmopolitan practices can provide the venues and vehicles for one to renew, or to become indigenous. In the perspective that I am adopting, the local still matters, and the global needs to be demystified along those grounds. I therefore agree with Friedman when he argues that "the global simply reflects the emergent properties of the articulation of numerous local processes" (2004, p. 180).

In what sense is the practice of articulating and expanding one's indigenous identity and culture becoming increasingly "cosmopolitan"? I say that the practice is cosmopolitan to the degree that it extends beyond the immediacy of the local; when intimacy becomes translocal (uniting Caribs from different territories in the Caribbean); when translocal relationships assume the forms of modern transnational organization (uniting Caribs from different territories in the Caribbean through the formation of the Caribbean Organization of Indigenous Peoples); when the communication of indigenous identity and politics widens to include nonindigenous audiences at home and abroad; where the everyday tools for communicating indigeneity are no longer the traditional ones, but expand to include cell phones with long-distance calling cards, blogs, faxes and email, airline travel to international conferences, talking on radio and appearing on television, being filmed for a BBC documentary, being interviewed by Condé Nast, playing host to eco-tourists; and, when "all our relations" expands to include peoples of different cultures in different parts of the world, because all of them in their own local contexts have been categorized, or categorize themselves, as indigenous. What we witness, and what I have described elsewhere, is the extent to which the symbols and discourse of indigenous groups in one part of the world (Canada, for example) can and do impact the symbols and discourse of indigenous groups in another part of the world (e.g., Trinidad) (see Forte, 2005). The Caribs of the pre-1492 era were by no means insular—any and all evidence points to intense inter-island trading, marriage, warfare, and the creation of a lingua franca known by scholars today as Island Carib. The Caribs of the post-1992 era, following the watershed produced by the Columbian Quincentennial for hemispheric communication and organization between indigenous communities and movements, still work within a wider transnational frame. Therefore, it is not that locality does not matter, but that it matters in different ways and it is no longer the only thing that matters.

The Universalist Aboriginal: An Aboriginal Lens on Universality

"*Ahakutiwa, alëlekatiwa, akuyawatiwa!* We awake, we laugh, we return!"—this is the ruling motto on the blog by Guanaguanare. Guanaguanare was the name of an Amerindian chief in Trinidad, plus the title of a locally sung Spanish song, and is also an Amerindian word for "the laughing gull," a seagull that is to be found in the Trinidad-Orinoco region.

I met Guanaguanare online, through her blog, while looking through a cluster of blogs by Trinidadians at home and abroad, mostly independent writers, multimedia artists, and political activists who have indicated personal genealogical descent or a broadly cultural appreciation of Carib indigeneity. Guanaguanare is a complex figure: identifying as indigenous, crossing boundaries between human and animal, between past and present, and she is also a patriotic nationalist, focused on home, yet resident abroad, concerned with justice and cultivating intelligent, appropriate and sustainable individual and national development, and almost never writing one word about where she lives now. Since I first met her online in late 2006, we have become close online collaborators, especially on issues of the ethnography of Trinidad, intellectual decolonization, and anti-imperialism.

Sensitive to her own situation as part of a dispersal of indigenous Trinidadians through migration, Guanaguanare identifies with a seed, specifically the *Catáhua* seed. As she explains, Catáhua is an Andean indigenous name for the Sandbox Tree, a tree that has the unusual habit of exploding its seed pods with a loud burst, mechanically dispersing the seeds as a result, rather than relying on wind or gravity. She writes about Trinidadians as Catáhua people, forcibly expelled and dispersed, and faced with identity choices. In her words (Guanaguanare, 2008a):

> The Sandbox tree that is our nation understands that too many seeds near the base of the tree does not allow for optimum growth, either for itself or for the seedlings to come. It arranges it so that its seeds and as well, its survival as a species, will have the best chance possible. There isn't sufficient light or food or space for us all here ... Catáhua people are deliberately pitched far and wide to near and distant shores. If circumstances allow you to return or if the "saudade" [longing] drives you to claw your way back, don't think yourself foolish and please do ignore the "What you come back here for?" comments. On the other hand, if you choose to or have no choice but to remain abroad, understand that even though you are not at the base of the tree which bore you, the life force that propelled you outwards hopes only that you will put down strong roots wherever you are. Trinbago is not only a physical location. It is also a way of thinking and being that can comfort and sustain. Expulsion is sometimes a survival mechanism.

This is the beginning part of her way of constructing an indigenous approach to universality that sometimes verges on leaving indigenous roots altogether, but only if one conceives of indigenous roots in territorial and spatial terms. She continues in separate writings, which are interspersed between her transcriptions of old time calypsos whose meanings she wishes to rescue, that the indigenous is *universal*. She does this by delinking indigeneity from land, especially land as *property*. In this manner, she reaffirms a classic indigenous, anti-capitalist ethos that land cannot be owned by anyone, while freeing up the indigene to move and travel and leave the land. In addition, she casts us all as one-time aboriginals, having been forced by circumstance to move. Furthermore, *we are all one*, in that we are all descended from common ancestors and share the same genetic makeup. As she puts it (Guanaguanare, 2008b):

> To say that I have aboriginal ancestry is to proclaim that I belong to the human race. Every single one of us is descended from an aboriginal. On the physical level, DNA markers are obsessive recorders and guardians of our genetic roots and meanderings. If, for my survival, due to the introduction of competition or threat, I must lay claim to a particular geographic location or cultural identity, I must also admit to myself that this aboriginality as location is also temporary, not written in stone, not bequeathed for eternity.
>
> I myself own no land and feel no desire to reclaim the specific lands that were "taken" from my ancestors. It does not mean that I do not feel the loss but this comes **NOT** from my not having access to the land of my ancestors. It comes simply from not having access to any land which I feel is the right of every human being who is a citizen of this earth. I do not believe that land should be owned privately and in perpetuity by anyone, and that includes myself.
>
> I instead want to put aboriginality before land. I want to put it before everything else by which we allow ourselves to be distracted. Long after religion and philosophy had been trying to convince us of the brotherhood of man, science confirmed that we did in fact all come from the same place, that we had the same parents. That this discovery was not met with greater universal rejoicing is an indication of our amnesia. I want to go back to the Guácara [cave], to remember the place where there was no doubt that we were **ONE**.

Overall, Guanaguanare's contributions are interesting, unusual, even revolutionary, a hybrid expression of nationalism, indigenism, and universalism, resulting in a nonethnocentric indigeneity. At first glance, this would make no sense, unless we are prepared to accept the presence of indigenous ways of being cosmopolitan, and cosmopolitan ways of being indigenous. For Guanaguanare, all of humanity is "indigenous" (and on the move)—either in an evolutionary sense that we all came out of Africa, or in a moral, humanistic sense that echoes the words of St. Augustine, that we are all citizens of the "City of God."

One must acknowledge that the universalist perspective on indigeneity is politically problematic for common indigenous discourses that tie identity and rights to land, and that the de-territorialization of indigeneity undermines the articulation of notions of indigenous difference rooted in land. Moreover, Guanaguanare's call would seem to contrast starkly with indigenous political projects of decolonization and self-determination that aim to regain control over land.

On the other hand, Guanaguanare's challenge is two fold. First, it invites us to rethink *everyone's* claim to *ownership* of land, and therefore it is not a challenge to land-rootedness or territoriality as much as it is a challenge to all parties to subvert the institutionalization, routinization, diffusion, and translation of capitalist *proprietary* relationships to land. As a philosophical and moral position, it is true that her position does not pay much regard to political practice and political consequences—which is not to say that it is above politics, as much as it is to recognize that she is thinking on a different plane than that on which the particular political contests of the day are situated. Second, Guanaguanare's perspective is, arguably, more attuned to the contemporary conditions of dispersion and loss of land that forces many indigenous *peoples* to become urban *persons*. In the Caribbean, indigenous peoples possess no land *as indigenous communities*, except in the case of the "Carib Reserve" in Dominica (whose fixed boundaries cannot satisfy the needs of a growing population). In North America, most aboriginal peoples are urbanized, and most of those possess no rights to reserve lands. The discourse of territoriality is thus also very problematic, having lost resonance with a great many persons who, like most other members of the working class, have no birthright to land. It is this injustice that is the focal point of concern for Guanaguanare, as well as the worry that identity politics will drive us to forget our common humanity, a commonality rooted in the most primordial aboriginality. At the very least, we have a debate on our hands, and it is a debate between indigenous persons.

In broader terms, Guanaguanare's narrative is helpful for shedding light at different angles on subjects we might have thought we understood or that we took for granted. Her narrative is not the expected one of "ontological devastation" that some might assume is the consequence of being "without social anchor or cognitive guarantee" (Rapport & Stade, 2007, p. 224). Instead, moving from an indigenous core outward, her sense of indigeneity becomes all encompassing, reanchoring everyone. Guanaguanare also offers some lessons for Trinidadians specifically, where "cosmopolitan" tends to involve forgetting the original Amerindian inhabitants of Trinidad (see Boomert, 1982). In contrast, Guanaguanare's approach is to mend the conceptual breach, to produce an indigenous cosmopolitanism that in the end is neither introverted nor exogenous.

Transnational Relationships: Aboriginal Universalism?

I see transnational inter-indigenous networking as a cosmo-political practice. It may be superficially cosmopolitan in appearance, or an instrumental cosmopolitan, as some might perceive it (Hannerz, 2004, p. 77), given that it follows the routes of cosmopolitan practice that I listed before: conferences, air travel, international organizations, communication, and coordination among indigenous peoples of multiple cultural backgrounds. Indeed, one would be right to question whether vehicles of interaction produce cosmopolitan results, assuming that we can agree on definitions, and further assuming that such results are beneficial to those concerned. I think there is more than just instrumental cosmopolitanism in the work of indigenous transnationalism, especially as it seems to be leading to the production of new indigenous networks that provide for new meanings, existing on the plane of international organization, neither entirely rooted in, nor entirely disconnected from, local settings.

Guanaguanare speaks of a universal aboriginality that both reaffirms indigenous identities and then embraces all other humans as sharing in an indigenously human identity, thereby coming close to classical notions of cosmopolitanism. We might also consider reversing the terms, giving us "aboriginal universalism." What would that involve?

Aboriginal universalism might be seen in the emergence of a transnational network of indigenous actors who meet in international fora and produce a common discourse of indigeneity, and where the actors find commonalities between their diverse histories and cultures. Here the Internet, indigenous assemblies, conferences, personal travel, even diaspora networks come to the fore as avenues and venues for the development of a comprehensive, supralocal indigenous metaculture. Under this heading I am speaking of encounters and exchanges between non-neighbors, what has come to be called the *transnational indigenous peoples' movement* (TIPM) (see Muehlebach, 2001; Tilley, 2002). Tilley defines the TIPM as "that global network of native peoples' movements and representatives—and of sympathetic institutions, non-governmental organizations (NGOs) and scholars—which, through decades of international conferences, has formulated certain framing norms for indigenous politics now expressed in several international legal instruments" (2002, p. 526). Tilley thinks that the TIPM has become an "omnipresent influence" in "indigenous ethnopolitics" around the world, by generating new financial, legal, and political resources that can be deployed in diverse local settings (2002, p. 526).

The TIPM has produced a language of indigenous rights that is quite abstract and remote from discourse "on the ground" in diverse local indigenous communities, tending as it does to represent the work of indigenous intellectuals and legal scholars. As Tilley notes, the discourse of the TIPM can tend to favor the more literate and less representative leaderships of indigenous communities (2002, p. 528). In the Caribbean case, it is not difficult to find certain Taíno leaders whose leadership exists more in different United Nations bodies than as representatives of any existing "indigenous community." Indeed, the strategy seems to be to first create representation at the UN and then hope that attracts enough impressed followers to form the semblance of a Taíno community. Some of these cases resemble the classic instances of ethnic entrepreneurship recognized by anthropologists in the 1960s as they began to unpack the notion of "tribe" (see Colson, 1968; Fried, 1968; and Moerman, 1968).[6] It may just be that what we witness is less stark, and more of a contrast between elite cosmopolitanism and banal or mundane cosmopolitanism (without intending these to be read as derogatory terms).

The production of TIPM discourse can be both attractive and powerful, in granting legitimacy to local leaders, and perhaps in vetting their legitimacy as indigenous as well:

> Latecomer indigenous peoples who seek to co-ordinate with the TIPM ... adopt the terms of TIPM discourse not only because it is attractive (dramatically dignifying long-despised "Indian" identities) but also because it constitutes the terms of admission to an international network of support and resources. In other words, to gain the international benefits of "being indigenous," a group must now fit a TIPM-inspired model of "being indigenous"—or face an extra burden of persuasion. (Tilley, 2002, p. 531)

The TIPM also sees the predominance of North American indigenous representations of indigeneity: "The incorporation of North American [Indian] religious imagery into indigenous emblematic art and ceremonies ... reflects a strategic sharing that has emerged from this transnational-identity project" (Tilley, 2002, p. 546). Given that the UN has been one of the primary loci for indigenous transnational activism, and given the proximity of Canadian and American indigenous nations to the UN in New York, plus the presence of many more financially well-endowed indigenous governments in North America that can afford travel and host hemispheric conferences of their own, it is not surprising to see North American narratives, symbols, and concerns dominating the TIPM.

The TIPM has made its influence felt at the local level in the Caribbean, especially among some of the more prominent actors with whom I collaborated, such as Ricardo Bharath, the head of the Santa Rosa Carib Community in Arima, Trinidad. To begin with, Ricardo has been the chair of a revitalized Caribbean Organization of Indigenous Peoples (COIP) since it gained new life in 2006, after being largely dormant for almost a decade. In its first incarnation, when it came into being in 1988, thanks in part to the activism and support of the Federation of Saskatchewan Indian Nations—which later funded Caribbean indigenous students to study in Regina at what was then called the

Saskatchewan Indian Federated College (now First Nations University) in 1992—COIP would become integrated into the now largely defunct World Council of Indigenous Peoples (WCIP), first established in 1975 by Chief George Manuel of British Columbia (see Palacio, 1989, 1992). COIP itself inspired the formation of new affiliated organizations in at least two other parts of the Caribbean: St. Vincent and Guyana. Desrey Fox, a Guyanese indigenous scholar and activist, attested to the fact that the Guyanese Organization of Indigenous Peoples (GOIP) emerged as a result of the formation of new associations such as COIP (1996, p. 88). Similarly, the Council for the Development of the Carib Community (CDCC) emerged in St. Vincent as a direct result of the formation of COIP, which itself came into being from a founding conference held in St. Vincent in August of 1987 (Roberts, 1996).

Figure 2.1: Standing, sixth from the left, is Ricardo Bharath (Carib, Trinidad); standing, ninth from the left, is Ovide Mercredi, Grand Chief of Canada's Assembly of First Nations; sitting, third from the left, is Suzan Campo (Carib, Trinidad).

This is the network of associations, presented in the brief genealogy above, which Ricardo has inherited as part of his practice, forming his horizons as first a local and now a regional indigenous activist. Beyond the Caribbean, Canadian First Nations have also exercised an influence (and this has been detailed already in Forte, 2005). By 1995, Ricardo and others in Trinidad's organized Carib Community began to publicly state that the proper way to refer to them was as "First Nations," saying that this was "the correct international designation, endorsed by the United Nations" ("Carib Community," 1995). The adoption of the "First Nations" designation is a result of this new transnational networking of indigenous peoples.

For the Carib Community of Trinidad, these transnational indigenous connections have been repeatedly renewed since they were invited by Ovide Mercredi, Grand Chief of the Assembly of First Nations, to attend a hemispheric indigenous gathering in Ottawa in 1991, proudly memorialized in the photograph above from one of the photo albums held at the Carib Centre, signed by Mercredi to one of Trinidad's Carib participants, "best friends in a common struggle." Since then, Trinidad's Caribs have also formalized ties with the Assembly of Manitoba Chiefs, with a large delegation led by Grand Chief Rod Bushie visiting them in Arima in 1999 (see Forte, 2005).

As if to underscore the "peoples of the sea" narrative, one of the more momentous, headline-grabbing events in the regionalized resurgence of indigenous Caribbean identification came in the form of the two sailings of the Gli-Gli Carib Canoe. The project was conceived in 1994 by Aragorn Dick-Read, a Euro-Caribbean artist based in Tortola, and Jacob Frederick, a Carib artist and activist in Dominica. The idea was to symbolically relink indigenous communities throughout the Caribbean by using the same seafaring means emblematic of the ancestors of the now isolated Caribs. The voyage, which began on May 13, 1997, started from Dominica and proceeded south, stopping at most of the major islands, including Trinidad, on its way to Venezuela's Orinoco River Delta and then via river into Guyana (a second voyage, proceeding north from Dominica, was undertaken in 2007). The project would show how inter-island communication by sea was undertaken in the past, in precolonial and early colonial times. Hillary Frederick, then Chief of the Dominica Carib Territory, remarked at the 1997 launch of the canoe that its voyage would be the first in 500 years. The canoe itself was 35 feet long and felled from a single tree. A documentary was also filmed by Eugene Jarecki and aired in 1999 and 2000 on PBS in the United States and the BBC ("Gli-Gli," 2008).

Throughout the notes and reports produced during the voyage, and in some cases reproduced in the narration of the film, there is a constant dynamic relationship between strangeness and familiarity, between roots and distance, between similarity and difference. In the film the leader of the Dominican Carib crew, Jacob Frederick, said of his encounter with Trinidad's Caribs: "We are meeting our own flesh and blood ... meeting lost family ... this trip shows that blood is thicker than water ... blood is calling." When I met Jacob Frederick in Dominica in 1998 he told me that the Trinidadian Carib descendants he met impressed him, as "they are just like us." The same theme of similarity is voiced when the crew arrived in Guyana: "We meet as

Caribs ... to share our one-ness." Even so, those who listen carefully will hear their Guyanese indigenous hosts remarking, with some trepidation, that they initially feared the arrival of these "Black Caribs" because they thought "they had come to eat us." It was an astounding moment that seemed to produce a look of embarrassment on Frederick's face. Here were the descendants of their original Amazonian ancestors distancing themselves, by resorting to colonial ideas of race and colonial allegations of cannibalism. Throughout the voyage, the Gli-Gli crew note the variety, and difference, of the local traditions that are presented as "Carib," and register their unfamiliarity with some of these traditions, and the absence of those with which they were familiar back in Dominica (see Dick-Read, 1997).

Another personage in this story of indigenous transnationalism is Catherine Ramirez, a Trinidad Carib from the tiny mountain village of El Tucuche, resident of Miami Beach for the past 40 years, who announces herself as Trinidad and Tobago's Carib Queen of Miami. Catherine has plugged into a broad indigenous discourse, beyond the questions of rights and struggles for territory, attending world prayer days for peace, participating in powwow festivals, attaching herself to Seminole Indians, and speaking a generic language that I call "American indigenese": she interjects with "Aho!" in public ceremonies in Trinidad, and when I asked her from what language that came, after a moment of apprehension as to the motivations behind my question, she answered, "It's an indigenous word that all indigenous peoples understand." She will tell me on the telephone, "Tomorrow I am leading an important traditional, indigenous spiritual ceremony on sacred spiritual grounds, where there will be Navajo, Seminole, Oneida." Also active on the powwow circuit, an e-mail correspondent of mine, a Trinidadian self-identifying as Carib, resident in Toronto and married to a Mohawk, wrote in late 2006: "A few days ago I was ask to attend the largest powwow in North America at the Sky Dome in Toronto ... I would dance in my Mohawk regalia. But I have been wondering about my Carib regalia. What would that look like? The headdress? The colors? The feathers? What pattern? I wear red, black, white, and green. But I believe purple and yellow may be included." The intended message underlying the brief mention of the activities of these last two persons concerns the engagement of Caribbean indigenous persons, resident in the diaspora, who grow attached to indigenous movements and rituals that pertain to another people of another region—a bit different from Guanaguanare's story, as to my knowledge she has forged no "substitute" or adoptive connections with indigenous communities in her new home away from Trinidad.

What we see in Catherine Ramirez's case is an expansion of one's horizons, a departure from one's roots, travel within another circuit, but symbolically reunited with her roots through the internationalized meanings of the label "indigenous" itself, and the connections that have expanded outward from North America. Even Ricardo Bharath participated in a large international powwow, in 2005, that takes place annually at Toronto's Sky Dome. Ostensibly, one could assume that there is nothing to connect these diverse peoples culturally, coming from different territories, with their own unique histories and ancestral languages, and yet there they are, blending into a kaleidoscope of indigenous colors, sharing and exchanging. That is not localist indigeneity, nor is it a cosmopolitanism that is divorced from cultural roots, but something between the two. As this kind of phenomenon becomes increasingly common worldwide, we need to appreciate the fact that being indigenous in today's world is a translocal process with translocal content.

The Traveling Worlds of Eco-Tourism and Shamanic Conferences: The World at Home in the Indigene

How does travel relate to cosmopolitanism? Anthropologist Ulf Hannerz, a recognized specialist in areas of travel and global cultural flows, states that "the arena of cosmopolitan engagement is not always in itself necessarily transnational" and that "Not all sheer physical mobility automatically entails cosmopolitanism" (2007, pp. 71, 74). However, he adds, "when a great many people are on the move for one reason or another, cosmopolitanism is likely to grow, even if, for some, it is a reluctant cosmopolitanism" (Hannerz, 2004, p. 77). This is the essence of cosmopolitan patriotism: "the cosmopolitan patriot can entertain the possibility of a world in which everyone is a rooted cosmopolitan, attached to a home of one's own, with its own cultural particularities, but taking pleasure from the presence of other, different places that are home to other, different people" (Appiah, 1997, p. 618).

In Trinidad's Carib Community, the leading shaman is a man by the name of Cristo Adonis, and he is a very close friend. Cristo is also a singer, and once headed a band called "Los Niños del Mundo," the children of the world, whose logo was the globe itself. He also took an Amerindian middle name of some significance here—Atékosang, the traveler. The name was given to him by a Taíno visitor in 1997 because he felt that Cristo would soon travel far and wide, and would delight in it. And he was right. Cristo, from the small mountain village of Brasso Seco, had never traveled outside of Trinidad before 2000. As that year arrived, he found himself traveling to New York, Toronto, St. Kitts, Suriname, India, California, and Texas, all in the span of a few short years. Recently, a group of self-described rabbis and imams for peace, based in Jerusalem, invited him to Israel to help conduct inter-religious peace functions.

Travel also comes to Cristo, as he earns a living in part from leading tours of the rain forest for which he is acquiring some international repute. As just one example, in a lengthy 2004 article in *Condé Nast Traveler*, one of the passages about Cristo said the following:

> This is adventure, all right—the whole journey has been. Yet somehow the moment that most stays with me is the one up in the forest with Cristo. There I glimpsed, however briefly, something more—an ancestral essence of what the Caribbean was before reggae clubs, before resorts and adventure tourism, before pirates and conquistadors and slaves: Cristo, arms uplifted, singing to the rain. (Isaacson, 2004, n.p.)

Travel, and the New Age, also comes to Cristo by way of Trinidadians who practice New Age shamanism, some of who lived and practiced with the Sun Bear Tribe in North America.

In 2004 Cristo attended a gathering of shamans from diverse cultures, including those that some might call New Age, at a gathering in Big Bear, California. In 2006, a self-described "world council of elders of the ancient traditions and cultures" in India invited him to attend what was titled an "International Conference and Gathering of the Elders," which was organized by a body calling itself the International Center for Cultural Studies, headed by Babu Ram Gupta in Bensalem, Pennsylvania. The conference theme was "we are all related," and the motto was "children of the mother earth unite." Two hundred and thirty-five people from 37 different countries and 57 different tribes attended, from all continents.

I am not certain whether Cristo traveled as a cosmopolitan indigene, or as an indigenous cosmopolitan, but I think it is more the latter case. Let me illustrate with a simple phone conversation Cristo and I had, when he called me in my office at Concordia University in April of 2006 and told me of his trip to Jaipur and Pushkar in India. Cristo and I both share a great love for East Indian food. I like Trinidad's East Indian food, but I like even more the food I have had in what I call "Indian-Indian" restaurants and homes outside of Trinidad. I suspected he would have been seduced and sedated by the lovely diversity of Indian cuisine in India. What did he say? "I hated the food there ... real sick boy, for days and days, thank god I brought a suitcase full of cassava bread with me because that's all I ate for two weeks, and I was to have shared it among conference delegates, too bad." A self-proclaimed lover of Indian food, I also knew that Cristo was a quiet enthusiast of Indian culture, able to recite entire prayers in very fluid Hindi, attending Hindu prayers and ceremonies, having gone to a Hindu primary school, having had Hindu friends, kin, girlfriends ... it just did not seem like this was the Cristo I knew who was talking. I asked him, "What do you mean? Anyone who likes Indian food knows that the best place to have it is in India, such variety, done the way it should be done ... I would have thought that it would turn you off the much simpler, narrower range of Indo-Trinidadian cooking." His reply was, "Nah, it tasted awful, far too hot. And if you see poverty in India, oh boy! It was bad,

bad, bad, bad." I could only respond to him with a Trinidadian saying: "What don't kill does fatten."

A traveler, indeed one who constantly dreams about the next chance he will get to travel; someone who is quite well immersed in Trinidad's own cosmopolitan setting, and yet while he thought he would love Indian food, it's Indian food in India that he found repulsive. As cosmopolitan as he might seem in one sense, it is still the local emphasis, the local customs he is used to, that come first in his appreciation of all things in the world; he looks at the cosmos with interest, but he sees it through a native lens. He is thus what I would call an indigenous cosmopolitan.

Conclusion

Indigeneity in the Caribbean arises from processes and practices that make use of "globalized" cultural influences, that can take the "foreign" and render it indigenous, while building ongoing indigenous identification through transnational routes. Anthropologist Marshall Sahlins wrote that "most people find critical means of their own reproduction in beings and powers existing beyond their normal borders and their customary controls" (1999, p. 411). Indigenous, in the Caribbean, was always cosmopolitan, not a culture-free and place-free cosmopolitanism, but a lived and practiced one, within all of the constraints that practice presents in everyday life. Indigeneity and cosmopolitanism have not met only recently in Trinidad; in fact, the two have influenced each other for hundreds of years, and since colonialism indigenous peoples in the region have incorporated European cultural symbols, African practices and marriage partners, interacting in a multireligious milieu, becoming polyglots and developing rituals that take "the national" (that is, cultural influences from the other groups that constitute the wider society) and re-present it back to the nation (with some modifications) as "indigenous." This is what Hannerz calls a "thick," or "everyday," or "banal cosmopolitanism," rather than a thin and elite cosmopolitanism (2004, pp. 72-73). This is not a rationalist, individualist, and universalist cosmopolitanism, but rather the kind that is a "fusion of all cultures" (Friedman, 2004, p. 193).

Otherwise, I do not think that the activities and the engagements of the Caribs need to be judged by the cosmopolitan values of the liberal imagination. I see neither particularist and recalcitrant hostility to globalization by actors who, in the end, do not have feet nailed to the floorboards of localism, nor do I see a tidal wave of global currents washing away local difference, or creating some homogeneous stew of undifferentiated universality. We are not dealing in this chapter with a notion of cosmopolitanism that implies that all places are alike, but rather that similarities can be sought and built by rooted yet mobile actors—in other words, we are not dealing with sameness, but rather similarity, and not difference, but rather variation. I believe that the actors at the heart of this chapter have manifested what Hannerz defines as actual cosmopolitanism, from an anthropological perspective: "an openness toward divergent cultural experiences, a search for contrasts rather than uniformity, but not simply as a matter of appreciation a general readiness to make one's way into other cultures ... a cultivated skill in maneuvering more or less expertly with one of more cultures besides one's own" (2007, p. 70). He argues that we need to speak of cosmopolitanisms, in the plural, but warns that in doing so the concept of cosmopolitanism becomes so attenuated that it can become largely unrecognizable (Hannerz, 2004, p. 77). The one possible exception to this story is that of Guanaguanare.

In broader terms, we mostly see persons dealing with globalized possibilities (and constraints) and finding new ways of expressing indigeneity, just as their ancestors had to do in confronting early colonialism (Smith, Burke, & Ward, 2000, p. 6). The very deployment of the idea of "indigenous" is a way of marking difference, of reproducing diversity in the world-system, while at the same time diminishing difference among the peoples united under the idea that they are indigenous (see Muehlebach, 2001, p. 416). What we end up with is a world of increasingly cosmopolitan selves and increasingly cosmopolitan others, sharing some of the same instruments and organizations of cosmopolitan practice. In terms of cosmopolitan indigeneity, specifically, we have *cosmopolitan indigenes*, embedded in internationalized discourses of indigenous rights and actively participating in transnational networks (think of Ricardo in this chapter), as well as *indigenous cosmopolitans*, locals who make provincial use of the means and methods of traveling culture, without developing strong affinities with nonlocal partners or discourses.

Notes

1 This section is not meant to cover the same ground as the introductory chapter of this volume. The idea was to delineate the kind of conceptual map I had before when I first set out to produce this chapter, without desiring to produce a long expose or synthesis of previous literature.

2 Since this chapter was first drafted, I have become a close online collaborator with Guanaguanare.

3 In the previous version of this chapter, presented as a paper at the symposium, "Transnational Indigeneity: Contemporary Routes of Indigenous Signification and Interaction beyond Stereotypes of the Local or the Hype of the Global," held under the auspices of the Canadian Anthropology Society (University of Toronto, May 12, 2007), I included various non-Carib and non-Trinidadian actors, with greater space devoted to discussion of Caribbean indigenous participation in various fora of the United Nations. For the sake of brevity, and enhanced focus, I chose to reduce the actors in the story

presented here to a smaller group, all of who are Trinidadian, or with whom I have interacted personally.

4 The economy of Trinidad and Tobago is primarily industrial and export-oriented, with a heavy focus on petroleum extracting, petro-chemical processing, and light manufacturing, and recent attempts to diversify into tourism. The majority of the population is urban. The two main political parties in Trinidad are divided along lines of ethnicity, with the currently ruling People's National Movement tending to represent urban Afro-Trinidadians more, while the opposing United National Congress tends to be favored by Trinidadians of East Indian descent, many of them in rural settings or situated in small towns with very close proximity to agricultural areas. The country as a whole has a high rate of literacy, with extensive media saturation in the form of newspapers, television, radio, and increasingly the Internet as well.

5 This collection was designed to address the main themes of indigeneities versus cosmopolitanisms, as laid out by the organizers of the 2007 conference of the Canadian Anthropology Society: "The 'indigenous' and the 'cosmopolitan' seem to exist as oppositional formations in the imaginary field demarcated by the local and the global. While the former seems rooted, timeless, and traditional; the latter appears mobile, contemporary, and (post)modern. As recent work by anthropologists has shown, both of these characterizations are quite deceptive. 'Indigeneity' is a deeply current issue, which, over the past decade, has relentlessly forced itself onto social, political, and academic agendas across the planet. While the question of who is and who is not 'indigenous' was never innocent, it is becoming increasingly crucial in today's global and globalizing world. At the same time, the genealogy of the 'cosmopolitan' has been moved back in time. It now appears as a quasi-primordial reference point for a social and political vision beyond the nation-state and empire. Together, the 'indigenous' and the 'cosmopolitan' signify the tensions animating contemporary anthropology. As the discipline negotiates its long-standing commitment to local processes in a rapidly transnational world, both the 'indigenous' and the 'cosmopolitan' have emerged as crucial figures for analysis and debate."

6 Elizabeth Colson put this in very direct terms, saying that tribes "are largely the conscious creations of intellectuals and other active leaders who have had the greatest opportunity to participate in the larger political and social world.... It is the political leaders' need for loyal followings rather than any ethnic group's needs for self-expression that lies behind the mobilization of tribes and the manifestation of tribalism in contemporary Africa" (1968, pp. 203, 205).

References

Appadurai, A. (1997). Fieldwork in the Era of Globalization. *Anthropology and Humanism*, 22(1), 115-118.

———. (1999). Globalization and the Research Imagination. *International Social Science Journal*, 160, 229-238.

Appiah, K. A. (1997). Cosmopolitan Patriots. *Critical Inquiry*, 23(3), 617-639.

Baugh, E. (2006). Literary Theory and the Caribbean: Theory, Belief and Desire, or Designing Theory. *Shibboleths: Journal of Comparative Theory*, 1(1), 56-63. Retrieved February 26, 2008, from http://www.shibboleths.net/1/1/Baugh,Edward.pdf.

Benítez-Rojo, A. (1996). *The Repeating Island: The Caribbean and the Postmodern Perspective*. (James

E. Maraniss, Trans.) (2nd ed.). Durham, NC: Duke University Press.

Boomert, A. (1982). Our Amerindian Heritage. *Trinidad Naturalist*, 4(4), 26-38, 60.

The Carib Community of Arima. (1995, August 13) *Sunday Express* (Arimafest Supplement), p. 5.

Colson, E. (1968). Contemporary Tribes and the Development of Nationalism. In June Helm (Ed.), *Essays on the Problem of Tribe* (pp. 201-208). Seattle: American Ethnological Society, University of Washington Press.

Dash, J. M. (2006). Farming Bones and Writing Rocks: Rethinking a Caribbean Poetics of (Dis) location. *Shibboleths: Journal of Comparative Theory*, 1(1), 64-71. Retrieved February 26, 2008, from http://www.shibboleths.net/1/1/Dash,Michael.pdf.

Dick-Read, A. (1997). Summary report of the research carried out on the Gli-Gli Carib Canoe Project's recent expedition from Dominica to Guyana. Retrieved June 3, 2008, from http://www.aragornsstudio.com/SUMMARY%20REPORT.doc.

Forte, M. C. (2005). *Ruins of Absence, Presence of Caribs: (Post) colonial Representations of Aboriginality in Trinidad and Tobago*. Gainesville: University Press of Florida.

———. (2006). *Indigenous Resurgence in the Contemporary Caribbean: Amerindian Survival and Revival*. New York: Peter Lang.

Fox, D. (1996). Continuity and Change among the Amerindians of Guyana. In Rhoda Reddock (Ed.), *Ethnic Minorities in Caribbean Society* (pp. 9-105). St. Augustine, Trinidad: ISER, University of the West Indies.

Fried, M. (1968). On the Concepts of 'Tribe' and 'Tribal Society'. In June Helm (Ed.), *Essays on the Problem of Tribe* (pp. 3-20). Seattle: American Ethnological Society, University of Washington Press.

Friedman, J. (2004). Globalization. In David Nugent & Joan Vincent (Eds.), *A Companion to the Anthropology of Politics* (pp. 179-197). Oxford: Blackwell Publishing.

Geertz, C. (1996). Afterword. In Steven Feld & Keith Basso (Eds.), *Senses of Place* (pp. 259-262). Santa Fe, NM: School of American Research Press.

Gli-Gli Home Page. (2008). Retrieved June 3, 2008, from http://www.avirtualdominica.com/gligli/index.html.

Glissant, E. (1989). *Caribbean Discourse: Selected Essays* (J. Michael Dash, Trans.). Charlottesville: University of Virginia Press.

Guanaguanare. (2008a). Catáhua People. Retrieved June 8, 2008, from http://guanaguanaresingsat.blogspot.com/2006/11/cathua-people.html.

———. (2008b). Universal Aboriginality. Retrieved June 8, 2008, from http://guanaguanaresingsat.blogspot.com/2006/11/thirty-pieces-of-silver-1.html.

Hannerz, U. (1992). *Cultural Complexity: Studies in the Social Organization of Meaning*. New York: Columbia University Press.

———. (2004). Cosmopolitanism. In David Nugent & Joan Vincent (Eds.), *A Companion to the Anthropology of Politics* (pp. 69-85). Oxford: Blackwell.

Isaacson, R. (2004). Keep It Moving. *Condé Nast Traveler*, April. Retrieved May 1, 2007, from http://www.concierge.com/cntraveler/articles/detail?articleId=5815.

Khan, A. (2001). Journey to the Center of the Earth: The Caribbean as Master Symbol. *Cultural Anthropology*, 16(3), 271-302.

Moerman, M. (1968). Being Lue: Uses and Abuses of Ethnic Identification. In June Helm (Ed.), *Essays on the Problem of Tribe* (pp. 153-169). Seattle: American Ethnological Society, University of Washington Press.

Muehlebach, A. (2001). 'Making Place' at the United Nations: Indigenous Cultural Politics at the UN Working Group on Indigenous Populations. *Cultural Anthropology*, 16(3), 415-448.

Munasinghe, V. (2002). Nationalism in Hybrid Spaces: The Production of Impurity out of Purity. *American Ethnologist*, 29(3), 663-692.

Munasinghe, V. (2006). Theorizing World Culture Through the New World: East Indians and Creolization. *American Ethnologist*, 33(4), 588-592.

Ortiz, F. (1995). *Cuban Counterpoint: Tobacco and Sugar*. (Harriet de Onís, Trans.). Durham, NC: Duke University Press.

Palacio, J. O. (1989). Caribbean Indigenous Peoples' Journey Toward Self-discovery. *Cultural Survival Quarterly*, 13(3), 49-51.

——. (1992). The Sojourn Toward Self-discovery Among Caribbean Indigenous Peoples. *Caribbean Quarterly*, 38(2-3), 55-72.

Priam, M. (2005). La créolisation du monde: Présentation du domaine. Peuples & Monde, August 16. Retrieved March 11, 2008, from http://www.peuplesmonde.com/article.php3?id_article=308.

Rapport, N., & R. Stade. (2007). A Cosmopolitan Turn—or Return? *Social Anthropology*, 15(2), 223-235.

Roberts, S. L. (1996). The Integration of the Caribs into the Vincentian Society. Bachelor's thesis, University of the West Indies, St. Augustine, Trinidad.

Rodney, W. (1973). *How Europe Underdeveloped Africa*. London and Dar-Es-Salaam: Bogle-L'Ouverture Publications and Tanzania Publishing House.

Sahlins, M. (1999). Two or Three Things that I Know About Culture. *Journal of the Royal Anthropological Institute*, 5(3), 399-421.

Smith, C., H. Burke, & G. K. Ward. (2000). Globalization and Indigenous Peoples: Threat or Empowerment? In Claire Smith & Graeme K. Ward (Eds.), *Indigenous Cultures in an Interconnected World* (pp. 1-26). St. Leonards, Australia: Allen & Unwin.

Smith, M. G. (1965). *The Plural Society in the British West Indies*. Berkeley: University of California Press.

Tilley, V. Q. (2002). New Help or New Hegemony? The Transnational Indigenous Peoples' Movement and 'Being Indian'. *Journal of Latin American Studies*, 34(3), 525-554.

Walcott, D. (1992). The Antilles: Fragment of Epic Memory. Nobel Lecture, December 7. Retrieved March 21, 2008, from http://nobelprize.org/nobel_prizes/literature/laureates/1992/walcott-lecture.html.

Williams, E. E. (1970). *From Columbus to Castro: The History of the Caribbean, 1492-1969*. London: Andre Deutsch.

♦ CHAPTER THREE ♦

Aboriginal Hip Hoppers: Representin' Aboriginality in Cosmopolitan Worlds

Craig Proulx

Sampling the City and the Rez: Past and Present

The non-Aboriginal perception that Aboriginal people become somehow less authentically Aboriginal when they move from reserves to cities and beyond, or when ways of being in the world change on reserves, continues to limit the opening up of new spaces for, and acceptance of, changing forms of expressing and living aboriginality (Proulx, 2006; Peters, 2004, 1996; Lobo, 2001). The lack of understanding of historical Aboriginal urban contexts and intertribal integration of past Aboriginal peoples contributes to this problem (Forbes, 2001; Quinn, 1993). In addition, the lack of comprehension of current movements of Aboriginal peoples back and forth from reserves to cities and internationally for resource exploitation, health care, family visits, and simply excitement, among other reasons, continues to circumscribe how Aboriginality is understood (Proulx, 2006; Darnell, 2006; Buddle, 2005, p. 27; Peters, 2004, p. 5; Norris and Clatworthy, 2003; King, 2003). So does the predominant reserve-centric foci of non-Aboriginal policy makers (Podlasley, 2002). Lastly, Aboriginal peoples are still subject to the pizza test in determining whether they are authentically Aboriginal. For example, any modern practice such as eating pizza rather than, say caribou, disqualifies the practitioner from being authentically Aboriginal. See (McEachern, 1991) for one of the more egregious applications of the pizza test. In the context of this chapter the argument that, because Aboriginal peoples have appropriated a Black American musical form, they are somehow less authentically Aboriginal or, at the very least, nontraditional, is contested. This argument ignores widespread traditional and continuing Aboriginal practices of oral performance and how these traditions have incorporated, and continue to incorporate, external influences without becoming inauthentic. This chapter focuses on how Aboriginal hip hoppers are cosmopolitan, remain authentically Aboriginal despite involving themselves in a musical form that is not traditionally Aboriginal, and how they perform their aboriginality to themselves and others.

In this chapter I begin with some definitional clarification and follow by outlining a particular view on cosmopolitanism. I then discuss the historical urbanism and cosmopolitanism of Aboriginal peoples and a theory/outlook which, if adopted, could allow policy makers to move away from a reserve-centric focus. These ideas ground the rest of the chapter as I focus on how Aboriginal hip hoppers in cities, reserves, and those flowing back and forth, are involved in the creation of alternatively modern rooted cosmopolitanisms. An alternative modernity is "the social and discursive space in which the relationship between modernity and tradition is configured," often involving "a process of reconstructing tradition through new forms of public culture" (Knauft, 2002, pp. 25, 29). Issues surrounding the legitimacy of hip hop as an Aboriginal practice, the performance of traditions and authenticity, new forms of pedagogy, and the politics of Aboriginality will be investigated. I also discuss how Aboriginal hip hop through the Internet "reaches in" to internal Aboriginal publics as well as "reaches out" to external others (Landzelius, 2006, p. 5), both Aboriginal and non-Aboriginal, to communicate and educate about processes of colonialism, empowerment, and identification. In order to do this I analyze journalistic interviews with Aboriginal hip hoppers, an interview I conducted with Rex Smallboy of the Cree hip hop crew War Party, a sample of Aboriginal hip hop videos posted on YouTube, and the growing academic literature on hip hop around the world.

Definitional Issues

Controversy continues to rage on the Internet and beyond over whether there is a difference between hip hop and rap. Many see hip hop as a wider "culture" that has four elements—MCing, DJing, graffiti, and rapping (all defined below), while rap is seen more narrowly as poetry to music emphasizing spoken rhymes over heavily rhythmic backing tracks. Hip hop is praised for its concern with social justice, empowerment, and respect for difference while some forms of rap are condemned as misogynistic, violent, capitalist, and so on. Both sides condemn each other for selling out to corporate interests (Answerbag, 2007). I prefer the term *hip hop* because of its wider approach to social and political concerns. However, I also recognize that rap can capture these concerns without necessarily falling into the above traps.

Therefore, I use both terms, hip hop and rap, and their permutations, to refer to musicians, dancers, graffiti writers, and DJs who are involved in social projects of renewal, reclamation, empowerment, and various resistances to powerful socioeconomic forces across many contexts, spaces, and places.

It is also useful to note some of the key terms used to describe its practitioners and practices. Taking much of their style from Jamaican "toasting," the early rappers were comparable to "masters of ceremonies" (MCs) rather than musicians or singers. The term MC is still used in reference to artists who prefer the party-oriented music of the 1980s over contemporary styles (Center for Black Music Research, 2007). Breaking is a form of urban dance involving styles such as rocking, popping, and b-boying, usually performed to funk. It is also called break dancing (Answers.com, 2007). Freestylin' is to improvise vocally. This intuitive process is both a skill and an art form. While freestyling is popular among MC's, it appears in many other artistic circles and forms of expression (Africa Resource, 2007). "A beatboxer is a human drum machine who creates a beat for an emcee to deliver their rap over and for a breakdancer to dance to" (Stavrias, 2005, p. 45). When DJs take snippets from various songs or prerecorded sounds and the like to create a new soundtrack to rap over or breakdance to, they are sampling. To represent means to "remain true to one's community and to the ideals of the hip hop culture one belongs to" (Stavrias, 2005, p. 46). Last, flowing is an "attitude, a value judgment on style and a term of inclusion and exclusion in hip hop culture" and flow is defined by the individual rapper's knowledge of the local (Stavrias, 2005, p. 46).

Rooted Cosmopolitans

Cosmopolitanism has been defined in many different ways within and across disciplinary boundaries. It has been defined as a cognitive "state of mind" wherein a person's "allegiance is to the worldwide community of human beings" (Tarrow, 2005, p. 41). Since individual identities are not merely matters of individual choice and are largely produced in social relations with others, "it is through peoples' relations to significant others that cosmopolitan attitudes are shaped" (Tarrow, 2005, pp. 41-42). Embedded in some cosmopolitan definitions is the idea that being cosmopolitan necessarily demands that individuals are detached from their locality, their roots. Appiah (1997) pointed out that that detachment or rootlessness is not a necessary condition of being cosmopolitan. He maintained that one could still be patriotic about one's own home "with its own cultural particularities, but taking pleasure from the presence of the other, different places that are home to the other, different people" (Appiah, 1997, p. 616). Beck (2002, p. 19) points out that "cosmopolitanism means *rooted* cosmopolitanism, having 'roots' and 'wings' at the same time. ... There is no cosmopolitanism without localism." Tarrow, building on the ideas of rootedness, said:

> What is "rooted" in this conception is that, as cosmopolitans move physically and cognitively outside their origins, they continue to be linked to place, to the social networks that inhabit that space, and to the resources, experiences, and opportunities that place provides them with. (Tarrow, 2005, p. 42)

Podlasley (2002) might have framed this in terms of transnational migration as outlined below. However, as Roudometof (2005) makes clear: there is no reason to restrict cosmopolitanism to transnational peoples who experience separation between homeland and the place where they live.

I think that many Aboriginal peoples, moving back and forth from reserves and cities are rooted in the manner described above. I am not saying, however, that roots and identities based upon them must always be essentialized and judged through authenticity discourses. Hebdige (1987 in Malkki, 1992, p. 37) is clear that roots change:

> I have tried to show the roots themselves are in a state of constant flux and change. The roots don't stay in one place. They change shape. They change color. And they grow. There is no such thing as a pure point of origin ... but that does not mean there isn't a history.

The cultural particularities and networks of relations within reserves and cities root Aboriginal individuals en route, to a myriad of places, living with and relating, to the difference of Aboriginal and non-Aboriginal Others. Meaning, then, is generated relationally as local actors with specific histories and social and political circumstances interact with "translocal and mass-mediated commodities, images and processes" (Urla, 2001, p. 172). I am interested in how roots and routes are creatively reconfigured in emerging social, oppositional, and self-determinative projects of Aboriginal hip hoppers.

Cosmopolitanism in North and South America's Past

The sheer numbers of First Nations and tribes indicate that the Americas also had their share of premodern cosmopolitans (Forbes, 2001; Quinn, 1993). Forbes (2001), using archaeological and historical records, shows that Aboriginal peoples in North and South America lived urban as well as nonurban lives. Intertribal integration of Aboriginal peoples was common with different Aboriginal peoples living apart from their original communities and within different Aboriginal communities (Quinn, 1993). Aboriginal towns and cities existed in the premodern era that had enclaves of different Aboriginal peoples and nations encapsulated by the dominant Aboriginal group or nation who created these cities (Forbes, 2001; Tanner, 1987, 1989).

Many Aboriginal groups voluntarily or involuntarily merged yet retained their premerger identities within these new communities (Quinn, 1993). Additionally, many different Aboriginal nations had trading relations across wide geographical spaces (Quinn, 1993). Adoptions, mixed marriages, and bilingual and trilingual speakers across what became known as the Americas further indicate that Indigenous peoples were not "isolated, discrete, homogenous bodies" but crossed many borders and lived extensively among different indigenous Others (Quinn, 1993, p. 38). Hence, it is not surprising that many indigenous peoples in North and South America have always been cosmopolitan to one degree or another at various historical junctures. I now summarize an argument that applies transnationalist theory to Aboriginal peoples in cities, reserve/urban, and urban/reserve flows.

A Transnational as Opposed to a Reserve-centric Approach

Podlasley (2002), a member of the Pacific Northwest N'laka'pmx First Nation, decried policy makers' unwillingness "to address what it truly means to be aboriginal in a modern and increasingly mobile liberal democratic society" (p. 1). Specifically, he was addressing government's "reserve-centric perspective" and how policy makers remained "hobbled by their past notions of Aboriginality as an immobile and geographically remote concept." Podlasley pointed out the inattention, at that time, paid to Aboriginal experiences in cities and how they were linked to reserves. His interest was in how informal Aboriginal networks combining both urban and reserve elements outside of government were linked up and spreading through Canada (p. 5). The diversity of Aboriginal cultures and their interactions in cities resembled global expatriate communities that were not "astray portions" of their home communities but were "increasingly important extensions of their home-land based culture" (p. 6). Podlasley thought that urban Aboriginal communities were beginning to "exhibit similar education, knowledge, and capital flows as their transnational counterparts" because of their "multiple pan First Nations media, business organizations, and cultural events" (p. 7). In the end, he recommended that we "shift our societal lens [from] the on-off reserve situation to an international-level perspective of urban expatriate communities," thereby "reinterpreting aboriginality" (p. 8). I maintain that Podlasley's ideas productively combine with rooted cosmopolitanism theory enabling us to view Aboriginal cultural creativity, space, place, and movements within them through a lens undistorted by negative, largely non-Aboriginal, judgments based on cultural appropriation, invention of tradition, and authenticity discourses.

Sampling the City and the Rez: Aboriginal Hip Hoppers

Aboriginal hip hoppers from Canada, Shawn Desjarlais, Manik, and OS 12, and MC Wire from Australia illustrate rooted cosmopolitanism across multiple cross-cutting contexts. In the analysis that follows I intersperse relevant ideas based upon my interview with Rex Smallboy.

> Traditionally, indigenous peoples utilized oratory teachings, visual and performance arts to educate our young about our way of life. ... I feel that it is imperative that we begin to revitalize our traditional educational practices. ... I have found that hip-hop is a very powerful medium for affecting this kind of change. (DeJarlais, 2003, p. 1)

> From coast to coast, the majority of young people listen to hip hop, so we thought we would harness it. Hopefully, we can create awareness of the situation of our people through hip hop and the spoken word. Tribal Wizdom is about looking at issues to see why things are the way they are and how we can start helping our people. (Efron, 2001, p. 3)

> It's not just that it's Native hip hop but it's Native hip hop with the message of revolution and change. It's not just a game for us; it's not a gimmick. We participate, we take over government offices, we block off roads, we fight cops to protect the land. And as soon as there's a band or a group of Native people that needs support, we will always be there. (Efron, 2001, p. 2)

> I'm able to stay there [the rez] and be in the city [and] at the same time be a Native person, live our family values the way we live, ... I have all that and still be close to the city where I can do this rap thing. It's torn between two worlds, being Native and being a rapper. (Efron, 2001, p. 5)

The two Australian quotes are from MC Wire a Gumbaynggirr descendant from New South Wales.

> This is my lyrical healin'; I can't go and get scared anymore and I can't become a traditional man. I'm a modern-day black fella, this is still dreamtime for me. Hip hop is the new clapsticks; hip hop is the new corroboree. (NotaRpietro-Clarken, 2007, p. 2)

> Because I don't have a physical contact to traditional practices, my music helps me to maintain a sort of twisted dreaming. (Lobley, 2006, p. 2)

These quotes indicate that Aboriginal hip hop is not merely all "surface" and an "appropriation of externalized, commercial styles," nor is it only about commodity consumption (Holland, 2004, p. 2). Nor is it merely homage to the misogynism, blatant consumerism, and violence characteristic of some USA gansta rap. Rex Smallboy points out that "peoples are looking for something more than the over-saturated commercial product the industry shits out to the masses." Aboriginal hip hop has a "style that is distinct and significant to Australian [and Canadian] indigenous culture, politics, and resistance" (NotaRpietro-Clarken, 2007, p. 1). Chamberlain (2001) has shown how immigrant and disenfranchised non-Aboriginal rappers from various regions across Canada have created distinctive rap styles addressing the politics of local and regional concern. When I asked Smallboy why Aboriginal hip hop videos mix traditional images with modern ones like jingle dancers with break dancers he replied, "We always get this *we are trying to act black thing* [my emphasis added]. So it is to show we are trying to be ourselves." This indicates how Aboriginal hip hoppers create a distinctive style beyond the appropriation of externalized, commercial styles as Holland (2004) notes. Smallboy also points to how Aboriginal hip hop is "a way to reach out to people" to fight "the low morale, lack of faith, [and the] low sense of pride as individuals and as a nation" resulting from the continuing imposition of colonial projects upon Aboriginal peoples. He is also critical of and puzzled by native rappers who don't want to be seen as native or write about native issues:

> Yeah I get a lot of flak from other NATIVES [Smallboy's capitalization] in the rap scene who don't want to be looked at as a native rapper. And being proud to be native is something we have stood for. They don't think we should be writing about who we are and where we come from. It confuses me ... is it a form of self-hate? I don't know. (Smallboy personal communication, August 23, 2007)

Mitchell (2006) says that the oral traditions of Aboriginal culture have paved the way for a vibrant hip hop scene and hip hop, in turn, also helps to preserve indigenous languages in Australia. For example, the rapper Munki Mark raps in his grandmother's language Jardwadjali, the language of the Grampians in western Victoria and in Arrernte, spoken in Alice Springs (Mitchell, 2006). Munki Mark points to how hip hop is a modern means to transmit indigenous knowledge: "Aboriginal language was never a written language; it's always been an oral and visual language, stories passed down through rituals, corroborees, song, and dance. Hip hop fits in quite well with that" (Mitchell, 2006).

Hip hop transmits by combining and changing traditional performance and teaching styles through the use of unconventional global techniques such as MCing, breaking and freestylin', beatboxing and graffiti (NotaRpietro-Clarken, 2007, Stavrias, 2005). It is important to note, as Holland (2004) does, that Aboriginal youths, will by-and-large remain rooted if their roots and traditions are updated. Indeed, the "internal logic of sampling, representin', and flow" (Stavrias, 2005, p. 46) common to all hip hop lends itself to new forms of performance and senses of belonging. It lends itself to celebrations "of roots in place, neighborhood, home, family, and nation" (Mitchell, 1999, p. 86 in Stavrias, 2005, p. 46). Additionally, hip hop's sense of style helps update the performance of tradition. Hip hop is the means through which traditions can be understood, re-worked, re-presented and thereby made relevant to youth accustomed to non-Aboriginal informational delivery systems. Indeed, Aboriginal rappers are not losing their traditions as a result of their involvement with a globalizing musical form. Rather, I would suggest as (Urla, 2001, p. 173) does in a Basque context, that young Aboriginal people are involved in "a dynamic conversation about tradition, exploring and defining for themselves what it means to be [pan-Aboriginal or Cree for example] in the present."

Aboriginal hip hop is, as the quotes indicate, a serious art form, a mode of political expression and a means for cultural survival and production. Hip Hop seeks to promote change, to decolonize, to bridge pedagogical gaps between elders and youth while articulating a sense of place for youth within local and regional reserve contexts, in urban and international contexts, and the flows between them all. Rex Smallboy is clear that War Party's hip hop is about the need to restore what many Aboriginal people have lost. "When we write about native issues it is to make our young people proud of who they are. Like in the chorus from *Feeling Reserved*, we need to try to restore pride." As such, hip hop offers "insights into the politics, concerns, and dreams of urban [and reserve] Aboriginal Canadian youth" (Lashua, 2006, p. 1) through understanding how these youth link with other like-minded indigenous peoples who confront racism, poverty, and political marginalization around the world and regionally and locally (NotaRpietro-Clarken, 2007; Peeters, 2002; Urla, 2001).

So how are these links achieved? Two of the quotes above indicate that Aboriginal youth organizations exist, enabling youth not only to trade information about their favorite hip hop artists and to download hip hop at sites such as redhiphop.com, but also to be politically active in an educational and militant manner. Tribal Wizdom (TW) is a Native hip hop collective that puts on regular events around Vancouver. But entertainment is not its only goal. Education on issues such as residential schools and the multisited, continuing oppression of Aboriginal peoples comes through the medium of hip hop at these presentations (Efron, 2001). TW also helps to translate indigenous oral traditions into youth-friendly contemporary forms at a time when youth tend not to have time to sit and listen to elders or grass roots leaders (Peeters, 2002). In an interview with a female rapper, Peeters (2002, p. 9) discusses how the blending of First Nation songs and drumming and hip hop functions to "maintain and develop indigenous traditions, and as a way to present the ideas and values contained in traditional songs to a young urban audience." TW also tours reserves and urban Native communities across the country doing workshops on pressing social and political problems during the day, while at night those messages are reiterated through the performances of DJs, rappers, and poets (Efron, 2001). Tribal Wizdom is also a conduit for spreading the message of an international Aboriginal organization called the Native Youth Movement (NYM) (Efron, 2001).

Founded in 1991 in Winnipeg with multiple chapters across North America and publishing an urban youth magazine called *Redwire*, the NYM is a truly rooted cosmopolitan organization (Dejarlais, 2003). The aim of the NYM is to "empower and educate youth regarding the true history of indigenous peoples, our family roots, past and present social issues, human/Aboriginal rights, and cultural activities" (Dejarlais, 2003, p. 3). The NYM "is in opposition to all colonial forms of government" and its intention is to "educate Native youth on our current situation as colonized peoples so we can work together to liberate the earth and each other" (Efron, 2001, p. 2). This philosophy leads the NYM to be involved in direct actions such as occupations of government offices, roadblocks, and occupations of traditional territories (Desjarlais, 2003). As one of the quotes above indicates, the NYM's message is being spread through hip hop. One member of the NYM says getting the message across to youth through youth forums is not always successful as few youth come to them. But people come out when the NYM puts on hip hop shows (Peeters, 2002). Hence, as quoted above, "It's not just that it's Native hip hop, but it's Native hip hop with a message of revolution and change" (Efron, 2001, p. 2).

Not all hip hoppers, however, are overtly political or advocate direct action and revolution. Ostwelve (Os12) is more concerned about identity issues surrounding Aboriginal existence in the movement between the rez and the city. He is concerned about how one remains true to traditional culture and rez family life while partaking in the modern world of urban hip hop. He recognizes how living on the reserve grounds him and allows him to stay "connected to his culture while participating in Vancouver's hip hop scene" (Efron, 2001, p. 4). Os12, therefore, raps more about "philosophy and the supernatural rather than the political struggles of Native people" (Efron, 2001, p. 4). Sampling Os12's videos on YouTube, for example *Ostwelve in Soweto* (2006), his cosmopolitan side definitely comes through as he showcases South African freestyling and beatboxing in the Global Hip Hop Summit in Soweto, South Africa. Ostwelve, therefore, demonstrates a different approach to living at home and among Others that illustrates the simultaneous roots and wings of rooted cosmopolitanism (Beck, 2002, p. 19).

As the Global Hip Hop Summit in Soweto, South Africa, indicates, the combination of hip hop and indigenous traditions, invented or otherwise, has spread throughout the world. The Australian rapper quotes by MC Wire are noteworthy because he first talks about the need for urban peoples to heal from the wrongs perpetrated on Aboriginal peoples in the past as well as from current wrongs. MC Wire talks about how difficult it is to be traditional in a modern urban context. He directs us to how hip hop can enable a pan-Aboriginal reconstitution and re-presentation of de-territorialized traditions. He directs us to how dreamtime is conceived of and lived by urban Aboriginal peoples often severed from traditional knowledges and practices. Hence, the hybrid "pick and mix" of musical forms and traditional elements in the creation of individual and culture identities, whether pan-Aboriginal or culturally specific, is characteristic of a rooted cosmopolitanism that has a global reach for indigenous peoples (Nederveen Pieterse 2001 in Holland 2004, p. 3).

Rooted Cosmopolitanism in Aboriginal Videos on YouTube

Indigenous and diasporic peoples "de-centered from dominant institutions and idioms" are utilizing information communications technologies (ICTs) to root and route themselves (Landzelius, 2006, pp. 1-2). Landzelius introduces ethnographic research on how indigenous peoples in a globalizing world link the global and the local while "articulate[ing their] alterity across spatial, temporal, and cultural divides ... within global fields of power and discourse" (2006, p. 2). In particular, the Internet is a creative context wherein indigenous peoples' sense of home and place, their political and identity projects can be performed online in multiple ways and for varied purposes for a myriad of stakeholders both indigenous and nonindigenous. Two orientations to this performance of indigenous activism are provided. The first is "in-reach" wherein on-line signifying practices and messages focus on "an internal public comprised of fellow group members" (Landzelius, 2006, p. 5). The second is "out-reach" where the above are tailored to an "external public, which may target nonindigenous peoples and/or indigenous peoples from other groups" (Landzelius, 2006, p. 5). Both of these are relevant to the preceding and following discussions, particularly as they apply to new forms of oral transmission, pedagogy, and to the decolonization of both Aboriginal and non-Aboriginal minds. Aboriginal radio, films, and television are utilized in similar fashions as Aboriginal city dwellers with opportunities to learn and/or relearn Aboriginal traditions, to embed themselves within real or virtual community relations and to participate in cultural production (Buddle 2005, pp. 23-26).

Out of a total sample of fifty-two Aboriginal hip hop and rap videos viewed between May 2007 and August 2007, I have chosen seven because I think they represent the wide variety of styles and sociopolitical projects involved in Aboriginal hip hop today. I have focused on Aboriginal hip hop from Canada due to space constraints. Five of these videos are based on hip hop songs while the final two are historical retrospectives of workshops. I begin with the videos based on songs.

The first two videos I analyze are Manik 1derful's *Commercial Drive* (2006) and Northerners with Attitude's *Don't Call Me Eskimo* (2006). Commercial Drive is about life on one of the main streets in East Vancouver. Shot in front of businesses and parks that line the Drive including the iconic Joe's Café, Commercial Drive is densely urban and cosmopolitan. Manik raps about the diversity of people (culture vultures, fake spiritual ciphers, hippy kids etc.) and how Commercial Drive is "an independent business place. I love and hate this place." He relates the inhabitant's lifeways, both legitimate and illegitimate, and how they cope with street life:

> There ain't that many guns
> That's where the hobo comes to raise up their funds
> The best weed grows there
> We've got black, red, white, and even yellow players ...
> The weed dealers is huddling
> The brown kids are thuggin ...

Although these lyrics may allow non-Aboriginals to continue to hold stereotypical views of urban Aboriginal youths as gangstas, Manik in fact provides a broader and more informed view of the Drive:

> It's an international assortment of flavours and varieties.
> Different levels of importance for these new members of society ...
> Strange cultures interactin
> The native housing is from 8th and Pender street back me ...
> Where the kids come and watch me freestyle
> By the Mafia bosses playin bocce

What this video gives us is a look at how Aboriginal peoples mix into the cosmopolitan swirl of communities within a large North American city. In the interstices of cultures, drug economies, international business, and local poverty, among others, Manik grew up, went to school at Brittania, raised a family, and picnics with them in Grandview Park, all meaningful roots of Aboriginal life along the Drive. The Commercial Drive video, then, reaches out opening up a particular view of some "brown kids" adults and their families living lives far from the rez but still identifying as Aboriginal within the many other identities that flow around and through them. The video shows how Aboriginal lives are inextricably intertwined in this cosmopolitan set of lifeworlds and not merely stereotypical culture of poverty victims of globalizing forces.

While Commercial Drive illustrates an unsurprisingly cosmopolitan urban context, Northerners with Attitude's *Don't Call Me Eskimo* (2006) demonstrates how being cosmopolitan is not restricted to urban places. Just as Commercial Drive reaches out to wider audiences to talk about how Aboriginal life proceeds in Vancouver, so too does *Don't Call Me Eskimo* in breaking down Inuit life in a small, isolated northern village. Additionally, this video has a number of de-colonization projects that Commercial Drive lacks. This video explicitly seeks to educate southern non-Aboriginal peoples about the identity, history, daily life, and political projects of Northerners with Attitude and, by extension, Inuit throughout the north.

As the name *Don't Call Me Eskimo* suggests, deconstructing the commonly held misnomer *Eskimo* is the first project undertaken. The chorus of the rap makes this abundantly clear: "In the land of ice and snow. Don't call me Eskimo. Bad people aren't Negros. Don't call me Eskimo." Many non-Aboriginal peoples are unaware that Eskimo is a name imposed upon the Inuit by colonizers witnessing that meat was the main staple in the Inuit diet. Eskimo simply means meat-eater. One verse clearly teaches the history of how the Inuit came to be called meat-eaters while also pointing out that the Inuit lived differently prior to colonization and how colonization continues to negatively affect them:

> The name Eskimo came from the British
> Who came here to look for gold, oil, and fish
> The name means that I now eat meat
> But we are the people, our name Inuit
> And since the slave period we knew how to survive
> To eat country food would keep you alive
> But they brought tea and sugar and hard bread
> They got scurvy and ended up dead
> Now we're in houses, no more igloos ...

As stereotypes are often a single attribute negatively generalized to a whole group, Northerners with Attitude clearly point to the white stereotype of how Negros are inherently bad and connect it to the colonially based stereotype that an exclusively meat based diet is *primitive*. Throughout the rest of the video the Inuit are shown to have undergone massive, not altogether positive, changes in their diet and food-gathering strategies. While walking through a grocery store the MC bemoans how much it costs to buy imported food and later complains about the exorbitant cost of cigarettes:

> Stores too expensive
> Can't buy a thing
> Need major bling bling
> Fifty bucks a pack is makin me broke
> People don't say "hi."
> They say "Got smoke?"

It is interesting to note how imported consumer goods, for example cigarettes, can change local interactional etiquettes. The Inuit also, however, have many of the same concerns as other peoples around the world. They have problems with cash flow needed to buy the consumer goods that come to them from the global markets beyond their village, just as southern Aboriginal and non-Aboriginal peoples do.

Northerners with Attitude also educate southern viewers on Inuit views about the new colonialism of naïve environmentalism. In particular, Northerners with Attitude humorously deride Southern non-Inuit environmentalists who criticize Inuit hunting practices as environmentally destructive:

> It's our way of life to hunt for a seal
> Back off Greenpeace we just want some meals
> Don't tell us what to do Paul McCartney
> When we go clubbin' we're havin' a party.

Clearly, these Inuit are savvy about using the power of video not only to educate but also to agitate and to change stereotypical images of Inuit. They point out how Southerners can recolonize if they do not take the time to understand the local Inuit context and simply impose southern values that would create an even greater reliance on store bought foods and the financial hardship that purchasing store bought merchandise can bring. Hence, not only do Northerners with Attitude describe life in the North to those unfamiliar with it, they also reach out politically to show how both historically and currently, the local Inuit continue to be defined by global others and the consequences of this power-to-define.

Last, Northerners with Attitude tackle the stereotype of the *lazy Aboriginal* through re-presenting Inuit reliance on welfare. One standard stereotype about Aboriginal peoples is that they are lazy and purposefully take advantage of the largesse of non-Aboriginals that non-Aboriginals have worked hard to get for themselves (Proulx, 2003). In this verse Northerners with Attitude make it clear that welfare is not about cynical exploitation of an easy resource but rather a necessity for some who are victimized by the harsh realities of global economy:

> Lots of people here are nervous wrecks
> On the 1st and the 15th waiting for cheques
> *There's no choice with no work here* [my italics]
> Many people turn to drugs and despair
> Drug abusing violent dropouts who suck
> Inuit people gotta have pride
> You gotta listen to the words of the Elders
> It's the only way of our lives getting better ...

The fact that there is no work for many Inuit peoples is often overlooked by many non-Aboriginal peoples in their rush to condemn "laziness" and, thereby, underhandedly assert their cultural superiority. Northerners with Attitude outline reality for some Inuit and *reach in* to them about the necessity for them to learn from the Elders in order to make their lives better. But throughout this section Northerners with Attitude *reach out* and educate others in other parts of the world about their complicity in these relations of economic and cultural production. The images and messages in *Don't Call Me Eskimo* cannot simply be dismissed as merely art or as merely teenaged angst embodied in hip hop. They are relevant locally and globally and illustrate that northern peoples are cosmopolitan in their knowledge of their worlds, the outer worlds that impinge upon them, how they are changed by them, and how they can change them.

I have chosen the last three song-based hip hop videos, Tru Rez Crew's *I'm a Lucky One* (2003), Team Rezofficial's *Keep on Movin'* (2004), and War Party's *Feelin' Reserved* (2006), because they clearly illustrate the decolonizing political projects of rez-based hip hoppers. These include the continuing importance of local family relations within the increasingly cosmopolitan life on the rez and the promotion of empowerment for Aboriginal peoples caught in unhealthy lifeways and relations. All these videos indicate how learning from past mistakes is important but looking to the future to build new lives is central to these healing and empowering projects.

Tru Rez Crew in *I'm a Lucky One* clearly make these last points when they say at various points:

> Life is never fair, don't get caught in that snare ...
> Keep your heads held high and never look back ...
> Don't look back, don't you ever look back, no ...
> Gotta look to the future.

Tru Rez Crew maintain that strong familial role models helped them through tough times in their dedication at the beginning of the video:

> This is dedicated to those who rose above us
> Because they chose to love us
> And when we didn't push ourselves
> They were the first to shove us ...

The message is that, some Aboriginal peoples did not lose their parents to the despair of colonizing projects and that the legacy of those strong ones continues to positively affect some Aboriginal youth. In a sense this video breaks down the non-Aboriginal stereotype of Aboriginal reserves as completely and hopelessly dysfunctional by showing that lifestyles without, for example, crime and alcoholism are possible and that positive role models exist:

> I'm a lucky one
> My parents were always there.
> I'm amazed with their ways ...

The lyrics throughout the rest of the video attest to how the members of Tru Rez Crew became strong and how those viewing the video can also be strong and respect themselves and others. Hence, one of the central messages is the promotion of strong, healthy Aboriginal identities that enable people "to go to any reservation in the world" and to "respect every man and woman and boy and girl."

Team RezOfficial also promote similar messages in *Keep on Movin'* (2004). Here is sampling of the lyrics throughout the video:

> Let's just keep on movin'
> We're gonna make it through.
> I know you feel like I feel
> All my native people stand up now
> Cause I feel everyday man ...
> This is a message to my people to stay strong
> It goes out the youth and the Elders
> In the form of a song ...
> About this life we choose to follow
> We use our minds so our kids can have a better tomorrow.

The music and lyrics play out around the Team RezOfficial crew as they move through shots of kids and families playing. There is an explicit claim to educate both youth and Elders through hip hop music. Once again the promotion of positive identities, the need to stand strong against all of the colonially based ills that continue to confront Aboriginal peoples on reserves, and the call to look to a better future is clear.

War Party's *Feelin' Reserved* (2006) is the most overtly political of these three videos. *Feelin' Reserved* refers to how Cree on the Hobeema reserve are "living out the white man's lies." How rez and family life was negatively changed by non-Aboriginal colonial projects such as residential schools, alcohol and crack abuse leading to

> ... feelin' reserved
> living disturbed
> living a life we never deserved.

But this song is more than just a litany of the abuses suffered due continuing colonialism; it too looks to the future, restoring pride and family life.

> ... the native way of thinking
> Ain't the way of the old
> It's time to look to the future
> and let our story unfold
> I'm feelin' reserved
> Man that's how I'm livin'
> I gotta do with this mic I was given
> To try to get by
> No word of a lie
> We gotta try to restore pride.

Rex Smallboy represents the past, present, and future of "his residence" realizing "there's more to see than all this rock around me." He sees his music as a force for change:

> ... There ain't no way I'd rather be
> One love for my people
> Unite
> Instead of feelin' reserved
> My reserve feel me

"*My Reserve Feel Me*" is War Party's attempt to reach, educate, and empower the people of Hobbeema and those outside of the rez. In my interview with Smallboy I asked what he wanted his audience to see through War Party's hip hop. He replied: "Hope, inspiration, empowerment. To have faith and to dream past the reserve life" (Smallboy, personal communication, August 23, 2007).

In all three of these videos, traditional values are still valorized but so is the need to find new values to live by. There are clear attempts to provide new routes for identification and social relations that encompass those from the rez and beyond. In this sense these videos reach in to the past and its strong role models but also reach out to new forms of being in the world and role models who can lead people to these new forms. Hip hop is the vehicle through which these efforts and aims are communicated.

I now turn to *Connecting with Nunavut Youth Through Hip Hop* (2006). This video differs from the other videos herein as it is a retrospective record of a six day hip hop workshop coordinated by the breakdancing crew Canadian Floor Masters for the youth of Iqaluit rather than videos built around individual rap songs. What I am most interested in this video is how the local and traditional merge with the global and modern in the creation of cosmopolitan lived experience in one Nunavut school and community. I focus on how images of the local and the global are juxtaposed and on how the words and practices of the Floor Masters, Inuit, and non-Inuit youth, Inuit parents and Elders co-mingle in this performative creation.

Throughout the video, the camera continually reminds us about the cold isolation and disconnection of Iqaluit from global circuits. Interspersed between each instructional day are shots of the exterior of the school surrounded by large drifts of snow. Other shots include a pan over the frozen roofs of Iqaluit, shots of youths tobogganing and a severe snow storm that delays the final hip hop battle/performance. These images of isolation are all juxtaposed with the images of cosmopolitan connection inside the school as relationships are built through hip hop between the southern-based instructors and the youth, between the youths themselves, and between parents and Elders. For example, in one shot we see the cold, snow-banked, deserted, exterior of the school that cuts to the warm interior of the school wherein local youth are learning how to DJ at a set of turntables.

Of greater relevance are the images that serve to link the local/traditional with the global/modern. Inuksuks, human-like figures constructed with stones that can traditionally function to communicate directions, warnings of dangerous terrain, markers of death, the residence of spirits, places of judgment and where festivals are held, and serve as background and as new hybrid signifiers. An Inuksuk is embedded in the floor of the gymnasium over which hip hop instruction occurs and, as shown below, the local and traditional Inuit signifiers blend with global hip hop signifiers. Of particular relevance is the brief frame of a tableau comprised of an Inuksuk flanked by the silhouette of hip hoppers on either side. Here an older form of communication is conjoined with images of global communication embodied in the hip hopper silhouettes. Rather than geographic directions this tableau gives direction to new forms of performance combining fruitfully with the old. This illustrates how tradition can easily accommodate new forms and readings and how the global also appropriates the traditional. This hybrid signifier reaches into Iqaluit constructing new meanings upon an older multivalent symbol, while reaching out to the wider world beyond teaching youth about difference through the stylized posing of hip hop. In this way both the global and the local *represent* in hip hop terminology but are also *re-presented* for diverse audiences on YouTube.

Still more interesting are the actions of all the participants revealing how Iqaluit becomes a place of roots and routes. Day one closes with a demonstration of beatboxing by the Floor Masters accompanied by scratching on the turntables. Noteworthy is the addition of an Inuit throat singer to the musical mix. Day Three closes with another hybrid performance. Two young Inuit throat singers combine with a Floor Master beatboxer backed up with youth using traditional drums. While some might simply dismiss these additions as merely another world music synthesis, I see these performances as conscious attempts not only to instruct and provide pleasure but also in-reaching to the local youth showing how their musical traditions are not only timeless, but also timely. The techniques of throat singing have much in common with the techniques of beatboxing. Both use the breath and vocal chords, are percussive, and arose as a result of geographic (throat singing) and economic (beatboxing) necessity. Both are portable and require no instruments beyond the human voice. In a real sense local culture, often thought of as deteriorating and fading away under the pressure of intruding global forms, is shown as vibrantly alive and using global culture rather than only being used by it. It demonstrates how local musical forms can enhance global ones. The lived-experience of observing the combination of throat singing and traditional drumming with hip hop teaches Inuit youth the values of tradition in accessible and meaningful ways. These scenes reach out to other Aboriginal and non-Aboriginal peoples watching on YouTube, helping them to understand how the north is connected to them through hip hop. Knowledge of Inuit youth and place is garnered from the video. One comment posted by a viewer of this video says, "It's not often enough that the positive sides of the Canadian north are made visible, but you guys showed the warmth of the arctic. Keep showing the world what true hip hop is." Another posting says "Wish there was more like you spreading the love and knowledge ... Hip Hop has no boundaries."

In day two of the workshop we see three to four Inuit youth elevated above the gym floor speaking to the assembled workshop participants and Canadian Floor Masters below them. In keeping with the overall workshop message of positive, healthy behavior and thoughts, as well as consistent reinforcement that "you can do it if you work at it," comes a further exhortation and reinforcement by a young Inuit speaker. It pinpoints how the work ethic, strength, and perseverance of Inuit people of the past relate to the current workshop themes.

> We are here because the Inuit are very skilled. Because our ancestors were very, very strong people and they knew how to live in the harshest climate in the world. We owe that to them and we owe it to ourselves.

The audience applauds. This is followed by traditional songs and drumming performances and testimonials of Inuit youth on the positive experiences they are having.

Day Four brings a further example of how the traditional local and youth and parents and elders blend in a participatory performance of breakdancing. In this sequence the Inuit youth work the turntables and do various forms of hip hop dancing for an audience of bemused yet appreciative Inuit Elders. During this performance hip hop hat dancing takes place in the midst of a circle of youth playing traditional drums. Next, a gray-haired Inuit man demonstrates his drumming followed by a young girl who appears to be a novice at drumming who is, in turn, followed by one of the Floor Masters performing on a traditional drum. The audience applauds all their efforts. Finally, the Elders are shown trying out their own hip hop moves with the help of the Floor Masters and the Inuit workshop attendees. In one last frame one of the older Inuit women *represents* in an arms crossed pose with a gangsta expression on her face while wearing a hip hop hat used in the dances. She is joined by three of the Floor Masters who pose in a similar manner. This sequence ends with the Floor Masters thanking the Elders for participating and applause for their efforts from the youth.

Clearly, this sequence is richly hybrid. Not only is cross-cultural knowledge and experience flowing both ways, but it flows inter-generationally. Traditional musical practices dialogically communicate with hip hop practices across divergent cultural contexts creating new musical and cultural understandings. Difference and roots, the cultural particularities of the global/modern and local/traditional, are both valued, and pleasure taken from the presence of the other and other places (Appiah, 1997, p. 618). Divergent musical, performative, and pedagogical roots branch out combining and creating new routes to cosmopolitan relationality.

Another video record of a workshop is of interest here. The video is entitled *Tellin' It Like It Is* and, according to the posting accompanying the video, this clip is part of a larger soon to be released video by Beatboard, a Youth Leadership, New Media and Contemporary Arts Education Organization based in Vancouver and Victoria, BC, Canada, involving urban Aboriginal and Métis youth. Another posting on the video gives some context: "Urban Aboriginal and Métis identified youth get real about their perspectives on healthy living and cultural identity." The video itself documents the group doing a hip hop workshop that culminates in the participants MCing their own hip hop composition. The lyrics are as follows:

> Life can be a stress All the stereotypes.
> Our culture is strength
> Our culture is our life
> Indian, Chug, Half-Breed, and Drugs
> We're not stereotypes
> We're still standin' strong.

One of the central problems Aboriginal peoples everywhere face is that they do not, by and large, control the power to define who they are; non-Aboriginal peoples tend to have control over this technology of power (Proulx, 2003). As I have illustrated earlier, the use of negative stereotypes of Aboriginal peoples by non-Aboriginal peoples is pervasive in Canada, a country that publicly prides itself on being nonracist (Proulx, 2003). These stereotypes have a long history in Canada (Harding, 2006). Dislodging these stereotypes is difficult. It is particularly difficult when Aboriginal peoples themselves have internalized negative non-Aboriginal images of themselves (Proulx, 2003). It is clear that the youth had discussed among themselves their experiences with being stereotyped and these form the basis of their message. The product of this process is the video that both reaches in to other urban youth experiencing stereotyping and reaches out to non-Aboriginal audiences to educate and thereby eradicate non-Aboriginal stereotyping. Importantly, the message "We're still standin' strong" shows both themselves and outsiders that, despite how others have had the power to define them, they are not only strong enough to withstand this power but also strong enough to reclaim it and use it for a better purpose. Later in the video the youth individually speak words (strength, artistic, athletic, individual, and culture) that define who they really are, or hope to be, thereby showing that they are not mere stereotypes but real people with real potential, dreams, and relations. Once again hip hop is the medium through which the local is represented and simultaneously transmitted to global audiences through the cosmopolitan medium of YouTube.

Conclusion

Anthropologists have long been interested in hybridity in various forms such as syncretism, diffusion, and cultural appropriation. Pieterse (2001) defines hybridity as denoting "a wide variety of multiple identity, crossover, pick-n'-mix, boundary crossing experiences, and styles, reflecting increased migration, mobility, and global multiculturalism." Aboriginal youth are hybrid on at least three levels relevant to this discussion. First, they have grown up in a world of time-space compression (Harvey, 1990) on the reserves and reservations as satellite TV and the Internet have brought the consumer/information world to their doors changing how peoples understand themselves locally and in relation to the rest of the world. Hip hop was one such import. Second, many youth now live in cities where they are immersed in other cultures and information flows *both* non-Aboriginal and Aboriginal. For example, multiple Aboriginal traditions co-exist in cities that can be taken up and mixed in the creation of identities. Third, many Aboriginal youth move back and forth from cities to the rez, mixing traditional knowledges and practices with those of the wider world. Some Aboriginal youth, then, are boundary crossers who have numerous lifeways, knowledges, practices, and styles from which to pick-n'-mix in the creation of their identities. In essence they exemplify Du Bois's (1999, [1903]) double consciousness as First Nation/indigenous, as citizens of nation-states, as well as traditional and modernizing while flowing through reserves and largely non-Aboriginal cities. The hip hoppers and the videos discussed herein also illustrate double-edged projects of in-reach and out-reach through the "co-embedding of local and global and their co-implications for articulating identity" (Landzelius, 2006, p. 9). They also deal with revitalization at times promoting native customs, languages, and knowledge while, at other times, looking beyond traditional modes to achieve this end. Aboriginal hip hoppers, then, "explode common misconceptions that reduce 'traditional cultures' to synchronic, homogenous, fixed entities" (Landzelius, 2006, p. 13). Aboriginal hip hoppers exemplify "the arts of the re-mix" (Lashua, 2006, p. 6) not only in the use of technology to remix music and create new hybrid sounds, but also in mixing Aboriginal traditions with non-Aboriginal modernities to become alternatively modern cosmopolitans while remaining indigenous. Lashua elegantly describes this cosmopolitan mixing:

> Young people make and re-make culture through appropriating the cultural "raw materials" of life to construct meaning in their own specific cultural localities. In a

sense they are "sampling" from broader popular culture and re-working what they can take into their own specific local cultures. That is, the ways that young people sample drum rhythms and vocal segments from songs may be thought of as analogous to the ways they sample from broader cultures (such as styles from USA hip hop cultures), modify, or restructure it in some meaningful ways and re-work the "compositions" of their own daily lives including notions of identity. (2006, p. 6)

What I have shown is how Aboriginal hip hoppers are very much rooted cosmopolitans in that they have "feelings of loyalty and commitment to particular cultures and openness toward difference and otherness" (Roudometof, 2005, p. 122). Mitchell (2006) points out: "As hip hop has been globalized, it has also been indigenized and incorporated into local languages and cultural forms." Indeed one may speculate that new forms of indigeneity are arising from the actions of youthful hip hoppers mixing the traditional and the modern in cities, reserves, and across international boundaries. Aboriginal rappers, then, in both informal and formal networks help us understand "what it truly means to be Aboriginal in a modern and increasingly mobile liberal democratic society" (Podlasley, 2002, p. 1).

References

Africa Resource. (2007). Retrieved June 4, 2007, from http://www.africaresource.com/component/option,com_glossary/func,display/letter,All/Itemid,110/catid,9/page,1/

Answerbag. (2007). Retrieved June 10, 2007, from http://www.answerbag.com/q_view/1839

Answers.com. (2007). Retrieved June 15, 2007, from http://www.answers.com/topic/breaking

Appiah, A. K. (1997, Spring). Cosmopolitan Patriots. *Critical Inquiry*, 23(3), 617-639.

The Beatboard. (2006). *Tellin' It Like It Is*. Retrieved August 1, 2007, from http://youtube.com/watch?v=QHsPN8qgW4w

Beck, U. (2002). The Cosmopolitan Society and Its Enemies. *Theory, Culture & Society*, 19(1-2), 17-44.

Buddle, K. (2005). Aboriginal Cultural Capital Creation and Radio Production in Urban Ontario. *Canadian Journal of Communication*, 30 (1), 7-40.

Center for Black Music Research. (2007). Rap and Hip Hop Resources. Columbia College, Chicago, Illinois. Retrieved July 4, 2007, from http://www.colum.edu.cbmr/hiphop/#def

Chamberlain, R. (2001). Rap in Canada Bilingual and Multicultural. In T. Mitchell (ed.), *Global Noise: Rap and Hip Hop Outside of the USA* (pp. 306-325). Middletown, CT: Wesleyan University Press.

Connecting with Nunavut Youth through Hip Hop (2006) Iqaluit. February. Retrieved July 10, 2007, from http://www.youtube.com/watch?v=cy1qjPZ5iJI

Darnell, R. (2006). Ted Chamberlin Meets a Critic. *Postcolonial Text*, 2(3). Retrieved July 12, 2007, from http://postcolonial.org/index.php/pct/article/view/558/313

Desjarlais, S. (2003). Rediscovering Tribal Wizdom. *Wiretap*. Retrieved April 11, 2007, from http://www.wiretapmag.org/module/printversion/15530

Du Bois, W. E. B. (1999). *The Souls of Black Folk*. New York: Bartleby.Com. [Chicago: A.C.

McClurg & Co., 1903]

Efron, S. (2001). Native Hip-Hoppers Rap Out Their Message. *The Georgia Straight*, May 31. Retrieved April 12, 2007, from http://www.saraefron.com/stories/tribalwizdom.shtml

Forbes, J. (2001). The Urban Tradition among Native Americans. In S. Lobo and K. Peters. (Eds.), *American Indians and the Urban Experience* (pp. 5-25). New York: Altamira Press.

Harding, R. (2006). Historical Representations of Aboriginal People in Canadian News Media. *Discourse and Society*, 17(2), 205-235.

Harvey, D. (1990). *The Condition of Postmodernity: An Enquiry into the Origins of Cultural Change.* Cambridge, MA: Blackwell Publishing.

Hebdige, D. (1987) *Cut 'n' Mix: Culture, Identity and Caribbean Music.* Cambridge, UK: Cambridge University Press.

King, T. (2003). *The Truth about Stories: A Native Narrative.* Toronto: House of Anansi Press.

Knauft, B. M. (2002). Critically Modern: An Introduction. In B. M. Knauft. (Ed.), *Critically Modern: Alternatives, Alterities, Anthropologies* (pp. 1-54). Bloomington, IN: Indiana University Press.

Landzelius, K. (2006). Introduction: Native on the Net. In K. Landzelius (Ed.), *Native on the Net: Indigenous and Diasporic Peoples in the Virtual Age* (pp. 1-42). London and New York: Routledge.

Lashua, B. (2006). The Arts of the Remix: Ethnography of Rap. *Anthropology Matters Journal.* 8(2). Retrieved May 12, 2007, from http:www.anthropologymatters.com

Lobley, K. (2006). Rock the Block. *The Sydney Morning Herald.* Retrieved June 19, 2007, from http://www.smh.com.au/news/gig-reviews/rock-the-block/2006/05/05/1146335896305.html#

Lobo, S. (2001). Is Urban a Person or a Place? Characteristics of Urban Indian Country. In S. Lobo and K. Peters (Eds.), *American Indians and the Urban Experience* (pp. 73-85). New York: Altamira Press.

Lobo, S. and K. Peters. (2001). *American Indians and the Urban Experience.* New York: Altamira Press.

Malkki, L. (1992). National Geographic: The Rooting of Peoples and the Territorialization of National Identity among Scholars and Refugees. *Cultural Anthropology*, 7(1), 24-44.

Manik 1derful (2006). Commercial Drive. Retrieved July 28, 2007, from http://www.youtube.com/watch?v=RH_kqmJXYK8

McEachern, A. (1991). *Delgamuukw v. A.G.: Reasons for Judgment of the Honorable Chief Justice Allan McEachern.* Vancouver: Queen's Printer.

Mitchell, T. (1999). Another Root: Australian Hip Hop as Glocal Subculture—Re-territorializing Hip Hop. *Musical Visions: Selected Conference Proceedings from the 6th National Australian/New Zealand IASPM Conference and the Inaugural Arnhem Land Performance Conference.* Adelaide: Wakefield Press, 85-94.

———. (2006). The New Corroboree. *The Age.* Retrieved April 1, 2007, from http://www.theage.com.au/news/music/the-new-corroboree/2006/03/30/1143441270792.html?page=fullpage#

Nederveen P. J. (2001). Hybridity, So What? The Anti-hybridity Backlash and the Riddles of Recognition. *Theory, Culture and Society*, 18(2-3), 219-245.

Northerners with Attitude. (2006). *Don't Call Me Eskimo.* Retrieved July 8, 2007, from http://www.youtube.com/watch?v=tS8RZcKQwBA

Norris, M.J. and Clatworthy, S. (2003). "Aboriginal Mobility and Migration within Urban Canada: Outcomes, Factors and Implications." In D. Newhouse and E. Peters (Eds.), *Not*

Strangers in These Parts: Urban Aboriginal Peoples (pp. 51-78). Retrieved June 3, 2007, from http://dsp-psd.pwgsc.gc.ca/Collection/CP22-71-2003E.pdf

NotaRpietro-Clarken, C. (2007). Blackfella Beats and New Flows: The Undercurrents of Aboriginal Hip Hop Are Emerging as a Cultural Force. *Arena Magazine*, (87), February-March. Retrieved April 12, 2007, from http://www.arena.org.au/ARCHIVES/Mag%20Archive/Issue%2087/features87.htm

Ostwelve (2006). *Ostwelve in Soweto*. Retrieved August 12, 2007, from http://www.youtube.com/watch?v=0Y_x1CRKA30

Peeters, M. (2002). *Movement Music: Hip Hop and Aboriginal Youth Activism*. Retrieved April 19, 2007, from http://research2.csci.educ.ubc.ca/indigenation/mwalu.htm

Peters, E. (2004). *"Three Myths about Aboriginals in Cities."* March 25th, Canadian Federation for the Humanities and Social Sciences. Retrieved August 2, 2007, from http://www.fedcan.ca/english/pdf/fromold/breakfast-peters0304.pdf

———. (1996). "'Urban' and 'Aboriginal' a Contradiction? The Social Construction of Aboriginal Peoples in Relation to the City." In J. Caulfield and L. Peake (Eds.), *City Lives and City Forms: Critical Research and Canadian Urbanism* (pp. 47-61). Toronto, ON: University of Toronto Press.

Podlasley, M. (2002). *Canada's Domestic Expatriates: The Urban Aboriginal Population*. Retrieved April 9, 2005, from http://www.newliberalism.ca/resources/Podlasly.pdf

Proulx, C. (2003). *Reclaiming Aboriginal Justice, Community, and Identity*. Saskatoon: Purich Publishing Ltd.

———. Aboriginal Identification in North American Cities. *The Canadian Journal of Native Studies*, XXVI(2), 403-436.

Quinn, W. W. (1993). Intertribal Integration: The Ethnological Argument in Duro and Reina. *Ethnohistory*, 40(1), 34-39.

Roudometof, V. (2005). Transnationalism, Cosmopolitanism, and Glocalization. *Critical Sociology*, 53(1), 113-135.

Smallboy, Rex. 2007. Personal communication, August 23.

Stavrias, G. (2005). Droppin' Conscious Beats and Flows: Aboriginal Hip Hop and Youth Identity. *Australian Aboriginal Studies*, (2), 44-54.

Tanner, H. (1987). *Atlas of Great Lakes Indian History*. Norman: University of Oklahoma Press.

———. (1989). "Tribal Mixtures in Chicago Area Indian Villages." In T. Strauss (Ed.), *Indians of the Chicago Area* (pp. 21-25). Chicago: NAES College.

Tarrow, S. (2005). *The New Transnational Activism*. Cambridge, UK: Cambridge University Press.

Team Rezofficial. (2004.) *Keep on Movin'*. Retrieved August 1, 2007, from http://www.youtube.com/watch?v=3K82flp_HSI Arbor Records

Tru Rez Crew. (2003). *I'm a Lucky One*. Retrieved July 24, 2007, from http://www.youtube.com/watch?v=PIyCDr_ojV4

Urla, J. (2001). "We Are All Malcolm X!" Negu Gorriak, Hip Hop, and the Basque Political Imaginary." In T. Mitchell (Ed.), *Global Noise: Rap and Hip Hop Outside of the USA* (pp. 171-193). Middletown, CT: Wesleyan University Press.

War Party. (2006) *Feelin' Reserved*. Retrieved July 6, 2007, from http://www.youtube.com/watch?v=nvCleNb1vB4&mode=related&search=

◆ CHAPTER FOUR ◆

David Neel's *The Young Chief—Waxwaxam*: A Cosmopolitan Treatise

Carolyn Butler-Palmer

As other chapters in this collection indicate, indigenous cosmopolitanism may at first blush seem to be an incongruous, if not contradictory, expression. For some, the term "indigenous" conjures up ideas about cultural stasis or isolation, while the term "cosmopolitan" evokes a sense of cultural connectedness and mobility. The work of photojournalist, painter, and hereditary Kwagiutl carver David Neel (b. 1960) leans toward the latter, as exemplified by pieces such as a carved mask, *The Kuwaiti Smoke Creature* (1991), that was inspired by news images of the First Gulf War; a serigraph, *What One Man Can Do* (1990), that juxtaposes a portrait photograph of a First Nations leader with a 1990 news photograph of the man who brought tanks to a standstill in Tiananmen Square; and an acrylic-on-canvas painting of a Kwagiutl tale, *The Young Chief—Waxwaxam* (2000) (Neel, 2002, postcard), that makes references to The Four Sacred Directions of Thai Buddhism. This chapter focuses on the last of these images, *The Young Chief*, as a visual treatise about indigenous cosmopolitanism (figure 4.1).

My argument builds upon my analysis of *The Young Chief* and the theme of cosmopolitanism that I briefly touched on in the 2003 essay, "Paintings in the Present Tense," published in the Department of Indian and Northern Affairs Indian and Inuit Gallery's *Living Legends: The Artistic Process* exhibition catalogue (2003, pp. 17–25). The goals of "Paintings in the Present Tense" are to situate *The Young Chief* with respect to subsequent paintings in that series and to introduce Neel's cross-cultural engagement as cosmopolitanism. By contrast, this chapter refines the account of his cosmopolitanism as being informed by beliefs about human relations to the universe, particularly as associated with The Four Directions (Buddhist and indigenous) and the humanitarian ideals of photojournalism, a practice that photographer Cornell

Capa dubbed "concerned photography" (1968, n.p). Concerned photography is generally considered to be a practice of photography that corresponds with a prevalent political concern of the post-World War II era, which asserts that people have essential rights that go beyond national, cultural, religious, and ideological boundaries—a concern for humanity that is greater than an ideal of nationalism.

Neel often likens the practice of concerned photography to his conception of The Four Directions. But within the context of indigenous North America, The Sacred is guarded by silence; therefore, in contrast to my description of concerned photography, I cannot respectfully enunciate a working definition or description of The Four Directions without violating this sense of The Sacred. One of the difficulties of this chapter is to find a way of talking about something that cannot be verbalized. I do so, first by situating the figure of The Young Chief in regards to the history and practices of concerned photography. I then turn to the purple object, which I locate with respect to Buddhist rituals of pilgrimage. Thus, my discussions of concerned photography and practices of Thai Buddhism are intended to move us toward The Sacred—toward Neel's praxis of cosmopolitanism.

This chapter sets out to explain why Neel's cross-cultural aesthetic praxis in general and *The Young Chief* in particular are cosmopolitan, and further, that his humanitarian approach presents a cosmopolitan ethic. That Neel's work embraces The Four Directions and the tenets of concerned photography—concepts with very distinct cultural roots—in itself evidences a cosmopolitan sensibility.

Cosmopolitanisms: Human Mobility and the Ethics of World Citizenship

As a point of departure, I turn to my reasons for selecting the term "cosmopolitan," rather than another—for example, "hybridity," "creolization," or "globalization"—to describe Neel's cross-cultural engagements. A number of scholars, including philosopher Anthony Appiah in his 2006 book *Cosmopolitanism: Ethics in a World of Strangers*, locate the origins of the term "cosmopolitan" in the words of the Cynics of Ancient Greece, who originally wrote of "a citizen of the cosmos," in a controversial move that extended the limits of citizenship beyond what was then the more conventional view, that a person belonged to a single city, or *polis* (p. xiv). Appiah's analysis of the word cosmopolitanism goes on to show that the term "cosmopolitanism" accrued a sense of moral responsibility in the eighteenth century through writings of philosophers Kant and Voltaire (pp. xiv-xv). Appiah presents the cosmopolitan not only as a citizen of the universe, but also as a moral being.

Anthropologist James Clifford, in the prologue to his 1997 book *Routes: Travel and Translation in the Late Twentieth Century*, shifts definition in another direction. He positions his cosmopolitanism in opposition to the *ethnographic* conception of culture as village-centered, exemplified by Boas's paradigmatic study of the Kwagiutl (1997, pp. 18-25). As such, Clifford's cosmopolitanism reinvigorates the Cynics' challenge to what was the traditional *polis*-centered notion of citizenship. Clifford goes on to point out that his view of culture as cosmopolitan is complicated by the fact that different sorts of people—for example, pilgrims, nomads, exiles, tourists, family visitors, explorers, and the colonized—become mobile for very different reasons (pp. 31-36). He weaves the term into a project aimed at configuring a new, more fluid, model of culture: he sees cultures as "sites of dwelling and travel" (p. 31). In order to find a vocabulary that more accurately indexes the range of cultural sites that are consequently produced, Clifford turns to the rhetoric of cosmopolitanism and then coins the expression "discrepant cosmopolitan" to register what he sees as cosmopolitanism's plural nature (p. 36). Thus, in contrast to the sense of morality that is featured in Appiah's cosmopolitanism, Clifford's cosmopolitanism provides an elastic model of culture and argues for the recognition of differences.

My use of "cosmopolitanism" draws upon and combines several aspects of Appiah's and Clifford's differing uses. First, as I argue below, the constellation of Northwest Coast, Kwagiutl, Thai, and European aesthetics that *The Young Chief* maps shares ideas about multiple allegiances that are present in both Appiah's and Clifford's conceptions. In addition, I evoke the rhetoric of cosmopolitanism because I find that Neel's cross-cultural work introduces an ethic of human relations that corresponds to the moral imperative of Appiah's definition. Finally, I wish to preserve Clifford's sense of cosmopolitanism's potential, because, as he argues, people become mobile for many different reasons. In contrast to Clifford's cosmopolitanism, which seems to include any sort of human migration, I reserve the term cosmopolitanism to map movement that also manifests an ethic of cross-cultural engagement. Therefore, my treatment of cosmopolitanism includes three necessary components: mobility, morality, and multiplicity.

Situating Neel's work within theoretical discourses of cosmopolitanism troubles the standard interpretative convention that focuses on the Pacific Northwest, as exemplified by anthropologist Marjorie Halpin's "Afterword," an essay that appears in Neel's 1992 book, *Our Chiefs and Elders: Words and Photographs of Native Leaders*. Halpin's essay begins by connecting Neel and his practice of photography to his Kwagiutl ancestors and their practices of carving. She writes,

> David Neel was born in Vancouver in 1960 to Karen Clemenson, a non-Native, and David Neel [Sr.], the eldest son of Ellen Neel, the first woman carver on the

> Northwest Coast. Although the Neel family is in Fort Rupert Kwagiutl, Ellen Neel herself was born in the house of Chief Wakas at Alert Bay, the same house that was reconstructed in 1989 in the Grand Hall of the Canadian Museum of Civilization in Hull, Quebec. David Neel's father, grandmother, and great-grandfather, Charlie James, were all carvers, as is David Neel himself ... while Neel may be the first professional photographer in the family, it is a family that has excelled in the arts of image-making for generations. (p.183)

Halpin goes on to acknowledge Neel's debt to the work of the concerned photographers, and then positions his portrait photographs in opposition to three non-Native photographic genres of Native representation that she refers to as "the anthropological lens," "the noble savage," and "the before-and-after tradition" (pp.185–187). Cosmopolitanism does not deny the import of Neel's Kwagiutl family to his work and identity or the ability to compare his work to other genres, but rather, it acknowledges his multiple affiliations and underscores the ethical ideals of his cross-cultural engagements.

David Neel: Tales of Travel and Concerned Photography

Neel's cosmopolitan ethic emerged over the course of years and in conjunction with years of his own cross-cultural experiences. As with many aboriginal children reared in the 1960s, the forces of economic necessity and movement enabled by twentieth-century technology largely shaped Neel's childhood. A year after Neel's birth, in 1961, his father, David Neel Sr., died in an automobile accident (Nuytten, 1982, p.70). Shortly thereafter, the 17-year-old Karen Clemenson and her young son left Vancouver. They first moved to the interior of British Columbia and then on to Alberta. They finally settled in a suburb of Calgary, Alberta, about 700 miles away from the Neel family and from Vancouver, an important center of the then fledgling revival of Northwest Coast carving practices, which started to flourish once again after the government prohibition against indigenous possession of ceremonial objects, such as carved poles and masks, was quietly erased from federal statutes (Canadian Press, *The Vancouver Sun*, Sec. B., p. 7 and Neel, 1992, p. 13). Between 1978 and 1982, Neel majored in photojournalism and took classes in anthropology and fine art at Mount Royal College in Calgary, and then at the University of Kansas in Lawrence (Halpin, p. 184). While training as a professional photographer, Neel was introduced to the work of the first generation of concerned photographers such as W. Eugene Smith (1919–1978), Robert Capa (1913–1954), and Henri Cartier-Bresson (1908–2004) (Halpin, p. 184), mid-twentieth-century photojournalists who traveled the globe photographing the lives of people in places such as Mexico, Japan, the American South, and China.

Michael Ignatieff, in his essay for the 2003 book *Magnum Degrees*, argues that the work of these photojournalists is filled with moral strengths and limitations. He observes that, on the one hand, they espouse what he refers to as the same "liberal internationalist moral imagination" that underpins the founding of institutions such as the Universal Declaration of Human Rights and the Geneva Convention, a moral imagination that was coming to terms with humanity in the aftermath of World War II and the Holocaust (2000, p. 54). The concerned photographers intended to promote a sense of universal fraternity consistent with the widespread post–World War II era view that people have essential rights that go beyond national, cultural, religious, and ideological boundaries. Thus, concerned photography's goals closely parallel the movement and morality of Appiah's characterization of cosmopolitanism.

These mid-century photographers, Ignatieff goes on to argue, supported this moral imagination with photography's truth-value. He writes,

> [They] ... believed that horror might be stopped if we actually took the trouble to see what it really was ... [this] is part of a determined twentieth-century effort to deny war its rhetoric of glory and to stop the sentimentalizing of suffering. [Their] ... aesthetic ... became an ethic. (2003, p. 54)

Ignatieff notes that, on the other hand, their work is not beyond reproach. As evidence of this, he points to Roland Barthes (1912–1980) and his famous 1957 review of *The Family of Man Exhibition* that included photographs by Capa, Smith, and Cartier-Bresson. Ignatieff summarizes Barthes's criticisms of the exhibition:

> The illusion was to believe that human unity is more important than difference, that prejudice, class power and colonial oppression pale before our common humanity. But this photographic celebration of human universality, Barthes went on to say "tells us, literally, nothing. Worse, it hides the enduring historical injustice of the world." (2003, p. 55)

Ignatieff concludes that these photographs are ambiguous, because they "compress complex moments of suffering and injustice ... into necessarily simplified and abstracted visual icons" (2003, p. 54).

Neel's autobiographical accounts, however, suggest it was the worldliness and the humanitarian intent of these mid-century photojournalists that inspired his own artistic journeys (1992, p. 11). In 1982, Neel moved from Calgary, Alberta, to Dallas, Texas, where he spent several years photographing the people of the Freedman's Town and State-Thomas neighborhoods (Halpin, p. 184), as exemplified by his 1985 *Portrait of Lily-Bee and Mertel Holloway* (figure 4.2). Neel's photograph of Lily-Bee, a 50-year resident of Freedman's Town, with her daughter Mertel, warmly recalls the documentary style of Cartier-Bresson's photographic portraits of people from the four corners of the earth, surrounded by their collections of paintings, family photographs, and jewelry—

expressions of personal identity. With such references to concerned photography, Neel renders his work legible within an international practice of photography, and fashions an identity as a traveler and humanitarian. But the similarity between Cartier-Bresson's photographs and Neel's *Portrait of Lily-Bee and Mertel Holloway* also opens up the latter to the same sort of universalizing critique that Barthes applied to *The Family of Man* exhibit in 1957. Though, the fact that Lily-Bee and Mertel Holloway are looking directly at the photographer suggests a sense of intimacy between Neel and his subjects that is absent from the work of Cartier-Bresson.

Concerned Photography and the Ethics of Localization

The juxtaposition of Neel's *Portrait of Lily-Bee and Mertel Holloway* with his subsequent work reveals sensitivity to local aesthetic concerns, as he moves to different cultural and geographic locales. This sensitivity to local concerns, which is crucial to what I have labeled his cosmopolitan aesthetic, separates Neel's maturing practice of image-making from the universalizing assumptions of Cartier-Bresson, Smith, and Capa (Ignateiff, p. 55). Localization brings us closer to the recognition of difference, and so, provides clues to the moral underpinnings of Neel's cosmopolitanism ethic. To chart the changes in Neel's work, I first turn to his practice of photography in British Columbia and then to his work in Thailand with his creation of *The Young Chief*.

In 1986, one year after he created his *Portrait of Lily-Bee and Mertel Holloway*, Neel returned to British Columbia. Within a year, he started photographing prominent First Nations people residing in British Columbia, creating what quickly became his most acclaimed photo-essay, *Our Chiefs and Elders*, represented by the most celebrated image of the series, Neel's *Self-Portrait with Chief Charlie James Swanson* (figure 4.3). In contrast to the universalizing assumptions embedded in the mid-century work of Smith, Capa, and Cartier-Bresson, Neel's work reveals a personal style that is sensitive to issues of cross-cultural engagement, and specifically to local concerns about representation and display. For example, Neel's *Portrait of Lily-Bee and Mertel Holloway* shares much with his *Self-Portrait with Chief Charlie James Swanson*. Each of the photographs portrays a pair of people, an end table piled high with bric-a-brac, and a bisected circular object—a mirror or a clock—at the right edge. But Neel's portrait of the Holloways seems very intimate, as he presents the two women in casual attire, complementing the informal qualities of Lily-Bee's home. By contrast, Neel's *Self-Portrait with Chief Charlie James Swanson* seems more composed, partly because of the contrast between Neel's apparently daily attire and accoutrements—a Thunderbird T-shirt, a pair of jeans, and a camera in hand—and Swanson's regalia—a ceremonial robe, a headdress, and a chief's staff—which, of course, are not Swanson's house clothes. The latter's carefully arranged quality is amplified through references to the making of the photograph that are included within the image—lights, diffuser, and photographic screen—along with the echoing of the staff's top-most shape in the clips attached to the light standards.

This pair of photographs also reveals how Neel uses the medium of photography to define and protect indigenous space. In the former image, Neel provides us with a seemingly unedited view of Lily-Bee's home. He not only allows us to see her personal possessions, but he also seems to invite us right into the living room, to occupy the Holloways' space. By contrast, the Swanson image appears a more controlled scene. The placement of the screen affords only a glimpse of his personal effects and space, and, as a consequence, simultaneously directs our attention toward indigenous people and away from indigenous things. In the context of indigenous life in the Pacific Northwest, this is a significant intervention into the idea of the vanishing Indian perpetuated by non-Native photographers such as Edward S. Curtis (1868-1952). The idea of the vanishing Indian has served an apologetic political function for white expansion into what is presented as an empty land (Watson, 1994, p. 96 and Crosby, 2007, pp. 219-222). Neel's use of the screen disrupts and politicizes the convention of looking at indigenous British Columbia as an empty land, in some places cluttered with seemingly unattended carved and painted artifacts: Neel blocks the prying and colonizing eyes, an ongoing problem for indigenous people. Thus, the photographic screen doubles as an imposing emblem of his art while it shields the culture, allowing the viewer access only to what Neel and Swanson have cooperatively and deliberately chosen to show and to share with the viewer. Thus, Neel's *Self-Portrait with Chief Charlie James Swanson* is a statement about the recognition of difference that brings us toward Clifford's ideas about cosmopolitanism.

The Four Sacred Directions and the Ethics of Human Relations

As a representation of an enrobed, staff-bearing chief, Neel's painting, *The Young Chief—Waxwaxam*, recalls his photograph of Chief Charlie James Swanson, creating connections to Neel's localizing practice of concerned photography in the Northwest Coast. In another localizing move, *The Young Chief* also visualizes the Kwagiutl story of *Waxwaxam* (Butler-Palmer, 2003, pp. 17-25). In Neel's painting, the figure appears against a yellow backdrop in a tangerine-colored robe, holding a staff and wearing a bird-like mask of *Xo'los*— an Ancestor of "The Chief Surpassing," the English translation of *Waxwaxam*. With yellow and orange as the painting's dominant colors, Neel also honors the artistic legacies of his Kwagiutl ancestors. Neel's grandmother, Ellen Neel, is often credited with introducing yellow into the Kwagiutl palette, as her grandfather, Charlie James, is credited with the color orange (Hawthorne, 1967, p. 9). In Neel's painting, the character of The Young Chief is perhaps juggling a trio of objects—a blue Killer Whale, a green clam, and a purple, teardrop-shaped, object. The blue and green objects map different aspects of the Kwagiutl universe. Killer Whale, in blue, represents one of the Neel family crests—an emblem of the family's origins—a sign of their place in Kwagiutl society. The green clam recalls the poisonous clams of Ge'gaqe, which, as the narrative goes, were eaten by two of the Chief Surpassing's children (Neel, personal communication, 2003). The third element injects something new, something Buddhist, into the Kwagiutl tale of Waxwaxam.

Neel painted *The Young Chief* during the summer of 2002, shortly after he completed a journey to several of Thailand's Buddhist commemorative monuments. The oldest form of Buddhist monument, the *stupa*, is typically a dome-shaped structure that is usually understood to be a "world mountain" or "cosmogram," a map of the universe. A *stupa* is usually made of stone or rubble and may contain relics of the Buddha, or mark the site of a key event in the life of the Buddha. An "umbrella," situated at the top of the hemisphere, denotes the axis of the Buddhist universe, otherwise known as the Fifth Direction (Linduff, 1997, pp. 110–113). Architect Karl Döhring, however, has pointed out that the commemorative shrines of Thailand, usually referred to as *chedi*, are more typically bell-shaped structures, an architectural form that integrates the umbrella and dome components into a single structure (Döhring, 2000, pp. 5–8). As a site that commemorates the life of Buddha, the *stupa* or *chedi* plays an important role with respect to the Buddhist focus on the cultivation of inner states of consciousness or enlightenment, especially as such cultivation relates to place. Buddha advised his followers that they could work toward enlightenment by undertaking pilgrimages to four sites linked to important moments in his life.

Buddhist commemorative monuments are typically surrounded by structures that guide the pilgrims' encounters. Pilgrims enter into such ritual precincts through one of the four stone structures, which are positioned to denote the first Four Directions of the Buddhist universe, and they circumambulate the shrine in a clockwise direction, a ritual that Katherine Linduff describes as "symbolic of walking the Path of Life around the world" (p. 111). The third, teardrop-shaped purple element of *The Young Chief* is based on Neel's photographs of one of the four carved gates that surround one of the *chedis* he visited in Thailand (Neel, telephone interview, 2003). Although Neel's understanding of Buddhism, the associated rituals of pilgrimage, and the structure of commemorative shrines were likely enriched by his travels in Thailand, his understanding was also shaped by his prior study of Buddhist texts over several years (Neel, conversation with author, 2003). Against this backdrop, Neel's reference to one of the shrine's entryways as one of four elements in *The Young Chief* codes the painting as ritual precinct and suggests that Neel's journey to Thailand is a pilgrimage of sorts.

The Young Chief's purple element also calls attention to the Buddhist universe, specifically The Four Directions. This is not, however, the first time Neel has made reference to The Four Directions. Much of his earlier work makes related allusion, though more usually as The Four Directions are manifest within the indigenous cultures of North America. In a serigraph, aptly titled *The Four Directions* (1991), Neel maps the center of the universe with a large blue face surrounded by four faces and pairs of hands denoting the cardinal directions. In another of his serigraphs, *Number One Hero–Sitting Bull* (1993), Neel alludes to The Four Directions with a cross created from a pair of intersecting dollar bills in each of the image's four corners. Neel's most famous piece, *Life on the 18th Hole* (1990), is a serigraph that commemorates the 78-day standoff between Mohawk warriors and members of the Canadian police and military that took place near the town of Oka, Quebec, in the summer of 1990. During the standoff, peace pipes used at the 1973 siege at Wounded Knee were sent to the Mohawk at Oka and raised in recognition of The Four Directions (Obomsawin, 1995, and York & Pindera, 1991). In *Life on the 18th Hole*, Neel commemorates these ceremonies with a circular diagram surrounded by four outward-bound arrows, one in each of the serigraph's four corners.

In keeping with the convention of silence that surrounds The Sacred in indigenous North America, Neel also verbally signals the Four Directions with only a guarded voice (Smith, 2001, pp. 629-661). In fact, his only published written reference appears in his *Life on the 18th Hole* artist's statement. There, he describes his representation of The Four Directions in the following manner:

> The circle is the Circle of Life, the arrows The Four Directions, four being the number of balance and completeness. The red dots represent the blood of man ... the red, the yellow, the black, and the white man. Jointly they remind us of the common bond of all men. (1990, p. 1)

Some of Neel's words, such as "common bond of all men," allude to a sense of universal fraternity that inheres in Neel's conception of The Four Directions. But his use of the expression "the red, the yellow, the black, and the white man," in conjunction with his depiction of four distinct arrows, articulates a recognition of racial difference. The fact that the arrow is also a symbol of mobility suggests that his concept of The Four Directions involves movement. Together, Neel's words and text suggest that his conception of The Four Directions involves a sense of balance and movement toward those who are different.

Neel's description of The Four Directions in terms of color and movement is a useful instrument for locating additional meaning in *The Young Chief*. As I noted earlier in this section, *The Young Chief* is, to some extent, a reworking of Neel's *Self-Portrait with Chief Charlie James Swanson* and includes a shift from the medium of black-and-white photography to a medium of color—acrylic paint on canvas. The painting's yellow backdrop, then, refers to the work of Ellen Neel, but because yellow is also an allusion to one of The Four Sacred Directions, it simultaneously alludes to David Neel's movement in the yellow direction—his movement toward Thailand. The yellow backdrop as a symbol of Thailand also creates a link between the tangerine color of the chief's attire and the saffron-dyed robes worn by the Buddhist monks of Thailand, as well as to the work of Charlie James. With this shift toward color, Neel silently inflects his localizing aesthetic with some of The Four Directions' sacred properties, connecting two cultures while retaining their distinctive integrity, distinguishing his work further still from the universalizing assumptions of Smith, Capa, and Cartier-Bresson.

The Four Directions, vis-à-vis Neel's *Life on the 18th Hole* and its accompanying statement, similarly involves an ethic of human relations based on the recognition of differences, the movement toward others, and a resulting sense of balance. As noted earlier, *Life on the 18th Hole* was produced in 1990 at a time of conflict between the Mohawk nation of Kanesatake and the nation-state of Canada. I have argued that in that piece Neel offered up the concept of balance as an alternative to combat. Neel painted *The Young Chief* during the summer of 2002, within months of the terrorist attacks of September 11, 2001. At a time when nations around the globe were becoming increasingly militarized, Neel inserted a fourth element, a symbol of The Four Directions, into the Kwagiutl parable of *Waxwaxam*, once again asserting the conception of balance and peace, instead of war. *The Young Chief*, then, is not just a pastiche of cross-cultural connections; rather, it charts a means for harmonious co-existence in a world full of differences that have become amplified due to a more rapid rate of mobility.

Our understanding of *The Young Chief* can be greatly enhanced by incorporating the humanitarian goals of socially concerned photography and the recognition of difference associated with Neel's conception of The Four Directions. Through the comparisons of Neel's *Portrait of Lily-Bee and Mertel*, his *Self-Portrait with Chief Charlie James Swanson*, and *The Young Chief*, I have mapped Neel's movement between Texas, the Pacific Northwest, and Thailand and accompanying changes in his aesthetic praxis. Although *The Young Chief* marks a shift from the medium of photography to paint, it posits a belief in humankind and opposition to war much like the work of the concerned photographers. But instead of presenting a view of a singular world, *The Young Chief*, like Neel's *Self-Portrait with Chief Charlie James Swanson* and his *Portrait of Lily-*

Bee and Mertel Holloway, renders views of multiple worlds. As Neel's cosmopolitan aesthetic praxis develops, it presents locally specific modes by which the world is mapped, through photographs, Kwagiutl narratives, Buddhist references, and colors. Neel's cosmopolitan ethic is further illuminated by events that followed the making of *The Young Chief*. During the next few years, Neel undertook multiple journeys to Thailand, enriching his knowledge of the Thai people and landscape. Then, in the summer of 2005, he moved with his family to Bangkok. Neel's relocation to Thailand is one in a series of international moves, and suggests that, in the early twenty-first century, Neel may be circumambulating the earth, much as a Buddhist pilgrim symbolically "walks the Path of Life around the world." *The Young Chief*, then, evokes a cosmopolitanism, both aesthetic and ethical, that is indebted to concerned photography and to aspects of indigenous and Buddhist conceptions of The Four Directions.

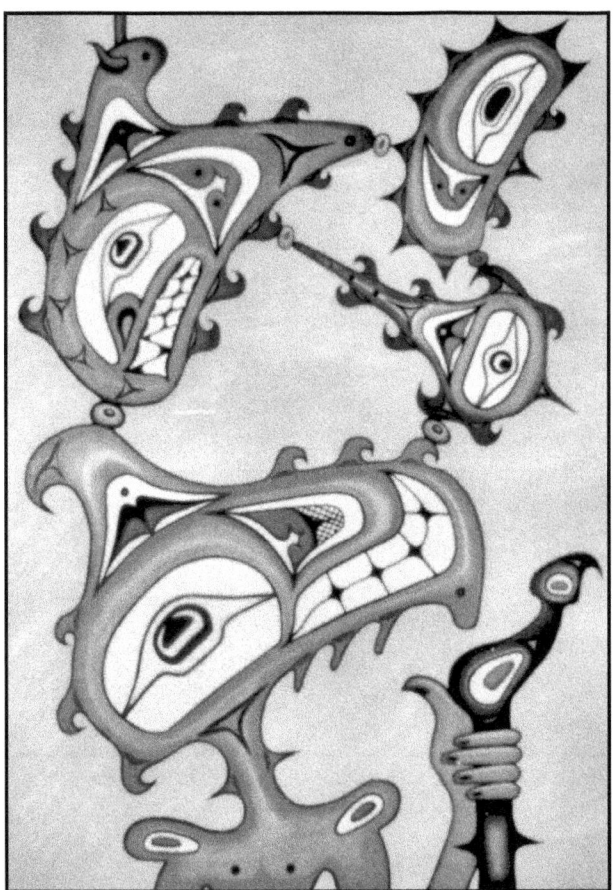

Figure 4.1: David Neel, *The Young Chief–Waxwaxam* (2002).
Reproduced with permission from the artist.

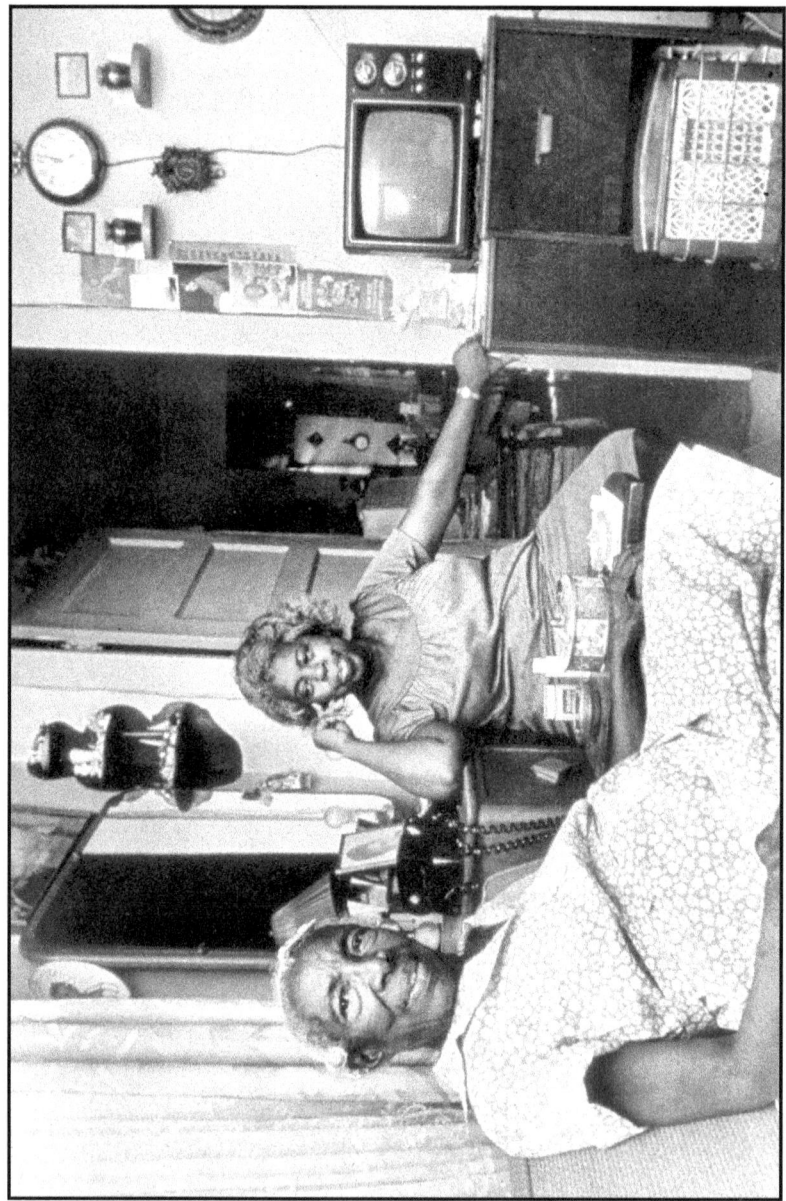

Figure 4.2: David Neel, *Portrait of Lily-Bee and Mertel Holloway* (1985). Reproduced with permission from the artist.

Figure 4.3: David Neel, *Self-Portrait with Chief Charlie James Swanson* (c.1990). Reproduced with permission from the artist.

References

Appiah, K. A. (2006). *Cosmopolitanism: Ethics in a World of Strangers*. New York: W. W. Norton.

Butler-Palmer, C. (2003). Paintings in the Present Tense. In Department of Indian and Northern Affairs, *Living Legends: The Artistic Process* (pp. 17-25). Gatineau, Quebec: Indian and Indian Art Gallery.

Canadian Press. (1991, April 1). Artist Aims to Reflect True Native Spirit in Masks. *The Vancouver Sun*, B-7.

Capa, C. (Ed.). (1968). *The Concerned Photographer*. New York: Grossman Publishers.

Clifford, J. (1997). *Routes: Travel and Translation in the Late Twentieth Century*. Cambridge MA: Harvard University Press.

Crosby, M. (2007). Construction of the Imaginary Indian. In J. O'Brian & P. White (Eds.), *Beyond Wilderness: The Group of Seven, Canadian Identity, and Contemporary Art* (pp. 219-222). Montreal: McGill-Queen's University Press.

Döhring, K. (2000). *Buddhist Stupa (Phra Chedi): Architecture of Thailand*. (E.J. Walter Tips, Trans.) Bangkok: White Lotus.

Halpin, M. (1992). Afterword. In David Neel (Ed.), *Our Chiefs and Elders: Words and Photographs of Native Leaders* (pp. 183-189). Vancouver: University of British Columbia Press.

Hawthorne, A. (1967). *Kwakiutl Art*. Seattle: University of Washington Press.

Ignatieff, M. (2003). *Magnum Degrees*. New York: Phaidon Press.

Linduff, K. M. (1997). Early Buddhist Art. In David Wilkins, Bernard Schultz, and Katheryn M. Linduff (Eds.), *Art Past/Art Present* (pp. 110-113). New York: Harry N. Abrams.

Neel, D. (1990). Artist statement: Life on the Eighteenth Hole [photocopy]. Life on the 18th Hole Preparation File. David Neel Studio, North Vancouver.

—— (Ed.). (1992). *Our Chiefs and Elders: Words and Photographs of Native Leaders*. Vancouver: University of British Columbia Press.

——. (2002). The Young Chief—Waxwaxam [postcard]. Meadville, Collection of the author.

Nuytten, P. (1982). *The Totem Carvers: Charlie James, Ellen Neel and Mungo Martin*. Vancouver: Panorama Press.

Obomsawin, A. (1995). Kanehsatake: 270 Years of Resistance [videorecording]. Ottawa: National Film Board of Canada.

Smith, T. E. (2001). Public Art between Cultures: The Aboriginal Memorial. *Critical Inquiry* (Summer), 629-661.

Watson, S. (1994). Race, Wilderness, and Territory and the Origins of Modern Canadian Landscape painting. *Semiotext(e)* (17), 96-104.

York, G. & L. Pindera. (1991). *People of the Pines: The Warriors of the Unknown Legacy of Oka*. Toronto: Little, Brown.

◆ CHAPTER FIVE ◆

Whither the Historicities of Alutiiq Heritage Work Are Drifting

Arthur Mason

Introduction: Narratives without Historicity

Several years ago, in the pages of *Current Anthropology*, James Clifford (2004) used the case study of Alutiiq Native identity and heritage on Kodiak Island,[1] Alaska, to make a larger point about the predicaments of indigenous people in the world today. Clifford pursues an intriguing theoretical exploration of external and internal conditions, forces, and historical circumstances that write the history of indigenous communities. He argues for taking into account the historicity of indigenous heritage and how indigenous consciousness was and is here to stay. Still, we are left with too general an account of the historicity of Alutiiq identity and heritage.

In this chapter I address Clifford's ambivalence with respect to Alutiiq historicity on Kodiak Island and his ambivalence about Alaskan ethnography more generally, by drawing attention to heritage work as a type of labor oriented toward creating new syntaxes of meaning. I argue that heritage work on Kodiak Island reorganizes spatial and temporal rhythms and thus contributes toward legitimizing new social orders, identities, and communal action. By examining the articulation of various heritage programs with local, national, and cosmopolitan visions, I situate Alaska Native identity and heritage within a larger historical sequence of struggles for gaining control over Kodiak's symbolic cultural order. From a broad point of view, this chapter is a call for ethnographic grounding in a scholarly field increasingly dominated by rather abstract and uniform perspectives on social transformations.

The concept of heritage invokes an idea of self-conscious tradition, what Ann Fienup-Riordan (2000) calls "conscious culture," performed in old and new public contexts against historical experiences of loss (p. 167). Heritage work includes such practices as oral historical research, cultural explanation through exhibits, interpretations of tourist sites, community-based archaeology, art production, marketing, and the like. Today, in Alaska, heritage work has become an integral part of creating a greater sense of Alaska Native self-awareness and identity. In this context, writes Clifford (2004), heritage work "responds to demands that originate both inside and outside indigenous communities, mediating new powers and attachments: relations with the land, among local groups, with the state, and with transnational forces" (p. 4).

As Clifford argues, community-based heritage work was present even prior to today's dramatically increased interest and political practice surrounding identity movements. For him this present moment exemplifies a "conjuncture" between corporate liberalism and indigenous heritage (p. 28). This is my argument too, but I feel that more attention could be paid in this context to what John and Jean Comaroff (1992) call the "endogenous historicity of local worlds" (p. 27). That is, by ignoring how new types of orderings of people emerge through heritage work, Clifford assumes that such developments can take place in the abstract and not be affected by particular local conditions. As such, Clifford avoids engagement with how Kodiak residents understand political authority to be intertwined in ways that depend on residents' own local histories of conflict and accommodation, and how these understandings, in turn, can transform a community's ideological self-sufficiency (e.g., Gledhill, 2000, p. 196).

Clifford sets up his narrative against a set of ethnographically inspired works, including my own (Mason, 2002, p. 13, 1996) that puts forth the argument about the emergence of an Alaska Native "identity industry." My work draws attention to a similarity between the kinds of state-centered technologies successful in constructing national sentiment (e.g., Anderson, 1992) and those used locally on Kodiak Island for developing an Alutiiq self-conscious identity (population maps, and archaeological and museum collections, e.g., Mason, 2008). Clifford (2004) believes that my work is "functionalist" by which he means that I have taken identity formation as a function of "corporate ideology [and] commodified tribal symbols" (p. 27), or in other words simply as a result of external forces acting upon an unconscious heritage, which only then becomes conscious of itself. This is a tragic misreading. In fact, my work attempts to frame identity and heritage as forms of political articulation and communal action that provide ways for Kodiak Islanders to secure a degree of autonomy from the nation-state (under certain conditions and up to a point) while pursuing alternative visions of modernity based on local tradition (although arguably *indigeneity* reflects a sense of active resistance that *tradition* does not, e.g., Braun, 2002, p. 92).

In this chapter I articulate my project more carefully by demonstrating how Alutiiq identity and heritage emerge out of a transitory moment when Kodiak's communal heritage work of the 1960s, which is oriented toward Russian tradition, shifts toward a newly understood indigenous culture of the 1980s and 1990s. This earlier Russian identification is sentimental, while the following, the Alutiiq indigenous culture, which becomes the dominant form during a post-land claims settlement period, emerges initially as a rationalized and interest driven form. Also, I argue that there is a drastic difference between these two periods of heritage work. In the Alutiiq heritage work of the post-land claims period, ideas about Alaska Native identity are further forged by economic and scientific practice that was not present before (as a dominant form).

As this relates to Clifford's narrow reading of my phrase identity industry, this transition suggests that the very technologies of identity formation and heritage work in Alaska are shifting and are now linked to the larger American political landscape, capitalism, scientific authority, and state intervention, as well as to local sentimentality and preservation of ancestral authority. Yes, indigenous identity and heritage work are open to negotiation; they are contingent, open and provocative, but there are specific conditionalities. On this point I agree with Clifford (2004) in subscribing to the Marxist argument that people do make history but in conditions not of their choosing (p. 14).

Heritage programs on Kodiak Island draw attention to three historically distinct visions: early twentieth-century Americana (1920s–1940s); nineteenth-century Russian American colonial (1960s–1980s), and; precontact "Alutiiq classical" (Crowell, 2001, p. 4) (1980s–present). The earliest form of heritage work on Kodiak that I encounter dates to the late 1920s and is referred to in a locally published Baptist newsletter. The passage is brief (see below). Still, it provides a perspective on the kind of heritage work taking place among Kodiak school children who as adults participate in the 1960s and 1980s Russian and Alutiiq heritage work programs, respectively.

The second quarter of the twentieth century also coincides with the birth of the first generation of Alutiiq Native leaders involved in the land claims movement of the 1960s. With congressional passage of the Alaska Native Claims Settlement Act (ANCSA) in 1971, the U.S. government ceded 44 million acres of land and nearly one billion dollars to Alaska Natives in the form of regional and village corporations. By reflecting on the kind of heritage work taking place in the 1920s and 1930s, one can learn of the milieu in which these future Native leaders were raised. Later in life, members of this "Alutiiq cohort" (Mason, 2002, p. 7) orchestrate two distinct communal heritage programs—the first taking place in the 1960s and oriented toward a Russian identity, and the second in the 1980s, oriented toward a newly formed Alutiiq identity.

Elsewhere, I argue (Mason, 1996, 2002) that members of the Alutiiq cohort share similar historical and personal developments and are descendants of prestigious nineteenth-century Russian-Native Creole families. These nineteenth-century burgher families (*meshchane*) possess political and cultural distinctions based predominantly on education, ancestry, and citizenship that differentiate them from other Kodiak families of the time. These distinctions separate the local population into what were relatively fixed and inherited social categories and in doing so prescribe life possibilities to those that occupy them. Thus, by focusing on heritage work programs, I demonstrate how descendents of Kodiak Creole families creatively secure visions of social order based on radically different ways of classifying social persons and of mediating their social interactions. In particular, I emphasize how these visions become realized through the *production of space* that organizes the activities of people in time and through space. As such, heritage work provides cultural categories and social relationships for everyday life.

Early Kodiak Heritage Work

The story of early twentieth-century heritage work on Kodiak Island begins in 1893, when the American Baptist missionary Ernest Roscoe establishes a missionary school on Woody Island, which is adjacent to the town of Kodiak. Some 25 years earlier, Russia had sold Alaska to the United States in 1867. Seeing the need for mission work in the new Alaska territory, the U.S. government requested leaders of various American denominations, including Moravian, Presbyterian, and Baptist, to select distinct regions of Alaska where each could work without interference from the other. The Baptist territory would comprise the region of today's Alutiiq cultural and linguistic area.

In 1908, the Baptist school on Woody Island consisted of 48 children. By 1924 it had over 75 children (Chaffin, 1967; Jacobs, 1995; Roscoe, 1992). At that time, Woody Island was alternatively referred to as Lesnoi. The word Lesnoi is the adjectival form of the Russian word for wooded area or forest (*les*). Until establishment of the Baptist mission, Russian was the language used among the local elite. These elite would consist of Russian orthodox priests as well as parents of the Alutiiq cohort, the descendents of prestigious nineteenth-century Russian-Native Creole families (Mason, 1996).

Establishment of the Baptist mission brought cultural change to Kodiak. Sanctioned by the U.S. territorial government, the missionaries' intellectual and religious work would soon possess a local official status. As such, their forms of knowledge and practice would soon begin to undermine the local authority once exercised by Russian priests. In truth, for Russian priests who elect to remain after the transfer of Alaska to the United States, increasing economic difficulty contributes to their deteriorating social and intellectual influence. Support from far-off Russia is insufficient to maintain earlier levels of educational service. These problems intensify in the post-1917 Russian revolutionary era.

This same period also marks a decline in Kodiak of Russian Imperial-style forms of etiquette. These elite forms would still be performed by the remaining Russian-Native Creole, whose social gatherings in the "parlors" of their Kodiak town homes are characterized in the diaries of newly arrived Americans as "old world customs" practiced by "half-breeds or Creoles, as they call themselves, speaking the Russian language and belonging to the Russo-Greek church" (Huggins, 1981, p. 132). The Baptist mission efforts to Americanize Kodiak Islanders include providing English language courses. Establishment of "a night school," Roscoe writes in his journal, began altering the vernacular of Kodiak "in a very few years from Russian to English" (Roscoe, 1992, p. 24).

With this background, let me now provide the reference to communal heritage work in the Baptist *Orphanage Newsletter* (1928) that I promised earlier. The newsletter was distributed among Kodiak Islanders and the quote is from the late 1920s,

> Our pupils are trying to get together a little school museum consisting of products and interesting specimens from various parts of the United States. They are willing to exchange Kodiak products for those from any part of the [United] States. Such a collection will be very helpful to them, especially in their study of geography. Think how much more real Texas and Nebraska will seem when seen through a ball of cotton and a big ear of yellow corn.

In this brief passage, we learn of Kodiak children participating in a particular type of educational and communal activity, what we might call Kodiak's first communal heritage work program. They are creating a museum and filling it with things—American things invested with the imagined realities of Nebraska and Texas as well as things "from any part of the [United] States." To understand the significance of this quote, let us begin with the museum. As a site for the display of cultural treasury and patrimony, the museum has long been identified as one technique for intimately linking together a population. The museum opens up space for thinking about domain, geography, language, community—what is both inside and outside the nation (Anderson, 1992). Thus, for Kodiak children of the early twentieth century, their "little school museum" is both technology and form for creating a new cultural experience—one of aesthetic fascination, temporal coincidence, and desire: "think how much more real Texas and Nebraska will seem" (*Orphanage Newsletter*, 1928).

Let us now examine their heritage work. Notice that the students exchange local Kodiak products willingly and in so doing they collect museum products "from any part of the [United] States." Through this exchange, the very locality of Kodiak, as symbolized in its artifacts, is distributed across Texas and Nebraska and thus, the locality of Kodiak circulates within the larger nation-state. Also, with the arrival of the little national treasures (ball of cotton, ear of corn) the national imaginings of the outside world circulate inside the self-enclosed understandings of the Kodiak community. Thus, from this first example of communal heritage work we can see how the locality of Kodiak begins to be appropriated into the unity of the nation-state while at the same time we can see the beginnings of deterioration in Kodiak's collective seclusion and inner ideological self-sufficiency.

Why do we learn of this museum activity in the first place? We become aware of this activity because it is published in the Baptist newsletter, which is circulated around Kodiak. Thus, this heritage work is also a public statement. It is an announcement of a new kind of cultural experience. And this new experience is taking place side by side with a number of other activities oriented toward creating new cultural experience. These other activities include the renaming of Lesnoi to Woody Island as well as creating a school for English learning that takes place in the night time, so adult Kodiak Islanders can participate after laboring in the day.

All these practices are introducing new conceptions of time and space, in which Kodiak's Russian locality and rhythms are being transformed. Russian place names are becoming American place names, people of different ages are becoming educated about new ideas in different times of the day and experiencing new kinds of spaces for congregating, speaking, and learning. Taken as a whole, these practices are creating a new syntax of meaning concerning Kodiak's local world, which involves redefining and recoding space and time. What we see here then is an entire combination of different kinds of techniques and forms oriented toward disrupting the spatial and temporal rhythms of Kodiak.

The geographer David Harvey (1990) points out that conceptions of time and space are necessarily created through material practices and processes that serve to reproduce social life. Each distinctive mode of production or social formation, Harvey argues, will embody a distinctive bundle of time and space practices and concepts. The history of social change, he states, is captured by the history of the conceptions of space and time and the ideological uses to which these conceptions might be put. In fact, Harvey concludes, ideological and political hegemony in any society depend on an ability to control the material context of personal and social experience. That is, materializations and meanings given to time and space are significant for the maintenance of political power. Thus, whoever possesses the ability to influence the production of Kodiak space and time also has the means to augment power. Moreover, because communal heritage work on Kodiak plays an important role in this production, it thus serves as an instrument to augment power.

I believe that these activities taking place on Kodiak in the early twentieth century that are disrupting the temporal and spatial order must be seen as techniques oriented toward a struggle for gaining control over Kodiak's symbolic cultural order. Early communal heritage work on Kodiak is part of the real and imaginary reorganization of space, time, and language that is taking place. This heritage work is creating a new mythology expressive of values and meanings associated with the American nation-state. As such, it serves as an advertisement and a reminder to Kodiak Islanders of the deterioration that characterizes the social order of Russian-Native Creole culture, the decay of its etiquettes, forms of knowledge, events, temporalities, localities, language, political statuses, and social relations. The sociologist Georg Simmel, writing about cultural deterioration at nearly the same time as the events on Kodiak, states that decay does not "sink the work of man into the formlessness of mere matter, [but rather creates new form] entirely meaningful, comprehensible, differentiated" (Simmel, 1959, p. 261). And that seems to be the message of these Kodiak schoolchildren involved in their heritage work, that there is a new symbolic cultural order coming.

Russian Heritage Work during the Cold War

During the mid-1990s, while living on Kodiak Island, I became aware of two historically different heritage programs whose artifacts reflect two radically distinct ways of marking social space. I had stumbled across two systems of symbolic interaction in which the world was organized around particular announcements.

In the first set of symbols, petroglyph designs as well as images of stone lamps and Native masks had become logos printed on T-shirts, baseball caps, coffee mugs, and jackets. The logos advertise various Alutiiq corporations established under the 1971 ANCSA. With passage of the ANCSA, Alutiiqs were ceded millions of acres of land and millions of dollars through the establishment of Native corporations. In the second set of symbols, visible throughout downtown Kodiak, Russian men's surnames—Rezanof, Shelikov, Baranov, Kashaverof—were displayed on plaques and statues that were themselves cemented into the ground or erected on poles as street signs.

Both sets of symbols index kin relationships between Kodiak Islanders and their Alutiiq or Russian forbears, respectively. They mark a relationship between Kodiak Islanders and objects of their social world. The petroglyph design, for example, suggests a place where Alutiiq forbears inhabited the island many years ago. The placement of the Russian men's names belongs to the period of the 1960s and 1970s and predates the Alutiiq corporate logos of the 1990s. Still, both sets of symbols were produced by members of the Alutiiq cohort and their children, many of who had become or are now governing members of the ANCSA Alutiiq corporations.

The geographical placement, immobility, and navigational capacity of the Russian surnames lie in stark contrast to the logos of the Alutiiq Native corporations, whose message stresses consumption, infinite reproduction, and mobility. The nonmovable street signs, plaques, and statues, for example, are part of a system of representation that freezes the flow of experience. The logo, by contrast, through its movement can weave places together, creating multitudes of Alutiiq space. The street signs, as permanent fixtures, localize. The logos, in their circulation, spatialize. The street signs represent a particular kind of norm in which the subject makes a movement across disciplinary space. The norm of the logo is liberated and localized outside this grid of control—outside of Kodiak Island altogether—for T-shirts, coffee cups, jackets, and baseball caps, can travel on a plane. What gave rise to these two different technologies and configurations for mapping both the Kodiak landscape and collective identities on Kodiak Island? What transition in social formation occurred on Kodiak from the 1960s to the 1990s as reflected in these forms of heritage work for representing time and space?

My explanation begins with a description of Kodiak's Russian heritage program during the 1960s, which must be seen as curiously self-enclosed, even by Alaskan standards. The positive meanings invoked by Russian heritage are at odds with what was taking place across America during the cold war period. Given that American communities were constructing bomb shelters as one response to the national sense of military and economic insecurity of the Cold War, it hardly seems the time to redefine public spaces, streets, and buildings by reference to the Russian state.

Within Alaska itself, promoting Russian heritage during the 1960s contradicts the sense of American national pride experienced by many Alaskans who were celebrating statehood status, achieved a few years prior, in 1959. With the shift from territorial status to statehood, Alaskans became full-fledged members of the United States, that is, they acquired two senatorial positions in Congress to become a serious partner in the nation-state's redistributive welfare process. From today's perspective, celebrating Kodiak's Russian past seems peculiar. It is at odds with an essential aspect of Alutiiq identity, given the historical fact that Russian colonization of Alaska during the eighteenth century ushered in a period of intense disruption and trauma among Kodiak peoples. Labor exploitation, massacres, and epidemics are well documented. For example, Russian wars of conquest coupled with the introduction of disease dramatically reduced Kodiak's population from 8,000 people in 1784 to 6,000 people in 1792 (Clark, 1984, pp. 186-187).

Yet, during the 1960s, Kodiak Islanders remapped their Russian kinship relations quite literally on to the village landscape. Under the direction of the local historical society, a merchant's house built by the Russians during the nineteenth century is renovated into a museum named after Alexander

Baranov, the first governor of Russian America. Town leaders introduce rhetorical techniques such as the naming of streets and the staging of a dramatization of Russian American life. In this play, titled *Cry of the Wild Ram* in honor of Baranov ("Baranov" signifies "ram" in Russian), Kodiak's Russian colony is reconstituted weekly. The play is advertised as "the largest civic endeavor the community has ever engaged in," involving some four hundred townspeople annually (Page, 1982, pp. 61-63).

Teresa Koreck (1991) suggests that naming within communities expresses different interests and histories as well as different visions of community. Some villagers may resist them; but these words signal material, social, economic, and political relationships. They mediate "new powers and attachments," to borrow the phrase from Clifford (2004, p. 4). I believe the reasons for celebrating Kodiak's Russian heritage during the cold war can be found in the cultural meanings invoked *at that time* by members of the Alutiiq cohort who led this program. Such meanings include the possible positive references of Russian colonization of Kodiak, references taken to be so profound that they are capable of glossing over negative associations. Let me begin by unpacking some of complicated positive meanings and then turn to the historical conditions within which they are invoked.

Of Enlightenment and Alaska Early Moderns

In the year 1821, the Russian state accorded the citizenship status of burgher[2] (*meshchanstvo*) to the Alaska Creole. In the nineteenth century when Alaska was a territory of Imperial Russia, Creole referred to the children of Russian men and indigenous Alaskan women. This group included members of the Kodiak Island community. At that time, the Creole of Kodiak Island was invested with the rights and privileges of Russian citizenship. Although this legal identification represented an ambiguous outsider status within the social framework of an activist state, for some Kodiak Creole, these privileges included traveling to St. Petersburg, Russia, where they enrolled in university and studied navigation, medicine, religion, and the arts.

The term "Creole" was introduced into the European Russian context sometime before 1816 for use exclusively in Alaska. In the 1821 Russian Imperial Charter authorizing activities of the Russian American Company, Alexander I (1777-1825), Emperor of Russia, decrees: "Creoles, who according to the latest information numbered 180 souls of male and 120 of female gender, and all those who should be born in the future are to ... constitute a separate estate under enjoyment of the following rules: [first] Creoles are Russian subjects ... [with] right[s] to governmental protection on the same basis as all subjects belonging to the *burgher estate* ... " (Black, 2004, p. 215, with emphasis).

While the juridical meaning of burgher functioned in a way as to endow a group of Alaskans with certain rights as citizens of Imperial Russia, the cultural connotations of this category as employed in Russia do not so readily convey this historical moment as experienced in Alaska. With the status of Russian citizenship came the rise of a new societal order. For the Creole of Kodiak Island, it coincided with the breaking of Native rank order and the introduction of a logic of class stratification, the values of civil rights, meritocracy, individualism, and credentials. Evidence of this can be seen through the emphasis placed by the Creole burgher on personal accomplishment, that is, self-legitimization by intellectual achievement.[3] The Creole burgher is also a subject of social mobility. Alexander Kashevarov, for whom one of the Kodiak street names is given, was educated as a ship navigator and rose to the position of commander of the Siberian port of Ayan (Oleksa, 1992, p. 151). His parents were a Kodiak Creole mother and a Russian father (Black, 2004, p. 214). Thus, Russian citizenship for the Kodiak Creole marked the threshold of their entrance into a particular kind of modernity.

It is precisely because I identify this moment as a threshold of modernity that I employ the term *burgher* to refer to the citizenship status (*meshchane*) of the Kodiak Creole. In the nineteenth century, the burgher signifies a sense of cosmopolitanism and transformation to modernity. In Central Europe, for example, the concept of burgher is bound to the twin concepts of maturity and reason—two words reflected on at length by German philosopher Immanuel Kant in his 1784 published response to the question "What is Enlightenment?" (Foucault, 1984a). Immanuel Kant, a professor of logic and metaphysics, was an eminent burgher himself.[4]

Elsewhere, I investigate the entry of Alutiiq life into history (Mason, n.d.). I demonstrate how, what I call the Alutiiq burgher, became Alaska's first home-grown early modern. While the Alutiiq burgher's historical appearance was assured by the introduction of the Russian American company on Kodiak Island, I point out that the subjectivity of this burgher remains an *indigenous* cosmopolitan. This social fact is never more clearly reflected upon at the time than in the criticisms expressed toward the company by the celebrated Alutiiq burgher Lt. Alexander Kashevarov. In 1861, during a debate on the future of the Alaskan colony, Lt. Kashevarov, then living in retirement in St. Petersburg, published several articles opposing the renewal of the Russian American company charter. He states: "Are we who were born in Russian America really supposed to consider forever the best interests of the Russian American Company as we have been taught from our childhood, and smother within ourselves every natural striving, every idea about the interests of our native land?" (Oleksa, 1992, p. 151).

Following from the above, I suggest that Russian citizenship for the Kodiak Creole was more than a bundle of political rights.[5] Their burgher identity presented certain conditions of possibility that signify the opportunity to obtain a European education and to hold a lead position with Alaska's Russian American trading company. Educational qualification has a "fixed value," which, being guaranteed by law, is freed from local limitations and temporal fluctuations (Bourdieu, 1990, p. 132). Thus, legitimized through the Russian legal apparatus, the Creole status was endowed with a permanence and opacity that lay beyond the reach of individual consciousness. In this way, the burgher status provided a mode of relating to the contemporary reality of the time through a certain relation of belonging. Following Michel Foucault (1984a), this mode or attitude would be similar to what the Greeks called an *ethos* (p. 39).

It is, in fact, this burgher ethos that newly arriving Americans to Kodiak during the nineteenth century find so disorienting and for which they seek to denigrate, but are also forced to identify as having a haughty character, as witnessed in the quote also presented earlier, "half-breeds or Creoles, as they call themselves, speaking the Russian language and belonging to the Russo-Greek church" (Huggins, 1981, p. 132).

Returning to the 1960s, by constructing heritage around the Creole burgher members of the Alutiiq cohort were invoking characteristics of an individual will oriented toward developing intellectual, scientific, and artistic achievement. This ethos was not directed solely toward material gain but was carried out as an obligation to Kodiak society for which members of the Alutiiq cohort would hold themselves responsible personally. In short, like their Creole forbearers of the nineteenth century, members of the Alutiiq cohort fashioned themselves as enlightened modern persons. It is particularly noteworthy that the Creole status was marked by patrilineal inheritance, hence the reference to Russian *male* names during the 1960s heritage work. In the nineteenth century, the child from a union of a Creole woman married or joined together with a non-Creole man would not be a member of the Creole burgher estate, but a member of the fathers' group. Children of a Creole man in all unions retained their fathers' privileged burgher status.

Kodiak Reconstruction

> Why can a street be completely rebuilt and still be the same? Because it does not constitute a purely material entity; it is based on certain conditions that are distinct from the materials that fit the conditions, e.g. its location with respect to other streets. (de Saussure, 1966 [1916], p. 109)

The story of how the nineteenth-century burgher ethos awakens begins with a crisis. The effects of the 1964 Alaska earthquake and tidal wave on Kodiak were transformative, causing millions of dollars in damage, loss of life, and complete destruction of Kodiak's downtown business community. In the wake of the disaster, federal and local governments seize control, tearing up streets while incorporating once commonly held property into private property (a process that James Scott [1998] associates with creating a "supralocal market" in land, p. 39). Kodiak becomes a city of plywood palaces where outside industry and government institutions experience undreamed of expansion, leaving some locals disenfranchised while providing new powers to others.

Occurring soon after the Alaska statehood, Kodiak reconstruction may be seen as a state-building policy in which the government seeks to consolidate authority at the local level through creation of new property rights, establishing subsistence regulations, linking the beneficiaries of locals directly to agencies, and creating new identities through which local communal ties might be replaced more fully by a national identity. Still, as Jennie Purnell (1999) argues, by refashioning the symbolic and institutional fabric of village life, state-building polices inevitably create new conflicts and intensify old ones "within communities, between communities and between communities and the state" (p. 179). They provide opportunities also for new alliances between local and state actors for the partial realization of local demands and agendas.

For descendants of Kodiak's honored families, this cosmos of disorder is ground zero for a new self-awareness about their collective identity. According to one member of this esteemed Alutiiq cohort, "The impetus [was] the past should be leveled—start out from scratch ... but the exposed historic Russian sites from the tidal wave 'woke us up'" (Kodiak Alutiiq, personal communication, 1995). As the quote suggests, the image of Russian heritage provokes a deep level awakening of Kodiak social life—a childhood memory of Creole identity as the basis of its grassroots re-creation. Thus, Russian heritage work during reconstruction can be seen as a type of reaction to increasing attempts by government structures to redefine appropriate social behavior—a reaction mounted on the sphere of a kin-based ethos.

And yet, while seeking to contain their kin-based lifeworld, Kodiak Islanders also manage to reestablish identification with the state. That is, they choose kinship with the Russian state. And from the moment of the Creole burgher's reappearance, members of the Alutiiq cohort "wake up." They are thus invested with the idea of a modern attitude that enables them to pave way for new historical relations for a world that is literally swept away. Stated differently, for Kodiak Islanders of the 1960s whose only reference to the modern is their colonial past, their entrance into a new modernity becomes a form of heritage work. Through their heritage work, the burgher in them awakes. Invested with the phantom of modernity's past, Kodiak Islanders invoke resemblance to enlightened ideas of honor, clarity, maturity. What Brackett Williams (1991, pp. 257–258) observes about the "ghostly constraint" of colonial identity that allows the Guyanese to "move on" applies here. Cast under the spell of this nineteenth-century attitude, Kodiak Islanders acquire existential equipment for (a double) crossing of modernity's threshold into self-conscious citizens of the American nation-state (i.e., moving forward by looking backward).

Roger Keesing (1992, pp. 216-217) argues that resistance and ancestral revelation are not solely romantic stances that have oppositional elements. They also entail motives of personal gain and political ambition. Thus, rather than feel threatened by the broader national context, heritage work ensures that entrance into the national community serves as a "liberating force" (Nugent, 1998, p. 9), but somewhat paradoxically, through conceptualizations of incorporation of gain within a system without seeming to challenge the system. Kodiak's reconstruction period serves as an example. It becomes recognized by local leaders as a strategic site through which to learn valuable lessons in dealing with federal agencies (Davis, 1979). As one member of the Alutiiq cohort states: "One of the lessons [learned] by those exposed [to the rebuilding effort], the business community, was how to utilize the government. [They have become] *less afraid and more knowledgeable, they know* now that there are literally hundreds of millions of dollars available. *It's all in knowing* how to get them" (Armstrong, 1978, p. 14, emphasis added; Davis, 1979, p. 54). That is, by entangling themselves with the enlightened burgher, Alutiiq leaders find *the courage, the audacity to know.*

> Ulwani! ("Inside")
> Ulwani! We yell ulwani when the fish begin jumping inside [the salmon net]. It means inside. When the fish jump, it means we've caught a lot of fish.
> —Alutiiq fisherman, Kodiak Island

From 1975 until 1982, practitioners of Kodiak communal heritage were primarily students of the Kodiak Aleutian Regional High School under the direction of instructor David Kubiak. In a series of 10 publications of approximately 40 pages each, and titled *Elwani Magazine: Inside the Life and Culture of Kodiak,* Kubiak and students bring together an impressive ensemble of the history, biographies, and customs of Kodiak Islanders. Elwani (alternatively written Ulwani) is an Alutiiq term meaning *inside.* The title reflects the self-enclosed meanings of Kodiak life. Students equipped with writing pads, cameras, and recorders entered into the homes of local elders and parents, recording Kodiak lifeways. The publication collection itself serves as a type of ethnographic genre. Anthropologist Nancy Yaw Davis (1984), for example, cites this material as ethnographic resource in her contribution to the *Smithsonian Handbook of North American Indians.*

This program represents a liminal period of Kodiak heritage work and can be seen as book-ended temporally by two seminal accounts of Kodiak lifeways gathered by Alaskan female author Yule Chaffin (1967; Chaffin, Krieger, & Rostad, 1983). Both Kubiak and Chaffin's efforts take place between two distinct authoritative heritage work programs carried out by members of the Alutiiq cohort and their descendants: Before the mid-1970s, a group of Kodiak Islanders focus their heritage work on promoting a Russian tradition; after the mid-1980s, members of this same group focus on an Alutiiq cultural identity. While the production of Elwani is centralized by its location at the high school, in comparison to the Alutiiq program that follows, it reflects a far less professionalized endeavor. It does not, for example, rely on theoretical principles of academic linguistics or culture. This is evident in an exchange between Elwani magazine publishers and Dr. Michael Krauss, linguist at the Alaska Native Language Center at University of Alaska, Fairbanks. In three separate formal requests by high school students to Krauss and his assistant Dr. Jeff Leer, Elwani publishers repeatedly ask why the linguists "call the language and the people of [the Kodiak] area Sugpiaq ... [when] the people we have talked to called their language Aleut" (Elwani 1976).

The letters and responses by the linguists are reproduced in one volume and illuminate the relationship of power and distance once exercised by scholars over the region. As one Alutiiq (Pullar, 1992) later recalls:

> [W]hen anthropologists began telling Alutiiq people that they were not Aleuts, but Eskimos, emotional responses included embarrassment, shame, and anger. The implication of the anthropological designation was a feeling that people were, in essence, being told "You people are so dumb that you don't even know who you are." (p. 185)

Still, the muse of Chaffin and Elwani practitioners as well as the term Aleut would soon pass. In 1978, during a week-long Alutiiq language workshop in Kodiak, sponsored by the Alaska Native Language Center, Kodiak English speakers are introduced to Alutiiq (Alutiiq is Aleut in indigenized form) (see Mason, 2008). The 1978 workshop was held for the purpose of "introducing the Alutiiq writing system to those who could be key people in language work in their villages" (Leer, 1978, p. 2).

Tradition through Optics of Loss

Soon after the Kodiak reconstruction, U.S. government negotiations with Alaska Natives over a land claims settlement began in earnest. Aware of the potential modernizing role from participating in the process, Kodiak leaders who previously had defined themselves through their Russian American ancestry began to identify themselves through their Native ancestry. Among their early activities was establishment of nonprofit associations "targeted directly" to fight for land claims settlement (Hank Eaton, personal communication, 1995; Pullar & Jordan, 1987).

During this period, Alutiiq leaders became uncertain about their new political identity and sought legal advice to determine the potential economic and social benefits as well as liabilities for participating in the land claims movement. According to one lawyer familiar with the time: "I can tell you what the conversations were [among] lawyers. ... Some of most prominent Native corporation leaders today, weren't sure about it and were asking their lawyers whether they should even sign up for the [land claims settlement] deal" (Ben Hancock, personal communication, 1997).

While determining what genealogies these leaders wished to write and how they should position themselves relative to others on Kodiak, certain town leaders began acquainting themselves with Alutiiqs from the surrounding region, forging new alliances and group identifications: According to one informant, the Alutiiq and judge Roy Madsen "would travel around to the [Alutiiq] villages, organize meetings, teach[ing] the Natives about the importance of the [land claims] settlement deal." The same informant, nodding her head in contemplative appreciation, concluded, "And I've always given him credit for that" (Kodiak Alutiiq, personal communication, 1997).

It is because of these efforts that members of the Alutiiq cohort became structurally situated historically, socially, and culturally to occupy the new economic positions established under the 1971 ANCSA. They became the first generation of Native corporate leaders to participate, along with other Native leaders across the state, in investment opportunities concerning 12 percent of Alaska land and large reserves of capital.

By the late 1970s, however, engaging opportunities as economic entrepreneurs began increasing a sense among Alutiiq leaders that recovery of a more fully Native existence seemed to recede further from their grasp. As one Native corporation founding member recalls: "We began to realize that there wasn't a heck of a lot on our people and as I say we were not interested in the Russian or American aspect of the history as much as we were becoming interested in our own Native history and how it came into being and where we fitted into the scheme of things before [the Europeans] ever landed here" (Hank Eaton, personal communication, 1995). This awareness was awakened in part by the political-social movements of the 1960s that embraced multiculturalism in America and also the arrival of various liberal intellectuals and professionals in Alaska.

This reflection led Kodiak leaders once again to choose specific practices and sites for how a particular awareness of the self could be realized. Employing linguistic maps, archaeological excavations, museum exhibitions, and with the assistance of archaeologists, historians, and educators, Alutiiq leaders utilized new equipment based on theoretical knowledge through which to invoke a local Native identity. According to one Kodiak Alutiiq attending Native corporation seminars on Alutiiq identity,

> At the Native corporation, there was more talk about [archaeological] artifacts and what artifacts really were. Before that I don't think I connected it to ancestry. You know—it was just something that happened to people before us, never really connecting—wow! ... That's where we come from. (Kodiak Alutiiq, personal communication, 1995)

Thus, movement toward rediscovery of a cultural past arose from an ethical paradox inherent in the profound corporatization of Native life. Native capitalist entrepreneurs began to see themselves as caretakers of an identity project and entered into alliances with academic expertise and state actors to protect (thus develop) Native heritage (e.g., Mason, 2008).

Conclusion: Heritage Episteme

As Kodiak's heritage programs suggest, politics at the level of the subject is likely involved in the struggle between official and popular nationalisms. The unsuccessful imposition of an official version of U.S. nationalism implies that power groups are not always able to colonize the very imaginations of the people over whom they seek to continue their rule. Thus, it is not enough to point out, as Benedict Anderson (1992) does, that the successful adoption, superimposition, and spread of official nationalism as a substitute for popular nationalism lay well within the capacity of ruling groups to accomplish. Still, ethnographic grounding is necessary in articulating the point.

After his *Current Anthropology* publication and in an e-mail conversation with me, James Clifford posed the question "What ingredients are linked together in the Alutiiq ethnogenesis? And what relative (causal?) weight should they be given?" (Clifford, e-mail communication, 2004). My ethnographic investigation suggests that such questions frame Alutiiq identity as inevitable, foreseen, and predetermined—a latency from which a "return to tradition" (Clifford, 2004, p. 32) is assured.

As I demonstrate above, Kodiak heritage work reflects a historical sequence of distinct yearnings by town elites for creating a sense of continuity, whereby points of origin are established and then trajectories through time and space are described, thereby legitimizing subjects as heir to specific origins. These shifting historical identifications suggest that Kodiak heritage work has a somewhat theatrical flair: actors take to the stage to proclaim a postulate of origins, and then, a historical moment later, they retake the stage to declare a new postulate. Each performance, as I indicate, attains official status through establishing spatial and temporal orders that articulate in complex ways with more general developments.

Does this make heritage work a two-way street where in one direction Kodiak Islanders are heading toward alienation or in the other direction toward authenticity? I hardly think so. Following Clifford's (1988) work on cultural revitalization, heritage work is a meaningful form of political articulation and communal action. It is a way for Kodiak Islanders to derive autonomy from larger forces over which they have little control and to pursue visions of modernity on the basis of their own popular culture. Still, my use of the phrase "postulate of origins" coined by Michel Foucault (1984b, pp. 76-100), suggests that origins can serve as sites of truth which, in turn, enable fields of knowledge to emerge.

During the 1990s, anthropologists and others viewed origins talk as alarmingly essentialist (Hale, 1994; Mouffe, 1993; Warren, 1998). Roger Keesing argued that origins talk provides a "systematic coherence, a pervasive sharedness, and an enduring quality that commits us to an essentialism of an extreme kind" (1994, p. 303). For my part, I see these postulates as partial practices for the constitution of new mythologies. The recent effort by Clifford included, such narratives without historicity assist actors in reshaping the normative and institutional relationships among property rights, religious practice, and local authority on Kodiak. They also contribute toward locally and temporally constituted fields of knowledge—what I call "heritage epistemes"—that are at once caught in and forged out of a conjuncture, as Clifford writes.

In this chapter, my interest in the location of heritage epistemes is historically and representationally broader than the framing of identity within the conflictive relationships between states and nations as suggested in the phrase "heritage politics" (i.e., attention to exacerbations of cultural globalization. See Gledhill, 2000, p. 162; Appadurai, 1990). I show how relations of spatial form, temporal process, and power, as well as modes of authority, serve in "topological arrangement" (Allen, 2004, p. 19). From this perspective, authority to be productive in social relations must be embodied in historically distinct bundles of time and space practices and concepts. The restructuring of spatial relations is key to establishing new social, economic, and political relations, including the distribution of control over how space is reproduced. The ability to influence the production of Kodiak space and time is an important means toward augmenting authority over personal and social experience. And because communal heritage work on Kodiak plays a unique role in this production, it thus serves as an instrument to augment power.

Notes

1. Kodiak Island is located in the Gulf of Alaska and is part of the Alutiiq cultural and linguistic area referred to by anthropologists as Pacific Eskimo during an earlier period of research (Clark, 1984).
2. Burgher signifies an intellectually formed middle class and may be contrasted to bourgeoisie that signifies an economically formed middle-class.
3. Contrast this with the precontact Kodiak Native "noble" class that accomplishes nothing in the sense in which others do, but for which the shaping of its distinguished and distinctive behavior is central to self-image and self justification (Clark, 1984, p. 186).
4. This generational shift in social position reflects the mobility project of the Central and Eastern European burgher as well as the Russian social middle-class categories or *soslovie* (Wirtschafter, 1994, 1997). Norbert Elias (1978, p. 20) writes, for example, that the whole burgher movement was one of upward mobility: Goethe's great grandfather "was a blacksmith, his grandfather a tailor." From similar social origins come Herder, Kant, Fichte, and many others of the Bildungs Bürghertum movement, the intellectually formed middle class.
5. Within the context of Imperial Russia, the Creole status was a juridically based social category (*soslovie*). It is true that the Russian concept of *meshchane* was derogatory. Still, by nineteenth century this category also represented a newer set of meanings that were associated with an enlightened socially progressive milieu (Wirtschafter, 1997, p. 64).

Acknowledgments

This chapter is based on my lectures at the Department of Social Anthropology, Norwegian University of Science and Technology, on February 26, 2007; Department of Anthropology, University of Alaska, at Fairbanks, on February 18, 2005; the Department of Cultural and Social History, University of Greenland, on October 12, 2004; and the Department of Eskimology and Arctic Studies, University of Copenhagen, on October 8, 2004. I thank my hosts on these occasions for their invitation and hospitality and their comments upon the arguments presented.

References

Allen, J. (2004). The Whereabouts of Power: Politics, Government and Space. *Geografiska Annaler*, 86(1), 19–32.

Anderson, B. (1992). *Imagined Communities: Reflections on the Origin and Spread of Nationalism.* London: Verso.

Appadurai, A. (1990). Disjuncture and Difference in the Global Cultural Economy. *Theory, Culture & Society*, 7(2), 295–310.

Armstrong, K. (1978). Unpublished interview with Nancy Yaw Davis. Armstrong papers, Kodiak, Alutiiq Museum Archives.

Black, L. (2004). *Russians in Alaska*. Fairbanks: University of Alaska Press.

Bourdieu, P. (1990). *The Logic of Practice*. Cambridge, MA: Polity Press.

Braun, B. (2002). *The Intemperate Rain Forest*. Minneapolis: University of Minnesota Press.

Chaffin, Y. (1967). *Koniag to King Crab.* Seattle, WA: Deseret News Press.

Chaffin, Y., T. Krieger, & M. Rostad. (1983). *Alaska's Konyag Country.* Columbia, MD: Pratt Publishing.

Clark, D. (1984). Pacific Eskimo: Historical Ethnography. In David Damas (Ed.), *Handbook of North American Indians, Arctic* (pp. 185-197). Washington, DC: Smithsonian Institution Press.

Clifford, J. (1988). *The Predicament of Culture: Twentieth-Century Ethnography, Literature, and Art.* Cambridge, MA: Harvard University Press.

———. (2004). Looking Several Ways: Anthropology and Native Heritage in Alaska. *Current Anthropology,* 45, 5-30.

Comaroff, J., & J. Comaroff. (1992). *Ethnography and the Historical Imagination.* Boulder, CO: Westview Press.

Crowell, A., (2001). Introduction. In A. Crowell, A. F. Steffian, G. & Pullar (Eds.), *Looking Both Ways: Heritage and Identity of the Alutiiq People* (pp. 3-19). Anchorage: University of Alaska Press.

Davis, N. Y. (1979). Kodiak Native Sociocultural Impacts, Western Gulf of Alaska Petroleum Development Scenarios. Technical Report No. 41. Prepared for USDOI, BLM, Alaska OCS Office.

———. (1984). Contemporary Pacific Eskimo. In David Damas (Ed.), *Handbook of North American Indians, Arctic* (pp. 198-204). Washington D.C.: Smithsonian Institution Press.

Elias, N. (1978). *The History of Manners, the Civilizing Process: Volume One.* New York: Pantheon Books.

Elwani Magazine: Inside the Life and Culture of Kodiak, (1976). Kodiak Aleutian Regional High School: Alaska.

Fienup-Riordan, A. (2000). *Hunting Tradition in a Changing World: Yup'ik Lives in Alaska Today.* New Brunswick, NJ: Rutgers University Press.

Foucault, M. (1984a). What Is Enlightenment? In Paul Rabinow (Ed.), *The Foucault Reader* (pp. 32-50). New York: Pantheon Books.

———. (1984b). Nietzsche, Genealogy, History. In Paul Rabinow (Ed.), *The Foucault Reader* (pp. 76-100). New York: Pantheon Books.

Gledhill, J. (2000). *Power and Its Disguises: Anthropological Perspectives on Politics.* London: Pluto Press.

Hale, C. R. (1994). Between Che Guevara and the Pachamama: Mestizos, Indians and Identity Politics in the Anti-Quincentenary Campaign. *Critique of Anthropology,* 14(1), 9-39.

Harvey, D. (1990). *The Condition of Postmodernity.* New York: Blackwell Publishing.

Huggins, E. (1981). *Kodiak and Afognak Life, 1868-1870* (R. A. Pierce, Ed.). Kingston, ON: Limestone Press.

Jacobs, J. (1995). *A School Teacher in Old Alaska: The Story of Hanna Breece.* Toronto, ON: Random House of Canada.

Keesing, R. M. (1992). *Custom and Confrontation: The Kwaio Struggle for Cultural Autonomy.* Chicago, IL: University of Chicago Press.

———. (1994). Theories of Culture Revisited. In Robert Borofsky (Ed.), *Assessing Cultural Anthropology* (pp. 301-310). New York: McGraw-Hill.

Koreck, T. M. (1991). Popular Subversions in Post-Revolutionary Mexico: Taking Up Reason in the Longitude of War. *Popular Culture, State Formation, and Revolutionary Mexico,* Center for United States-Mexican Studies, San Diego, California, as cited in Roseberry, W. (1994).

Hegemony and the Language of Contention. In G. M. Joseph & D. Nugent (Eds.), *Everyday Forms of State Formation: Revolution and the Negotiation of Rule in Modern Mexico* (pp. 355-366). Durham, NC, and London: Duke University Press.

Leer, J. (1978). *A Conversational Dictionary of Kodiak Alutiiq*. Fairbanks: University of Alaska, Native Language Center.

Mason, A. (n.d.). Enduring Status Capital and Sociological Form among Alaska Native Elites. Mimeograph.

——. (1996). In a Strange Turn of Events: How Alutiiq Cultural Pride Became a Commodity. M.A. Thesis, Department of Anthropology, University of Alaska, Fairbanks.

——. (2002). The Rise of an Alaska Native Bourgeoisie. *Inuit Studies*, 26, 5-22.

——. (2008). Vanguard Heritage Practice and the Import of Expertise. *Inuit Studies*, 32, 2.

Mouffe, C. (1993). *The Return of the Political*. London: Verso.

Nugent, D. (1998). The Morality of Modernity and the Travails of Tradition: Nationhood and the Subaltern in Northern Peru. *Critique of Anthropology*, 18(1), 7-33.

Oleksa, M. (1992). *Orthodox Alaska, a Theology of Mission*. Crestwood: St. Vladimir's Seminary. *Orphanage News Letter*, (1928). Baranov Museum: Alaska.

Page, R. (1982). *This Is Kodiak*. Kodiak: Page Photo & Printing.

Pullar, G. (1992). Ethnic Identity, Cultural Pride, and Generations of Baggage: A Personal Experience. *Arctic Anthropology*, 29(2), 182-191.

Pullar, G., & R. Jordan. (1987). The Kodiak Archaeological Project, 1983-86: Perspectives from the President of the Native Association and the Project Director. *Fifth Inuit Studies Conference*, Montreal, Quebec.

Purnell, J. (1999). *Popular Movements and State Formation in Revolutionary Mexico: The Agraristas and Cristeros of Michoacán*. Durham, NC: Duke University Press.

Roscoe, F. (1992). *From Humboldt to Kodiak: 1886-1895* (S. N. Roscoe, Ed.). Kingston, ON: The Limestone Press.

Saussure, F. d. (1966). *Course in General Linguistics* (C. Bally & A. Sechehaya, Eds.). New York: McGraw-Hill. (Original work published in 1916).

Scott, J. (1998). *Seeing Like a State: How Certain Schemes to Improve the Human Condition Have Failed*. New Haven, CT: Yale University Press.

Simmel, G. (1959). The Ruin. In Kurt Wolff (Ed.), *Georg Simmel 1858-1918* (pp. 259-266). Columbus: Ohio State University Press.

Warren, K. B. (1998). *Indigenous Movements and Their Critics: Pan-Maya Activism in Guatemala*. Princeton, NJ: Princeton University Press.

Williams, B. (1991). *Stains of My Name, War in My Veins: Guyana and the Politics of Cultural Struggle*. Durham, NC: Duke University Press.

Wirtschafter, E. (1994). *Structures of Society: Imperial Russia's People of Various Ranks*. Dekalb: Northern Illinois University Press.

——. (1997). *Social Identity in Imperial Russia*. Dekalb: Northern Illinois University Press.

◆ CHAPTER SIX ◆

The Alto Balsas Nahuas: Transnational Indigeneity and Interactions in the World of Arts and Crafts, the Politics of Resistance, and the Global Labor Market

Frans J. Schryer[*]

Alto Balsas Nahuas is a label that refers to a group (Nahuas) and the region they inhabit (Upper Balsas, named after a river) in the state of Guerrero, Mexico. The Alto Balsas Nahuas epitomize the indigenous and the local; they speak an Amerindian language (Nahuatl) and have their own way of life, characterized by customs and institutions typical of Mesoamerica.[1] They have occupied a specific territory for the past 800 years. They also use camcorders, travel a lot, and reside in towns and cities throughout Mexico. Moreover, they work in a wide range of occupations in urban centers and live in 18 different American states (García, 2006). Nahuas may speak English as well as Spanish and some have picked up a few words of French or Korean. They are a good example of indigenous cosmopolitans[2] who go back and forth between their home villages in Guerrero and other parts of North America, including the United States. Many interact with people from other parts of the world. One can refer to their cross-border lives as an example of transnational indigeneity. Transnational indigeneity also implies the development of new forms of identity and cultural expressions of indigenous people that transcend national borders.

This chapter will use the example of the Alto Balsas Nahuas to critically examine different aspects of transnational indigeneity within the world of art and crafts, the politics of resistance, and the labor market, paying attention to how people from this region are represented and to the patterns of social interaction within each of these social fields. Each social field will be treated as a site of social interaction and signification, along the lines of Pierre Bourdieu. Bourdieu sees social fields as semiautonomous, partially overlapping, spheres of social life, each with its own logic of practice.[3] I am particularly interested in the connection between groups and fields, a topic I explore in a journal article where I argue that a group reputation may have greater salience in some fields of action than in others (Schryer, 2001). In the case of the Alto Balsas Nahuas I apply this theoretical perspective to examine the reputation of this indigenous group and the involvement of its members in several social fields. Their group name does not have the same connotations and it does not evoke the same images in the world of arts and crafts, in the politics of resistance, or in the global labor market. Nor does the involvement of its members in these overlapping social fields take the same form at the local, regional, or international levels. Yet, despite this multidimensionality in the engagement of Nahuas in different social fields, they are portrayed as a homogeneous group in media and scholarly accounts. The Alto Balsas Nahuas are not what they may appear to be, yet we cannot ignore how they are portrayed.

An Overview of the Alto Balsas

The Alto Balsas region in the state of Guerrero is an extension of the Iguala valley, whose largest population center is the city of Iguala. The villages in the Alto Balsas came to the attention of a broader public in the early 1990s with a social movement to stop the building of a hydroelectric dam in San Juan Tetelcingo, the name of a village located about one kilometer from the place where the old paved highway from Mexico City, the national capital, to the port city of Acapulco crosses the Balsas River. An organization set up in response to this threat received lots of press coverage and still has a presence in the World Wide Web.[4] Around the time of this, indigenous social movement the region became one of interest to anthropologists and other researchers who chose it as their object of study. Their writings, directed to an academic audience, were published in both North America and Europe. However, this was not the only way, nor was it the first time, that its inhabitants became known to outsiders. Some people may be more familiar with the crafts they sell to tourists in the major beach towns and urban craft markets in Mexico. Few people know that the majority of Alto Balsas Nahuas, including former artisans, are currently working as undocumented migrants, in an increasingly global economy.

Historical background

The lives of the Alto Balsas Nahuas have been shaped by worldwide social, political, and economic forces for at least the last couple of hundred years. Spanish-speaking people (whether mestizos or Europeans) did not settle in any of the villages in the region under study. Nor did their inhabitants lose control over their own territory. One reason for this lack of past incursions is that the land, prone to periodic drought, was not as attractive to outsiders.[5] Yet, despite their marginal geographical location, the inhabitants of the Alto Balsas have always had contact with the rest of Mexico. Because people could only cultivate one crop of maize per year, they had to find other ways to make a living. Throughout the colonial era, and during the nineteenth century, men worked as mule skinners. A trail that ran through the Alto Balsas was the only route to transport the goods originating in the Philippines, as well as the Andean countries, destined for Europe. Spanish galleons arrived in the port of Acapulco once a year, and the goods had to be unloaded, then put on mules. The Alto Balsas Nahuas knew how to get pack animals and people across the sometimes turbulent Balsas river in the first stage of a long overland journey to Mexico City and then to Veracruz, where the merchandise was again loaded onto ships that crossed the Atlantic.

The Nahuas not only worked as mule skinners and loaders, they also engaged in trading of their own. Right up to 1930, Nahua itinerant merchants made a three-day journey to the coast to obtain salt along the coast (the Costa Chica of Guerrero), which they would later sell in the highlands. These merchants loaded up their donkeys with onions, grown on the banks of the Balsas River, and pinole, made from dried corn.[6] They traded these food items for the salt that small-scale producers on the coast extracted from sea water. Another form of trade was to go to the neighboring *montaña* region to buy pineapples (piña), mangos, and *chico zapote* for sale at fairs held in Cuetzala or Tacupulco, located in yet another region. This type of trade continued up until the end of the 1940s. Today only a few older men recall the names of the hamlets they used to pass in their travels to the coast. The salt and piña trade disappeared because of the building of the highway I mentioned earlier.

An upsurge of tourism by Americans after the World War II created opportunities in the form of a commercial outlet for local craft production. What makes the Alto Balsas craft industry unique is that artisans market their own products. This ability to sell in other regions can in part be explained in terms of dispositions going back to the salt trade. The people who started producing crafts for sale made frequent trips to other parts of Mexico to sell directly to consumers, without middlemen. With the expansion of craft production, family members started earning more money, which enabled them to start building first adobe and later cement houses with multiple stories and arches. A boom in the craft industry lasted right up until the end of the 1980s, when increasing competition and lower demand made this a less lucrative form of livelihood. Nevertheless craft production and the marketing of crafts continued to be a viable way of making a living. The selling of crafts provided Alto Balsas Nahuas with greater exposure to the outside world, as they came into contact with tourists from many countries. Craft vendors without schooling learned Spanish and sometimes a few words of English. In some villages young women became familiar with Mexico City and other urban centers where they learned Spanish by working as maids. Other women became more sophisticated through ongoing interactions with foreigners when selling crafts at beach resorts. A combination of travel to other parts of Mexico and the gradual expansion of schools in their home region, starting as early as the 1970s, enabled the Nahuas to hold their own when interacting with outsiders.

Despite the lack of roads, most villages in the Alto Balsas did have at least one-room elementary schools going back to the early 1950s. Teachers paid by the government, who did not speak Nahuatl, tried to impart lessons in Spanish. A priest, who believed in the importance of education, set up private parochial schools in several villages, with assistance for students of parents who could not afford to pay. He helped promising students to continue their education in boarding schools in a neighboring region. By 1990 several villages could boast that they had native sons who had made a name for themselves in the outside world. Xalitla counted half a dozen young professionals, including three anthropologists, an economist, and several teachers. A man from San Juan Tetelcingo had studied law and occupied an important government position at the national level. These more educated Nahuas had university degrees and worked in the state capital or in Mexico City.

Educated leaders, increasing levels of bilingualism, and familiarity with the rest of Mexico enabled the inhabitants of the region to defend themselves when faced with the threat of a potentially harmful development project, the proposed dam. A successful nonviolent struggle resulted in the cancellation of this dam in 1992. However, the impact of broader changes resulting from the North American Free Trade Agreement (NAFTA) and neoliberal policies, presented new challenges throughout the rest of the 1990s. The removal of subsidies led to a decline in agriculture. Simultaneously, the market for local crafts, which had become increasingly competitive, reached a point of saturation. Craft production and selling crafts in other parts of Mexico was no longer a viable option for most young people looking for a way of making a living. Consequently, more and more of them had to start working for wages, this time as migratory laborers in the United States. Even well-established artisan-vendors headed north.

The Alto Balsas Nahuas as Seen by Anthropologists

The short history just presented was written from a political economy perspective, with an emphasis on the ways people make a living plus comments on migration, education, and politics. Such an approach leaves out many other aspects of social life; neither does it provide a good idea of how people see themselves. An overview of their culture using an anthropological approach can provide a more complete picture. To sum up, villages in the Alto Balsas are typical of other places in Mesoamerica whose inhabitants are indigenous. They have a cargo system, also known as a civil-religious hierarchy, an institution that involves obligatory public service as part of the duties that confer rights of membership in a community and access to land. Most of the land is communally owned, with individual usufruct rights. Most people are nominally Roman Catholic, but they practice a syncretic form of Christianity that includes many elements from a pre-Columbian belief system. Most households are patrilocal since couples usually move to the house of the man's parents. Courtship and marriage require the services of an intermediary whose task is to persuade the girl's parents to allow her to leave their household, or to placate them if a couple has already eloped. The Nahuas are endogamous, although some people do find their life partners in other villages. They also have a form of fictive kinship, known as *compadrazgo*,[7] which is characteristic of Latin America as a whole. Each village has a strong sense of local identity, and one can identify from which village people come by the way they speak the Nahuatl language.

Anthropologists who have written about the Nahuas tend to focus on ceremonial life, religious beliefs, and kinship. A well-illustrated electronic document written in Spanish for the general public[8] can be used to demonstrate how such anthropologists portray the Alto Balsas. While acknowledging the influence of European and other cultures, this document represents the Alto Balsas Nahuas as indigenous people who have maintained a traditional way of life despite their constant travels. The emphasis is on communalism, the cultural importance of feasts for patron saints (with their associated rituals), and proximity to the land. It does not mention that the cultivation of maize and beans has been largely abandoned in all but one of the villages of the region. Nor does it comment on the almost total dependence on migratory labor in the United States. Yet such an idealized view of the Nahua way of life represents the norms and world view that is an integral part of group identity. How people see themselves and how they are represented by anthropologists can be mutually reinforcing. Indigenous political leaders often use the findings of anthropologists, including anthropological archaeologists, to define or redefine who they are, as we shall see later. However the influence can go the other way. The very term "Alto Balsas Nahuas," used to refer to a regionally based ethnic group was originally coined by Nahuas themselves at a time when they were engaged in their struggle to prevent the building of the Tetelcingo dam.

The Politics of Resistance: The Struggle against the Building of a Dam

The social movement against the building of a dam must be placed in the broader context of how the indigenous people of the Alto Balsas fit into the administrative structures of the Mexican state, and their prior dealings with government officials. The Alto Balsas Nahuas did not, and still do not, constitute a single administrative unit. Nor did they have a sense of belonging to a specific geographical or ethnic unit beyond their individual villages. The 16 villages (*pueblos*) located on both sides of this section of the Balsas River (from San Juan Tetelcingo to San Francisco) belong to four different *municipios* (the Mexican equivalent of counties), whose respective centers (*cabeceras*) are geographically inaccessible. The mestizos who live in these administrative centers dominated the administration of the municipios and paid little heed to the demands for public services in Nahua villages. Nor did Nahua village authorities act together until they had to defend their common interests.

When it became apparent that the federal government planned to build a hydroelectric dam that would flood most of their territory, resulting in the relocation of several villages, leaders from these villages set up an organization to represent the whole region. Over the span of just two years, their organization, initially unknown to anyone outside of the Alto Balsas region, became well known to political activists at both the national and international levels. The name Alto Balsas Nahuas was also adopted by people in academia and other social fields. Yet today very few people who live in this region know about its existence, neither do they identify themselves as Nahuas of the Alto Balsas. In order to understand this discrepancy, it is necessary to trace the origins and evolution of an organization that continued to exist beyond the political struggle culminating in the official cancellation of the Tetelcingo dam project. At the same time we cannot overlook the symbolism and connotations of the group name that was born in this struggle.

The chronology of the fight against the dam

When a group of people decided to stop the building of this large hydroelectric project, most outsiders would have considered this an impossible task. No social movement of indigenous people had ever succeeded in doing so anywhere in Mexico or Central America. Past dams were built without prior consultation and with little advance notice. Indeed, people in the Alto Balsas only found out about the Tetelcingo dam project when someone leaked several documents to village authorities (Hindley, 1996, p. 46). Even then, the state-owned Federal Electricity Commission (CFE) denied that a dam was about to be built. The project would have gone ahead were it not for the actions of a group of Nahua professionals who had maintained close ties with their home villagers. They disseminated information about the impending dam project by visiting most villages that would be affected. They also presided over local meetings, followed by larger assemblies attended by the authorities of numerous villages, resulting in the founding of the Consejo de Pueblos Nahuas del Alto Balsas (CPNAB, for "Council for the Nahua Towns of the Upper Balsas"). Its organizational structure was multitiered, consisting of elected officers, including a general secretary, a group of *comisionados* (official representatives) who formed a working team, and local (village-based) support committees (Hindley, 1996; 1987–1988). The *comisionados* consisted of the Nahua professionals, who did the planning and represented the CPNAB to the outside world. Their fluency in Spanish and connections with politicians and well-known intellectuals, in addition to their higher level of education, made them the ideal people to write petitions and letters. In choosing the name Alto Balsas these indigenous professionals appropriated a term hitherto used only by hydraulic engineers working for the government, in order to create a new regional identity.

The biggest challenge for the founders of the CPNAB was to get state and national officials to take them seriously. These Nahua leaders were not recognized as legitimate political actors since their organization was not part of any existing government institutions. In order to gain recognition they formed alliances with, or sought the support of, other organizations and well-known individuals. Their first political ally was the municipal president (*presidente municipal*) of Copalillo, a Nahuatl-speaking municipio bordering on the region under study. It was the only indigenous municipio in that part of Guerrero run by Nahuas themselves, after a minority of teachers and professionals gained political control of the municipal administration (during the 1980s), in contrast to the complete monopoly of political power held by the mestizo mayors in the Alto Balsas (Hindley, 1996, p. 12). The first public act of protest of the CPNAB involved their participation in a demonstration in the state capital, Chilpancingo, on November 28, 1990. There they joined several already established organizations from different parts of the state that had links with the Workers' Revolutionary Party, the political party to which the leaders of Copalillo belonged. This ability to choose political allies, even if those allies had no inherent indigenous ideology, demonstrates the sophistication of the Nahua leaders of the CPNAB—indigenous cosmopolitans at home in university campuses and government offices. They were also well versed in the language of indigenous rights used in Latin American countries and other parts of the world.

To better understand the challenges faced by the leaders of the movement against the dam, and the tactics they used in their struggle, one must keep in mind the nature of the Mexican political system in the early 1990s. Mexico still had a de facto one party political system, although several independent political parties were starting to make headway in gaining power at the local level. Nevertheless, repression of overt and public opposition to the government was still a possibility. At the same time, the Mexican state, and its ruling party, the Institutional Revolutionary Party (PRI), allowed a certain level of dissent and preferred to co-opt any opposition rather than use overt repression. The man in power in 1990, Carlos Salinas de Gortari, was a neo-populist. He used left-wing language and presented himself to the outside world as a defender of indigenous rights. In 1990 his government had ratified the International Labor Organization's Convention 169 (on Indigenous and Tribal Peoples) (Overmyer-Velásquez, 2003, p. 12) and subsequently recognized the pluricultural nature of the Mexican Nation. Quite aware of the discourse used by the government, the CPNAB leaders emphasized the indigenous nature of their movement. They spoke of the need for greater indigenous autonomy, and pointed out that the Tetelcingo dam would destroy their cultural heritage, couching their demands for both recognition and government action in terms of the same language of respect for cultural differences and native rights used by the federal government. The leaders of the CPNAB did not challenge the legitimacy of the government and they downplayed any links with opposition parties. Yet in order to be able to openly challenge authorities of the CFE without impunity, the CPNAB depended on support from opposition political parties, including the newly formed PRD (Party of the Democratic Revolution) that had some bargaining power at the state level. The leaders of the CPNAB also welcomed the presence of foreign scholars at local rallies and meetings to ensure their safety (Hindley, 1996, p. 28).

In order to get the government's attention, as well as broad-based support, the CPNAB needed media exposure. They got their first press coverage within Guerrero when they participated in the demonstration in Chilpancingo. But the CPNAB needed to become much better-known at the national and international levels, and find strategic allies at both levels before they could hope to have any influence on the decision-making process that could result in a cancellation of the dam project. Their first breakthrough came on February 18, 1991, when a leading national newspaper, *La Jornada*, published a full-page declaration by the CPNAB. This declaration included the signature of a group of one hundred prominent Mexican artists, writers, and intellectual leaders, including Octavio Paz. The CPNAB received international exposure when their representatives started traveling abroad. One of them denounced the Tetelcingo dam at the Non-Governmental Conference on the Environment and Development in Paris (in December 1991). The following year someone else traveled to Rio de Janeiro to attend the World Conference of Indigenous People on the Environment, Development and Territory, and an international forum of NGOs. During these trips CPNAB representatives made valuable contacts with indigenous leaders from other countries. In Mexico they received support from an NGO who offered to help the Nahua organization formulate a development plan that would be an alternative to the mega dam project.[9]

While these high profile Nahua leaders were busy attending conferences, writing policy documents, and looking for further support, local leaders became involved in a confrontation with several new protagonists. The CPNAB went beyond lobbying to stop the building of the Tetelcingo dam to also play an advocacy role. For example, several villages asked the CPNAB to be their official representative in a series of negotiations with the Mexican Petroleum Corporation (PEMEX) when it started exploratory drilling in the region. The CPNAB also got involved in negotiating with, and then confronting, a private construction company whose fleet of trucks carried heavy equipment back and forth along an unpaved road between Xalitla and the site of a large construction camp set up to build a huge bridge for a new highway between Acapulco and Mexico City. This project was particularly disruptive for the villages of Oapan and San Miguel Tecuixiapan, since a fleet of large trucks and heavy equipment passed through the center of these two villages.[10] Local inhabitants saw a direct link between this construction project and the projected dam since it soon became apparent that this new bridge was going to be higher than the water level if a large area was inundated. The village of Oapan, together with supporters from neighboring villages, set up a roadblock that lasted more than two weeks (starting January 25, 1992) resulting in the state governor signing a letter stating that the dam project was cancelled. For the next couple of months, CPNAB representatives entered into face-to-face negotiations with the state government in order to provide compensation for the damages caused by road construction, and a variety of development projects, including paving the road from Xalitla to San Francisco.

The outcome of the roadblock in Oapan represented a partial victory for the organization, but the governor's signature was no guarantee that the dam would not be built. The next tactic, promoted by several Nahua professionals, was to link their struggle against the dam project with the broader international indigenous movement to oppose official celebrations of the 500th anniversary of Columbus' arrival in the Americas. They collaborated with the Consejo Mexicano de Quinientos Años de Resistencia Indígena. A CPNAB contingent attended a meeting on September 14, 1991, which saw the launching of the Guerrero branch of this international movement (Hindley, 1996, p. 196). They called themselves the Consejo Guerrerense de 500 Años de Resistencia India, Negra y Popular (CG500ARI), the first autonomous state-level indigenous organization in the state of Guerrero. This organization was to outlast both its national and international counterparts following the protest against official celebrations that took place in 1992. By joining this state organization in an 11-day march on Mexico City in October of that year, the CPNAB finally attained its main objective, the definitive cancellation of the dam. They were successful in part because the Mexican president, Carlos Salinas de Gortari, who portrayed himself as a champion of indigenous rights, needed to present a good image to the rest of the world. This victory illustrates that the globalization of native rights movements, a form of transnational indigeneity, can be advantageous for indigenous people engaged in local struggles (Hindley, 1996). It also helped to have experienced, well-educated leaders.

Although the immediate threat of the dam was gone, the organization's leaders, whose original goal was to stop the construction of the dam, continued to work for the social and economic development of their region. However, frictions among two rival groups, which had already surfaced during the preceding two years, prevented the CPNAB from functioning effectively. The leaders of these factions were the professionals from Xalitla mentioned earlier (Hémond, 2004). This factional dispute was shaped by competing loyalties to rival political parties. One faction became ever more closely allied to the PRD while their rivals had close contacts with the official PRI. Even PRD supporters were internally divided. The secretary general of the organization, a school teacher from Oapan who was the person most actively involved in negotiations with the state government, and subsequently with Mexico's Institute of Indigenous Affairs, was at loggerheads with the president from Xalitla (Hindley, 1996, pp. 253, 262-263), even though they both had strong ties with the same political party. Thus ironically, while Mexico's political system was moving toward a more open system that allowed competing political parties, the CPNAB lost their autonomy as well as their unity as an indigenous organization.

The factional dispute within the CPNAB came to a head one year after the cancellation of the dam, resulting in the creation of another organization with the same name, adding only the ending "Guerrero," resulting in confusion among their supporters (Celestino, 2005, pp. 54-55). The head of one of these rival organizations assumed an important post on the national level, as federal deputy (a member of Mexico's Chamber of Deputies).[11] Today there are still two rival organizations of Alto Balsas Nahuas, at least on paper, although only one of them is represented on the World Wide Web. Neither of these organizations has much of a presence in the local political arena. However, the organization is still a functioning entity in the political field at the international level; in 2002 the leader of one of the CPNAB factions was part of a global movement in opposition to the Plan Panama, a multibillion dollar development project for Colombia, Central America, and seven Mexican states, including Guerrero. This project, which included plans to build more hydroelectric dams, was championed by Vincente Fox, the president of Mexico who came to power in 2001.[12]

Figure 6.1: Office of the Consejo de Pueblos Nahuas del Alto Balsas, Mexico

The way the CPNAB is represented

Very few people beyond a handful of anthropologists are aware that there are two organizations with the name CPNAB. Those who look at Web and written sources get the impression that there is a single organization representing more than 30 Nahua pueblos. As far as the broader public in Mexico and the rest of the world is concerned, the people living in, or originating from, these villages constitute a single, cohesive indigenous group. This representation belies the diverse, as well as politically divided, nature of the Alto Balsas region. Even during the struggle to prevent the building of the dam in the 1990s, which saw a high level of political and social solidarity, the term Consejo de Pueblos Nahuas del Alto Balsas glossed over the fact that these pueblos belong to two subregions whose populations had little prior or subsequent contact with each other. The leaders of these two subregions worked together during the two years of struggle against the dam project, and they chose a name and symbols that made the rest of the world believe these regions had more in common than they did. After 1994 there was no more contact between the leaders of these subregions nor was there ever any form of exchange between their respective populations, separated by a deep gorge. Yet the CPNAB continued to present itself as representative of a much larger, united region of Nahuas. Paradoxically, increasing engagement with the wider world at the national and international levels helped to reinforce the illusion of a homogenous community.

The success of the movement against the dam was as much the product of an ideological struggle as it was the outcome of using such tactics as roadblocks and demonstrations or making political alliances, hence the importance of the rhetorical strategies and the symbols used by the CPNAB leaders. We also need to take into account the way these leaders used the findings of archaeologists to present the argument that Alto Balsas Nahuas can trace their descent back to people who lived there thousands of years ago (Hémond, 2003, p. 333), much older than the Nahuatl-speaking Coixcas who did not arrive in the region until the twelfth century.[13] Nor can we overlook how debates within archaeology became intertwined with the fight over the dam. One archaeologist who had excavated a site in the region argued that it was the oldest ceremonial site in Mesoamerica, and hence a valuable part of the heritage not only of the Alto Balsas region, but all of Mexico. She became a vehement critic of the proposed dam project and supported the movement. In contrast, the director of the National Institute of Anthropology and History (INAH) for Guerrero, who was put in charge of official archaeological rescue operations in preparation for the future dam reservoir, argued that the site was not that old or significant (Hindley, 1996, p. 92).

The use of symbols based on Mexico's prehistory has been an integral part of the formation of a Mexican national identity for a long time. Hence it is not surprising that the leaders of the CPNAB chose as a logo for their letterhead a picture that could be immediately identified by a broader Mexican public: an Olmec head surrounded by an amate-style garland of flowers. It did not matter that the Olmec statue on which the logo is based comes from an entirely different region of Mexico. At the same time the use of the words Nahua and Alto Balsas enabled these political leaders to bring into existence a new collective identity with salience at the national and international levels in a surprisingly short period. CPNAB leaders started to represent themselves as members of a unique indigenous group, the Nahuas of the Alto Balsas, as opposed to other Nahuas in other parts of Guerrero. This new label was likewise used by Nahua professionals when they attended international conferences. Subsequently anthropologists, as well as economists and specialists in ecology, turned this newly defined ethnic group into an object of study (Hémond, 2003, p. 333). However, the reputation and relevance of this newly created indigenous group, and of the organization that bears its name, are not the same everywhere and at all times.

We have seen that the struggle against the dam involved mobilizations and events that took place simultaneously at the local level, in the state of Guerrero, and in the national capital. The movement also had an important international dimension, and the name of the organization created to carry out this struggle has since become a global icon. For both indigenous and nonindigenous political activists, the name Alto Balsas Nahuas became a symbol of the struggle of indigenous peoples against globalization. However the relative importance of, and impact of, the organization set up to represent the indigenous people of the Alto Balsas Nahua, changed over time. Initially the CPNAB involved a large number of leaders at the local level, including village authorities, and had the support of the vast majority of the population. Fifteen years later it had minimal local support and no involvement of village authorities. In contrast, the organization and the group it represents have maintained their reputation among politically active people in different parts of the world. One of its leaders continues to make contacts with groups fighting for native rights in other parts of the Americas and beyond, showing up at numerous international conferences wearing the traditional garments no longer worn by indigenous people in his home region. In contrast, people who spend most of their time living and working in the villages of the Alto Balsas are less likely to identify as *indígenas* (native people) (much less as Alto Balsas Nahuas) than the Nahua professionals who represent them at the national and international levels.[14]

Today most young people in the Alto Balsas region do not remember the struggle against the dam that took place over a decade ago, nor would they recognize the name Pueblos Nahuas del Alto Balsas. For many older people this name now has negative connotations because of internal splits in the movement. However, although the CPNAB as an organization exists only on paper at the local level, its name has not lost relevance in the subfield of international politics. Moreover, the group name Alto Balsas Nahuas, derived from the title of the organization set up for a political struggle, has taken on a separate life of its own and is now used in other social fields. Political activists and intellectuals in Mexico City and other places in Mexico still use the group name Alto Balsas Nahuas; they see members of this group as politically mobilized indigenous people.[15] For anthropologists and art critics this group label has different connotations. For this reason we need to take a closer look at the Alto Balsas Nahuas and their international connections in social fields other than the politics of resistance.

Alto Balsas Nahuas in the World of Arts and Crafts

We saw earlier that a commercial craft industry is a recent phenomenon in the Alto Balsas. What had been minor craft production for local use was transformed into production for sale to outsiders in a relatively short period of time and became the main source of income for the majority of households.

This social field, the world of art and crafts, has its own dynamics. It involves a different set of social relations, not to mention such cultural dimensions as aesthetics and the notion of artistic talent that imply a different type of group identity. This social field has its own social hierarchies, including the distinction between art and crafts. Even ethnic categories take on a different connotation. In the case of the Alto Balsas Nahuas, their incorporation into the world of arts and crafts also took on an international dimension, not only because clients from other countries admired and bought what the Nahuas created, but also because of links with art critics and gallery owners in other parts of the world. The involvement of Alto Balsas Nahuas in the international field of arts and crafts thus represents another facet of the process of transnational indigeneity. At the same time it is impossible to ignore the relationship between the world of art and the politics of resistance, since these two social fields are not completely autonomous or unconnected to each other.

Figure 6.2: An example of an Amate (bark painting), Mexico

The history of the incorporations of Nahuas in the field of art and crafts

Before 1950 everyone living in the Alto Balsas grew maize and other crops, such as sesame seeds, both to eat and to sell. Craft production was a sideline.

Women in several villages made jars for holding water and pots for straining the lime water used to soak corn. Men made firecrackers (*cohuetes*) used in local religious celebrations, or burned wood to make charcoal. All of these objects were for home use although some were sold or traded in neighboring villages. In the early 1950s craft production was modified so that artisans' products could be sold to outsiders. Initially several men in Ameyaltepec experimented with painting designs once applied to clayware on other surfaces. The most successful medium turned out to be bark paper (*amate*) once used by the Aztecs.[16] For several years, three families were involved in painting amates on commission, but gradually more people, both men and women, learned the craft. While one person in each family was more adept at drawing the designs, the whole family was involved in filling in the colors with water-based, and later acrylic, paints. Painting amates also started in San Agustin Oapan and spread to other villages. Each village developed its own style. Other forms of craft production were invented. Some villages specialized in making masks, carving wooden figurines, or painting amate-type scenes on ashtrays and bowls. As early as 1960 most of the villages specialized in the production of some form of crafts for sale to tourists and middle-class Mexicans, of which the best known and most original was the painting of amates.[17] Indeed, long before the creation of the label "Nahuas of the Alto Balsas," the inhabitants of this region were known as *amateros*.[18]

Craft production transformed the way people made a living. Initially the production and selling of craft objects and works of art took place during the dry season when no one could work in the fields. Most of the artisans, both men and women, spent part of the year selling their artwork in other parts of Mexico. Over time some of these craftsmen-vendors returned home for shorter periods of time and left agricultural work in the hands of friends and relatives. Some artisans now spend more time in Cuernavaca, Cancún, or San Miguel de Allende (all places well known to tourists) than they do at home. However, it requires talent and perseverance to achieve success in the field of arts and crafts. A minority of amate painters, who developed their own individual styles, became well known and were commissioned to paint for wealthy patrons. Owners of art galleries took an interest in their work and brought Nahua artists to the attention of art lovers and art collectors in Mexico and abroad. These amate painters were incorporated into the subfield of museum art when their paintings were discovered by international art collectors who became sponsors of better-known amate painters (Cowen, 2005, pp. 41–71). Several painters set up studios. Less well-known craftsmen and artists of the Alto Balsas attended local and national competitions where they have also achieved recognition for their work.

Nahua artisans see themselves as creative artisans and take pride in the fact that they do everything by hand.[19] However, they need to be pragmatic since the production of amate paintings, making clay necklaces, or carving masks have become an important source of income. Starting as early as the 1970s, increasing competition for access to customers resulted in lower prices. In order to survive economically, many Nahuas started selling crafts originating in other regions, including jewelry made from semiprecious stones imported from Asia (Good, 1988, p. 40). Over time two types of differentiation took place. Some artisans specialized in buying and selling the crafts produced by others, leading to a gap in standards of living between vendors and producers who could not afford to travel to sell their goods. At the same time a handful of more skilled painters with an upper-class, often foreign, clientele became professional artists, while other amate painters made lower-quality products for sale to wholesalers. A more recent development in the field of arts and crafts is not only to sell one's work to tourists but to provide lessons in how to paint pottery in tourist resorts. This became the specialty of a group of artisans from San Juan Tetelcingo who now live in a small colony of migrants near Playa del Carmen on the Mayan Riviera (Morales, 2007).

Art and the politics of resistance

For Alto Balsas Nahuas craft production and politics are not associated with the same people. None of the leaders of the movement against the dam were artists or craftsmen. Nevertheless these two social fields (art and politics) are interlinked to some extent. During the two years of political mobilization many artisans supported the CPNAB and amate painters were recruited for the cause. One of the unique features of the social movement was the use of artwork during marches and demonstrations; the banners used in the protest march in Chilpancingo in 1990 were decorated with bark paintings. In first petitioning Salinas, the Mexican president, during his visit to Iguala, CPNAB representatives referred to the contribution of amates and other crafts of the region to Mexico's heritage:

> We have given a lot to our country, so much so that currently on the television one of our bark paintings appears with the words "Mexico se pinta solo," thus showing that our art is considered part of the patrimony of all Mexicans. (CPNAB 2/12/90c, quoted in Hindley, 1996, p. 120)

Later during the campaign, their national support committee organized an exhibit in the Frida Kahlo gallery in Mexico City in order to attract more media coverage. The exhibit, designed to tell the story of an indigenous society under threat from the dam, included Alto Balsas crafts alongside the work of Jorge Claro and Fernando Soto, well-known photographers whose images of the Alto Balsas depict the same gentle, pastoral society portrayed in Nahua bark paintings (Hindley, 1996, p. 160). Nahua artists from Oapan also used amate-type designs to cover the construction company vehicles delayed by a symbolic demonstration of power at the end of the weeklong roadblock to protest the actions of the company building the new bridge across the Balsas River (Hindley, 1996, p. 266).

One cannot leave out the role of scholars in linking these two social fields. When a group of academic sympathizers organized a seminar at the Autonomous University of Guerrero in May of 1991, in partnership with the CPNAB, their publicity poster had an amate design (Hindley, 1996, p. 181). Earlier an American anthropologist persuaded better-known Nahua artists to depict the fight against the building of the dam and the threat of being flooded in their paintings (Cowen, 2005, p. 127). He arranged for their work to be included in a book titled *The Amate Tradition: Innovation and Dissent in Mexican Art*, published by the Mexican Fine Arts Museum in Chicago (Amith, 1995). This connection between art and politics is also evident in *Peindre la révolte* (Hémond, 2003), a book dealing with the Alto Balsas published in France.

The symbols of Alto Balsas art also reinforce ethnic and regional identity. Nahua artists portray the same idealized way of life presented in some scholarly publications. Nahua visual artists depict a traditional way of life, showing only the tile and thatch-roofed houses that have almost disappeared. These images, another manifestation of transnational indigeneity, are an integral part of the group identity of Nahuas now living abroad. Similarly, artists currently living in other parts of Mexico visit their home region as a source of inspiration.

The reputation and identity of the *Amateros*

An important aspect of any group is how its members are perceived in different social fields. In the subfield of the politics of resistance at the global level, Alto Balsas Nahuas have come to be known as militant opponents of the Mexican government and neoliberalism. They have a different kind of reputation in the world of arts and crafts. The presence of artisan-vendors from the Alto Balsas in the beach towns and markets of Mexico came to the attention of a broader public as early as the 1960s. They were seen as creative Indian craftsmen and became known as "the amateros from Guerrero." Film crews from Japan and Europe have come to the Alto Balsas region to record amate painters at work. Some Mexicans, aware of how well Alto Balsas artists and vendors have done for themselves, have created yet another image, that of "rich artisans." In some parts of Mexico, where Nahuas sell replicas of archaeological artifacts, they have gained the reputation of being shrewd and cunning. A customer in Mexico City told me he admires the ability of people from the village of Xalitla to deceive even anthropologists by selling false stone figures.

The logic of each social field shapes the way people see themselves. In order to make a living, itinerant vendors have to sell products other than what their own families produce at home. Yet to be successful vendors, it is important that they present themselves as authentic native artists, even when they are selling crafts produced in sweat shops in nonnative regions. This tension between the commercial and the aesthetic dimension of craft production is also evident in the world of "pure" art. It is difficult to make a clear-cut distinction between "high" art and folk art, or between art and crafts. The subfields of museum art, handicrafts, and the marketing of art and crafts are closely intertwined. In both cases, how artists, art vendor, and craftspeople see themselves, and how they are perceived by others, are mutually reinforcing. American and European tourists and foreign art dealers have expectations of the Nahua artists and craft vendors with whom they interact. However, the experiences and the stereotyped impressions of these artists and vendors are not the same as those associated with Nahuas involved in the labor market, where transnational indigeneity takes a different form.

The Labor Market and International Migration

The participation of Nahuas in labor markets outside their home region has fluctuated and become transformed over time. Prior to the craft industry boom men worked as seasonal migratory laborers in neighboring regions, in both Guerrero and Morelos. They were a source of cheap labor and subject to discrimination directed against native people. These workers moved to other parts of Mexico during the dry season (in the winter), coming back to grow corn during the wet season that starts in June. Starting around 1950 some men went to work in the United States, usually for periods lasting between 3 to 6 months. Unlike in other parts of Mexico, this international migration did not become significant until several decades later. By 2008 the majority of people in some Nahua pueblos were living and working in the United States.

The arrival of Nahuas from Guerrero is only one (and the latest) component of a diverse indigenous Mexican presence in the United States.[20] The awareness that there are indigenous Mexicans, as opposed to mestizo Mexicans, was not reflected in American census data until the year 2000 with the inclusion on the category "Hispanic American Indians" (Huizar & Cedra, 2004). Within the United States, Mexican groups, especially from Oaxaca, have developed their own hometown, as well as broader regional, associations, some of which have organized people in both the United States and Mexico (Fox & Rivera-Salgado, 2004). The Nahuas have not yet done so. However, the ongoing social interactions between Nahua international migratory laborers and people in their home villages, plus the emergence of new forms of indigenous identity in the United States are also a form of transnational indigeneity.

Life and work in the United States

When Alto Balsas Nahuas first started working in the United States, they were transported to their work destination as part of the *bracero* program,[21] a program resulting from an agreement between the two countries. When international migration resumed in the 1980s, the undocumented migrant workers from the Alto Balsas had to pay someone to be smuggled across the border. These men are called *coyotes*. In 1986, the U.S. government introduced legislation that provided an amnesty to any undocumented workers who could prove that they had already been working and living in the United States for several years. This legislation enabled some Nahuas to become official U.S. residents, although the majority of migrants continued to be part of an underground economy. International migration from the Alto Balsas region picked up throughout the 1990s.

Prior to "9/11" it was relatively easy for Nahua workers to cross the border. They would normally stay for at least one year before returning to Mexico, although most later went back to the United States. In contrast, after the events of 2001, those who leave their villages to work in the United States remain for as long as four or five years at a time, given the risks and costs[22] associated with reentry. Some people have not been back to Mexico for over 10 years. Ironically, the small percentage of international migratory laborers who have work permits ("papers"), and in some cases American citizenship, travel to Mexico regularly, while the vast majority of undocumented workers stay away from home the longest. Nevertheless, greater vigilance on the border and stricter laws designed to reduce the entry of undocumented migrants have not stemmed the flow of undocumented workers.

Despite the increasing costs associated with crossing the border, Alto Balsas Nahuas continue emigrating. Even those who earn minimal wages can save enough money in four to five years to build a house in Mexico. Remittances sent from migrants in the United States allow families in Alto Balsas to hold luxurious weddings and birthday parties. All of these events are recorded with camcorders, which enable family members to feel connected. The use of such electronic devices by migrants and people at home indicate the level of sophistication in technical knowledge by members of transnational indigenous communities. Of course, not everyone is able to buy a camcorder. Some migrants return with no money at all and others pay dearly for attempting to cross the border without documents. In 2005, two boys from Ahuehuepan died of dehydration while walking across the desert in Arizona. Nevertheless, most teenagers, both male and female, still leave to seek their fortunes in "*el*

Norte" as soon as they have finished high school. Only the older people and children stay at home, and you will find few people between the ages of 16 and 35.

Today one can find Nahuas from the Alto Balsas all over the United States (García Ortega, 2006) but they do not all go to the same places since every Nahua pueblo has its preferred destination. For example, the majority of those who emigrate from San Juan Tetelcingo live and work in Ontario, California, while people from Ahuehuepan are more likely to end up in Lincoln, Los Angeles, or Sacramento, California. One is more likely to find people from Ahuelicán in Houston, Texas. Some Nahuas from these and other villages also work in Chicago, Illinois, or in Atlanta, Georgia. Within each city Nahuas are dispersed in different neighborhoods although they also cluster in certain areas. For example, in Houston, Texas, people from San Miguel Tecuixiapan live on or near Beechnut and Brissonnet streets, in Houston's Bellaire area, while those from San Juan Tetelcingo live in the town of Katy, just outside of Houston.

When it comes to social contact with migrants from different Nahua villages who happen to live in the same American city, people associate with and still marry primarily those from their hometown. A strong local identity and village endogamy is thus reproduced in the American context. Migrants come home for festive celebrations, to get married, or whenever it is their turn to provide public service. Relations between children of different ages, even if they are born in the United States, also follow traditional patterns.[23] However, Nahuas in American cities are aware of the presence of migrants from other parts of the Alto Balsas and they cooperate and socialize across village lines. In Houston, Nahua migrants from different villages originally lived in the same apartment building on Wirt Street. Men from Oapan play basketball together with men from Ahuelicán. Several families from San Miguel Tecuixiapan and Ahuelicán visit each other regularly after they became acquainted as a result of an inter-village marriage. Around the time of the social movement in opposition to the dam, a new awareness of a common region also became apparent in an American setting. In 1991, a group of migrants from Xalitla who were working in Los Angeles formed an international support committee for the CPNAB (Hindley, 1996, p. 89).

While Nahuas continue to speak Nahuatl among themselves in the United States, and in telephone conversations with those at home, they have become more cosmopolitan as a result of their experience working outside of Mexico. The first transborder migrants spoke little Spanish but improved their Spanish in the United States through contact with other Mexican workers who are not indigenous. Most of the managers and overseers in these workplaces also use Spanish. However children born in the United States or those who attend elementary school quickly learn English. I have met Nahua children and teenagers who speak three languages fluently. Even children who have never left Mexico pick up a few words of English from their returning cousins. Such children, who ride on the backs of donkeys in their home village, are familiar with the malls and housing complexes of metropolitan centers in the United States from watching videos brought back by older relatives. This awareness of, and links with, relatives in the United States, is as much a part of transnational indigeneity as the use of Nahuatl by those who have become American citizens.

Indigenous migrants learn new skills in the places where they work. Starting as early as 1983, migrants from both Maxela and Ahuelicán started working for department stores and supermarkets (especially the Fiesta and Kroger chains) where they can work their way up from stocker to assistant manager. A minority of Nahua migrants in Houston found jobs in landscaping or works in restaurants. These migrants were often able to apply previous skills. The expansion of primary and, after 1994, secondary education in the Alto Balsas means that international migrants nowadays are literate. Others learned about bricklaying in Mexico before migrating. Unfortunately people who were skilled artisans in Mexico are not able to apply what they knew how to do best in the United States. I am aware of only one case where a Nahua amate painter was able to use his artistic talents at least for a while.

The case of the amate painter is a man from Maxela who came to the United States in the 1980s. His first job, in Houston, was as a carpenter's assistant. Like so many others who worked in construction, his jobs never lasted more than a few weeks at a time. Next he got a full-time job in a small ceramics factory, specializing in garden ornaments and interlocking patio stones. One day his boss noticed that the man from Maxela was drawing pictures of birds and flowers on a scrap of paper during one of his breaks. He had learned how to paint amates and pottery in Mexico since he was 8 years old. His American employer recognized his talents, and for the next couple of years his new employee drew all of the designs for molds used in a new line of patio stones. The artist started earning 350 dollars a week instead of the one or two hundred dollars that the regular workers earned. He did this for several years until the government fined the owner for employing undocumented immigrants. The owner sold the factory to someone who started manufacturing a new line of products and the Nahua men had to find work elsewhere. The next job of the man from Maxela was washing the cars that came from the assembly line of a new Ford auto plant, until he found work in a supermarket.

The Nahuas who continued to flow into Houston at the turn of the century and beyond continue to work for the most part for chains of large grocery and department stores. These latest newcomers are often the children of former migrants who have since returned to Mexico. Nowadays young women from the Alto Balsas also migrate to, and find jobs in, Houston. A man I interviewed in San Juan Tetelcingo told me he had four daughters in the United States and I met all of them in Houston. One of them works in a fast-food restaurant and she has done babysitting. Her sister works for a supermarket, shelving, as does her husband, a man from Ameyaltepec whom she met in Houston. The entry of women into a wide range of occupations is altering gender roles among Nahuas in both the United States and the Alto Balsas. For example, women now drive cars in both settings, something that was unthinkable even 10 years ago.

The vast majority of the men and women who live and work in the United States do not have work permits, so the immigration authorities could have them deported at any time. When someone reported to the United States immigration authorities that a man working for a store was an undocumented migrant, he was not only deported, but had to sign a declaration that he would not return for at least another 10 years. He went back to Ahuelicán where he is now an artisan, traveling to other parts of Mexico and exporting crafts for other artisans. In order to avoid being caught, other Nahuas nowadays borrow the work permits or identity cards of other migrants.[24] These migrants, better educated and more familiar with urban life, are thus finding ways to bypass the legal restrictions and bureaucratic regulations designed to thwart undocumented migration.

Group identities and reputation

International migration and globalization have resulted in new forms of identity and group labels. Nahuas refer to White Americans as "bolillos" (white buns). Even the few Nahua migrants in Houston who now have American citizenships do not consider themselves as "real Americans," unlike their children born and raised in Houston. Such children see themselves as Mexicans rather than as *indígenas* even if they speak the Nahuatl language. Variations and changes in group identity and corresponding lifestyle are also apparent in the field of religion. Most Nahua migrants in Houston are Catholics and many homes have the same altars and pictures of saints as in Mexico. They attend masses at several parishes, some of which have Mexican priests. Those who belonged to Protestant denominations in Mexico had no trouble finding an equivalent Spanish-speaking church. However, such American religious institutions have also had a direct influence on indigenous communities in Mexico. One man from Ahuelicán first became a Pentecostal in Houston where he joined a large Spanish-speaking congregation. He studied to be a pastor. When he went back to Ahuelicán several years later he started proselytizing and set up a small Pentecostal congregation. There are close connections, partly based on kinship, between the Nahua Pentecostals in Ahuelicán and Houston.[25]

Indigenous identities and group loyalties can take new forms in a transnational setting. Unlike one of the professionals from Xalitla who frequently attends international meetings of indigenous peoples from the United States and other countries, undocumented Nahua migrants have no contact whatsoever with American native peoples. This does not mean that the revival of an indigenous heritage and new forms of pan-indigenous identity will not happen in the context of big American cities, albeit in surprising ways. One man from Ahuelicán who lives in Houston has taken on an Aztec identity as a result of his contact with Jo Harper, an American writer not of Mexican descent.[26] This writer was initially surprised that the Nahua migrants she met did not know the history of ancient Mexico. When she realized they spoke Nahuatl, she told them they were direct descendent of Aztecs and showed them several history books. This was a consciousness-raising event. One of these men now refers to himself as an Aztec whenever he meets Americans not of Mexican descent.[27] This new identity was reinforced when he met a group of Chicanos (Americans of Mexican descent) who see themselves as Aztecs, even though they might not have any Nahua heritage, as opposed to some other form of Native American ancestry. One day an American dance group specializing in Aztec dances arrived in town. They was amazed to discover there were migrants in Houston who spoke Nahuatl and asked the man from Ahuelicán who identifies as an Aztec to give them Nahuatl lessons. This man, who came to Houston in the 1980s, is now an American citizen and speaks fluent English. A younger cousin who is an undocumented immigrant with strong ties to Ahuelicán also refers to himself as an Aztec.

Whether or not this new Aztec identity, combined with an interest in Aztec dancing, will become more prevalent among Nahua migrants is hard to say.[28] It is more likely that people from the Alto Balsas living in Mexico will adopt the group identity of Nahua, a category used by anthropologists to label all indigenous people who speak the Nahuatl language. I know several bilingual teachers who see themselves as Nahuas, and suspect this group name may become more prevalent among professionals whose mother tongue is Nahuatl, especially if they interact with other Nahuatl-speaking people at political meetings for indigenous people, academic conferences, or workshops for bilingual teachers from different regions. Such teachers and other Nahua professionals in Mexico are not likely to become undocumented migratory workers in the United States even though they would initially be earning higher wages if they did.[29]

The patterns of social interaction, identity formation, and group stereotyping associated with international migratory labor are distinct from those of internal migratory labor or people who stay. In two villages of the Alto Balsas where people never adopted craft production, people have continued to work as seasonal agricultural laborers in other parts of Mexico, where they still face prejudice directly against indigenous people. In contrast, the Nahuas who move back and forth between Guerrero and the United States are no longer seen as country bumpkins by fellow Mexicans. Indeed, they are regarded as cosmopolitan travelers. They may also be seen as rich vendors, artists, and craftsmen because of their villages of origin. Yet Americans see them as no different from other Mexican workers in the Unites States. Some people despise Nahuas as illegal immigrants who should be deported. Only within specific situations in the United States, such as for educational institutions, are people from the Alto Balsas seen as the repositories of Mexican indigenous knowledge. Jo Harper, the writer referred to earlier, bases much of her creative writing on the stories Nahua migrants have told her.

Nahuas who are spending a good part of their lives in the United States continue to be citizens of pueblos in the Alto Balsas. Through ongoing contacts with relatives at home, remittances, and participation in their home towns upon returning (or in between trips), they are gradually modifying the physical appearance plus some aspects of Nahua culture such as gender roles and governance. At the same time Nahua villages keep exporting more young people who have been brought up in Mexico and socialized as members of indigenous communities. Unlike their parents or grandfathers, they know what to expect when they leave to go to the United States. Most have jobs waiting for them, since American employers utilize the family ties or existing Nahua workers to recruit more workers. Older Nahuas who prefer to stay in the United States are helping to ensure the survival of the Nahuatl language and culture among the Nahua children born and raised outside of Mexico. Many of those children will end up spending time in the Alto Balsas when their parents or older siblings take them home for visits, and sometimes to stay. The Nahuas from the Alto Balsas are now part of a fully transnational indigenous community.

Conclusion

The Alto Balsas Nahuas are an example of the complexity and multidimensionality of transnational indigeneity. The experience of Nahuas involved in a movement of resistance against the Mexican state was not the same as that of those who carved out a niche in the world of crafts. Nor are the dynamics of social interaction of Nahuas within the world of politics, or their efforts to gain recognition in the field of art, the same as those associated with the struggle for seeking new forms of livelihood in the United States. The way that Nahuas are represented by outsiders, including scholars, is also different in each of these transnational social fields.

Despite the diversity of experiences of indigenous people originating from this part of Guerrero, they have become part of a single social group well known to anthropologists, art dealers, and political activists. As is the case with any group label, the name Alto Balsas Nahuas, with its connotations of homogeneity and commonality, gives the impression that its members share a single way of life and a single social identity. Its representatives portray this group as one with a long history. Yet the label "Alto Balsas" came into existence only recently. The label was born as an ethnic category within the field of politics, and then adopted in other fields such as academia (hence my use of the label in this chapter). The name has also come to the attention of native activists in the United States and Canada. However, as a group label, Alto Balsas Nahuas is somewhat unusual. Unlike such group names as Mexican, *indígena* or mestizo, the majority of the people, and even political leaders who live in the Alto Balsas region today, do not use, or identify with, that label. The Alto Balsas Nahuas are currently better known to people outside of their region of origin than in the places where members of this group reside. Moreover, the label Nahuas del Alto Balsas is better known, and has more relevance, in the field of national and international politics, as well as in academia, than in some other social fields.

When it comes to the world of commerce, education, or religion, the name Alto Balsas (unlike e.g., Guerrero or Mexico) is not associated in peoples' minds with a particular ethnic or linguistic group. Tourists and art lovers are more likely to talk about the *amateros* of Guerrero, while people in the city of Iguala talk about "the pueblos of the river." Nor does the term "Alto Balsas Nahuas" have the same connotations even in those fields where it is well known. Political activists see Alto Balsas Nahuas as an ethnic group engaged in a struggle against globalization, as part of a worldwide movement against globalization. In contrast, for most anthropologists and other scholars, it is a convenient label to refer to a specific group of people and a geographical region regardless of the level of participation of their inhabitants in a global political movement. Anthropologists talk about, and accept the reality of, the Alto Balsas as both a region and a group of people. Yet the meaning of this label has been contested and is subject to competing interpretations. Anthropologists, including Nahua anthropologists, will continue to debate the question of what it means to be an Alto Balsas Nahua or to what extent we can generalize about a Nahua culture or way of life.

Notes

* The author started doing research on this region in 2001. A little over 10 months of fieldwork was conducted in the village of Ahuehuepan, for periods lasting two or three months each, with shorter visits, anywhere from one day to several weeks, to Xalitla, San Juan Tetelcingo, Ameyaltepec, Oapan, Ahuelicán, and San Miguel. Interviews were also conducted in several cities in Mexico and the United States.

1. Mesoamerica refers to those parts of Central America and Mexico that were characterized by complex state level societies before the arrival of Europeans.
2. The adjective cosmopolitan, which connotes urban sophistication and familiarity and ability to feel at home with people from different countries and cultural backgrounds, is usually seen as the opposite of local or parochial.
3. The concept of social field (*champs d'action* in French) is part of a broader conceptual framework that includes the notion of habitus and different forms of capital (economic, social, and cultural). Bourdieu (1990, pp. 87–88; 191–192) considers each social field to be relatively autonomous to a greater or lesser extent.
4. See "El Consejo de Pueblos Nahuas del Alto Balsas, Guerrero A.C." in *Tlahui-politic* 2(2), 1996. Retrieved September 8, 2007, from http://www.tlahui.com/cpnab.htm
5. In contrast, the indigenous people in the rest of the Iguala valley lost most of their land shortly after the arrival of the Spaniards. For a comprehensive treatment of the colonial history of this part of Guerrero, see Jonathan Amith (2005).
6. Most of this information about economic history was obtained through interviews with people in Ahuehuepan. The history of the salt trade is also covered in an article by Catherine Good (1995) who did earlier fieldwork in Ameyaltepec.
7. *Compadrazgo* (literally co-parenthood) refers to the relationship between the biological parents of a child and their child's godfather (*padrino*) and godmother (*madrina*) on the occasion of a baptism, confirmation, or wedding. Unlike the Catholicism practiced in Europe and other parts of the world, the relationship between the adults (*compadres* for men and *comadres* for women) in Latin America is even more important than that between the child and godparents. Men can also become compadres on the occasion of secular ceremonies such as a school graduation. Compadres and comadres treat each other with respect and are expected to help each other.
8. This document, titled "Nahuas del Alto Balsas," was written by Catherine Good Eshelman and Guadalupe Barrientos Lopez (2004). It is available from a Mexican government Web site, retrieved May 2, 2007, from http://www.cdi.gob.mx.
9. This organization, CEA (*Grupo de Estudios Ambientales*), subsequently entered into an agreement to conduct such a study, which never advanced much because of lack of resources (Celestino, 2005, pp. 55-56).
10. The death of a young man hit by this company's truck triggered off a blockage of the construction road and the subsequent evacuation of its workers (Hindley, 1996, pp. 210-211).
11. This lower house of Mexican congress includes a number of deputies (*plurinominal*) who are selected by political parties that have won a certain percentage of the popular vote. This man was chosen as representative of the PRD as well as the *Consejo Guerrense* (CG500ARI).
12. The only sign of any participation at the local level was a poster prominently displayed in the central square of San Miguel Tecuixiapan, this leader's hometown. This poster gives the false impression to any outside visitors that the whole Alto Balsas region is actively involved in, and aware of, the Plan Panama. In 2005 Fox gave his word to, by phone, to a CPNAB leader that the Tetelcingo dam project would not be resurrected, but he was not willing to put this in writing (Celestino, 2005, p. 56).
13. A good overview of the prehistory of the Mezcala region, based on archaeological work, is provided by Louise Paradis (1995).
14. People at the local level, with the exception of two villages, are more likely to speak Nahuatl, while the Alto Balsas leader best known internationally speaks no Nahuatl whatsoever. This leader grew up in Xalitla at a time when most parents no longer spoke

Nahuatl to their children. Some of the leaders of the opposing faction, who also grew up in Xalitla, did learn Nahuatl from their parents or through self-study later in life.

15 I first heard about this view of the CPNAB from several Mexican students whom I met in Canada. In a subsequent trip to an academic institution, I was told the same thing by a well-known Mexican scholar.

16 In 1950 amate paper, used by shamans to create cutouts used for ritual purposes, was only produced in the Otomí village of San Pablito Pahuatlán, located in the state of Puebla. With the introduction of amate paintings, producers from San Pablito started traveling to the Alto Balas region to sell sheets of paper to Nahua artisans. For a comprehensive history of the development of the amate industry in the Alto Balsas, with a focus on Ameyaltepec, see Good (1988).

17 A Mexican specialist who knew about the artists from the village of Ameyaltepec recommended that an American anthropology student go there to do research on the aesthetic values and art style of an indigenous village that resulted in a doctoral dissertation and an article in a leading anthropological journal (Golde, 1963, 1973).

18 Painting on bark paper (amates) distinguishes the artisans in the Alto Balsas region from artisans in Copalillo who specialize in the production of hammocks, or the people from the neighboring Montaña region who make embroidered blouses.

19 These artists criticize other artists who depend too much on mechanical devices in the production process. For example, in the village of Ahuelicán, several amate painters use seals to stamp Aztec calendars or Grecian-style outlines before painting additional details by hand (Hémond, 2003, 272). In other villages, after the introduction of electricity, craftsmen started using electric motors to polish wooden figures prior to painting in order to increase the level of production.

20 I am so far not aware of any migrants from the Alto Balsas region in Canada although mestizos from other parts of Guerrero do work there, mainly in agriculture.

21 The bracero program was started toward the end of World War II to deal with labor shortages, especially in agriculture. The program lasted until the mid-1960s.

22 Human smugglers charged $3,000 in 2007 instead of the $1,500 they charged in 2002.

23 When children of Nahua parents speak English among each other, they use the Nahuatl words "*wewe*" y "*pipi*" to address an older brother or an older sister.

24 They give half of their earnings to the person who lent the papers. This is highly risky since they could both be deported. Increased border security has not stopped the flow of undocumented migrants into the United States.

25 However, not everyone in the same family changes their religion. Neither the husband of the formerly non-Roman Catholic woman in Houston nor her son converted.

26 Jo Harper is an award-winning writer of juvenile fiction.Several of her books are based on the life history of the young Nahua men from Ahuelicán whom she got to know in Houston (see the acknowledgment in *Delfino's Journey* 2001).

27 This case is based on my own encounter with him, as well as conversations with Jo Harper, while staying in Houston.

28 In Mexico City there are also Aztec dancers who perform in the main square. They belong to a group of young people who want to go back to a lifestyle (such as vegetarianism) that they believe was associated with the Aztecs of Tenochtitlán (the name of the capital of the Aztec empire located on the same site as current downtown Mexico City).

29 Unfortunately, despite the expansion of high schools in the Alto Balsas region, the number of Nahua students who opt to continue their studies in Mexico is likely to drop

over time. Teachers in the Alto Balsas region, including Nahua teachers, complain that most of their pupils do not have aspirations to become doctors, lawyers, or engineers in Mexico, much less teachers. They prefer to go off to the Unites States immediately after high school so that they can earn dollars.

References

Amith, J. (Ed.) (1995). *The Amate Tradition* (Innovation and Dissent in Mexican Art). Chicago: Mexican Fine Arts Center Museum.

———. (2005). *The Möbius Strip: A Spatial History of Colonial Society in Guerrero, Mexico.* Stanford, CA: Stanford University Press.

Bourdieu, P. (1990). *In Other Words: Essays toward a Reflexive Sociology* (Matthew Adamson, Trans.). Stanford, CA: Stanford University Press (original work published 1987).

Celestino, E. (2005). El proyecto hidroeléctrico San Juan Tetelcingo, Guerrero? Cancelado o suspendido? *Diario de campo, suplemento* 33 (June), 53–57. Retrieved September 10, 2007, from http://www.antropologia.inah.gob.mx/pdf/pdf_diario/junio_05/supl_junio_05.pdf

Cowen, T. (2005). *Markets and Cultural Voices* (Liberty vs. Power in the Lives of Mexican Amate Painters). Ann Arbor: University of Michigan Press.

Fox, J. & G. Rivera-Salgado. (2004). Building Civil Society among Indigenous Migrants. In Fox, J. & Rivera-Salgado, G. (Eds.), *Indigenous Mexican Migrants in the United States* (pp. 1–65). La Jolla, CA: Center for U.S.-Mexican Studies/ Center for Comparative Immigration Studies.

García Ortega, M. (2006). Región tradicional y capitales migratorios internacionales. Diásporas nahuas entre el Alto Balsas, Los Ángeles y Houston. A paper presented at the Second Round Table (Mesa Redonda, titled "*El conocimiento antropológico e histórico sobre Guerrero*") in August. In Taxco, Guerrero.

Golde, P. (1963). Aesthetic Values and Art Style in a Nahua Pottery Producing Village. PhD Dissertation. Harvard University.

Good, C. (1988). *Haciendo la lucha (arte y comercio nahuas de Guerrero)*. Mexico: Fondo de Cultural Económica.

———. (1995). Salt Production and Commerce in Guerrero, Mexico: An Ethnographic Contribution to Historical Reconstruction. *Ancient Mesoamerica*, 6, 1–13.

Good Eshelman, C. & G. Barrientos López. (2004). Nahuas del Alto Balsos (pueblos indígenas del México contemporáneo). Retrieved, August 20, 2007, from http://www.cdi.gob.mx

Harper, J. (2001). *Delfino's Journey*. Lubbock, TX: Texas Tech University Press.

Hémond, A. (2003). *Peindre la révolte* (Esthétique et résistance culturelle au Mexique). Paris: CNRS Editions.

———. (2004). Factions et parties politiques: La mécanique des groupes dans un village indien du Mexique. *Ateliers*, 27, 111–146.

Hindley, J. (1996). Indigenous Mobilization, Political Reform and Development in Mexico: The Struggle of the Nahua People of the Alto Balsas, Guerrero. Doctoral thesis, Department of Geography, University of Essex.

Morales, B. (2007). Classes Paint Your Own ... (Produccción y commercialization artesanal por los migrantes nahuas de San Juan Tetelcingo en Playa del Carmen, Quintana Roo). *Regiones* (suplemento de antropología), 30, 5–9.

Overmyer-Velásquez, R. (2003). The Self-determination of Indigenous Peoples and the Limits of United Nations Advocacy in Guerrero, Mexico (1998–2000). *Identities: Global Studies in*

Power and Culture, 10, 9-29.

Paradis, L. (1995). The Pre-Columbian History of the Mezcala Region. In J. Amith (Ed.), *The Amate Tradition: Innovation and Dissent in Mexican Art* (pp. 113-128). Chicago, IL: Mexican Fine Arts Center Museum.

Schryer, F. (2001). Multiple Hierarchies and the Duplex Nature of Groups. *Journal of the Royal Anthropological Institute* 7, 705-21.

♦ CHAPTER SEVEN ♦

Transnational Migration and Indigeneity in Canada: A Case Study of Urban Inuit

Julie-Ann Tomiak and Donna Patrick

In this chapter, we focus on urban Inuit as a transnational population. We explore how dominant constructions of Inuitness rooted in the Arctic North are simultaneously mobilized and challenged, producing new Inuit identities through discourses and practices circulating in and across different locales. In looking at Inuit community-building in Ottawa, an urban center in Southern Canada, we seek to problematize commonsensical and essentialist notions of Indigeneity as firmly rooted in place or as "spatially incarcerated" (Malkki, 1997, pp. 58–59). Our case study examines the complexities of the reterritorialization of Inuit difference. As we shall see, the processes of Inuit transnationalism, like the movement of other Indigenous peoples to cities away from their home communities, effectively complicate taken-for-granted relationships between identity, place, and difference (Gupta & Ferguson, 1997).

While transnationalism has been widely discussed in anthropological research, this "boom time for the anthropology of migration" (Vertovec, 2007, p. 962) has largely excluded systematic investigations of transnational Indigeneity. Indigeneity and transnationalism are conventionally conceptualized as incompatible, much as Indigeneity and cosmopolitanism are (introduction, this volume). This is because Indigeneity is generally understood as being tied to, and legitimated by, a single locale, whereas both transnationalism and cosmopolitanism entail mobility between locales. However, as our analysis demonstrates, the social, geographical, and cultural complexities of urban Inuit experiences make a compelling case for transnational migration within a nation-state. This chapter focuses on the ways in which urban Inuitness has been constituted transnationally and locally in discourses, historical and political processes, and institutional practices.

We begin with a brief discussion of urban Indigeneity and cosmopolitanism and how various understandings of the latter concept, including "rooted cosmopolitanism" (Appiah, 1997) and "banal cosmopolitanism" (Hannerz, 2007), relate to this case study. In the next section, we contextualize our discussion of the spatialized construction of Inuitness and the (re)territorializations of Inuit identities in urban contexts within the larger picture of urban Indigeneity. We use an analytical framework that situates Inuit in a highly uneven urban Aboriginal[1] landscape. Stressing the role of state practices related to the allocation of resources for Aboriginal-specific services, we problematize the "urban Aboriginal" category as a simultaneously homogenizing and hierarchizing construct that has marginalized Inuit and their urban experiences. In the third section, we provide a brief description of the Inuit community in Ottawa, home to the largest urban Inuit population in Southern Canada. Finally, we discuss how Inuit identities have been constructed in relation to dominant notions of Inuit as geographically and culturally situated in the territorial North, or Arctic,[2] and what this means for Inuit who reside outside of traditional Inuit homelands. Drawing on interview data, we explore these spatial and discursive positionings as constitutive of struggles over representation, categorization, and social justice. And we illustrate some of the ways in which "rootedness," transnational connectedness, and symbolic resources linked to the Arctic play a central role in Inuit community-building in Ottawa.[3]

Indigeneity and Cosmopolitanisms

It has been suggested that cosmopolitanism "is often considered an elite characteristic" (Hannerz, 2007, p. 73)–a privilege accorded to mobile global subjects. It assumes a structural division of labor between "elite cosmopolitans and subordinate locals" (p. 75), or a division "of 'haves' who move and 'have nots' who stay put" (p. 76). Among other things, cosmopolitans also are said to share a sense of belonging as "citizens of the world." Given these characterizations, cosmopolitanism does not appear at first glance to be a useful lens to look at the processes of transnational migration involving Indigenous peoples who, as we shall see, have neither the material resources to constitute a mobile elite nor the inclination toward "global commonality." For the most part, urban Indigenous peoples continue to assert their difference, which is often crucial in mobilizing resources and spaces for marginalized Indigenous migrants. This assertion of difference runs counter to global, homogenizing orientations of cosmopolitanism. In short, there are a number of problematic assumptions inherent in the dominant conceptualization of the term (Nashashibi, 2007) that render its usefulness open to debate.

At the very least, the notion of cosmopolitanism "needs to be considered in the plural" (Pollock, Bhabha, Breckenridge, & Chakrabarty, 2002, p. 8) since there appears to be a range of actors, practices, and projects that are described as "cosmopolitan" (Vertovec & Cohen, 2002). One form of cosmopolitanism that might be worth exploring in an analysis of urban Indigeneity is the concept of "rooted cosmopolitans"—a term used to describe the experiences of migrants who remain attached to places of origins (Tarrow, 2005, p. 42). As defined by Appiah (1997, p. 618), a rooted cosmopolitan is someone who is "[...] attached to a home of one's own, with its own cultural particularities, but taking pleasure from the presence of other, different places that are home to other, different people." While the notion of "rootedness" may indeed be applicable to urban Indigenous experiences, it is nevertheless unclear what the analytical purchase of "cosmopolitan" would be, especially with regard to urban Inuit. This is largely because the majority of the participants in our study would not characterize themselves as mobile elites with "cosmopolitan" tastes. For the most part, their symbolic capital (in the Bourdieuan sense) is not akin to the "cosmopolitan tastes and knowledge ... of competitive elite games of distinction" (Hannerz, 2007, p. 74), although in some cases it is decidedly "urban." That is, the Inuit we encounter in Ottawa, like other urban dwellers, possess a range of Southern-oriented linguistic and cultural capital, and have diverse urban social networks that differentiate members of the group. However, rather than unifying as "cosmopolitans," the salient unifying category for all is "Inuit."

A second type of cosmopolitanism that might be useful in characterizing urban Indigeneity is modeled after Michael Billig's concept of "banal nationalism." Hannerz (2007) develops the notion of "banal cosmopolitanism" in providing a space for the "recurrent practices and experiences of everyday life" that have come to characterize urban existence. Here he mentions the numerous border-crossings in the process of becoming "at home in the world," including involvement with different places, cultures, and nations and the "hybrid" or "creolized" practices that result (Hannerz, 2007, p. 73). This cosmopolitanism as "everyday practice" that "anyone can join" seems to transcend the elite aspects of the concept, but it still fails to account for the socioeconomic realities of urban Inuit.

A third type of cosmopolitanism that we might call "technological cosmopolitanism" may have some potential in characterizing aspects of urban Indigeneity. This concerns access to new media technologies and the connectedness to the broader world that results. Particularly for Inuit, the telephone and the Internet, including e-mail, webcam, and instant messaging, have become part of maintaining their "rootedness" by communicating with friends and relatives in the Arctic. However, like other migrant populations, this connectivity does not necessarily lead to more "cosmopolitanism" or a sense of "global citizenship," since it entails maintaining local ties.

In the context of urban Indigeneity, and urban Inuit in particular, the concept of cosmopolitanism seems to be more problematic than useful. For one thing, it tends to neglect the unequal structural relationships and political economic forces that shape urban Inuitness. Cosmopolitanism further tends to feed into universalizing discourses and can thus subvert assertions of Indigenous differences and political claims against the settler state. This is exemplified in the overarching liberalism of the "cosmopolitan ideal," as articulated by Appiah (1997, p. 622): "The cosmopolitan ideal—take your roots with you—is one in which people are free to choose the local forms of human life within which they will live." This "ideal" overemphasizes individual choice and becomes problematic when applied to migrants who have been displaced and marginalized. In particular, people affected by historical and ongoing processes of colonialism may, in fact, have little choice regarding their life conditions in urban settings or the circumstances that prompted them to leave their home communities in the first place. As our case study illustrates, for Inuit in Ottawa the ability to freely choose local forms of life is tightly circumscribed by the constant struggle to access resources to create community spaces where Inuit identities are valorized and connections to the Arctic can be maintained.

In light of these critiques, we turn to transnationalism as a set of grounded processes that characterize the urban Inuit experiences discussed in this chapter. As noted, "the image of transnational migrants as deterritorialized, free-floating people represented by the now popular academic adage 'neither here nor there' deserves closer scrutiny" (Guarnizo & Smith, 1998, p. 11). Guarnizo and Smith stress that the translocal realities of migrants are not placeless. Rather, they remain situated historically and geographically, and continue to be structured by unequal power relations. Thus, power asymmetries continue to play out in and through the process of "transnational social formation" (Guarnizo & Smith, 1998, p. 27). As we shall see in the next section, this is a useful way of conceptualizing the processes involved for Inuit who move to urban centers in Southern Canada.

Urban Indigeneity, Inuit Transnationalism, and Struggles for Recognition

Indigenous experiences in cities are under-researched in Canada, despite the fact that more than half of Indigenous people live in urban areas (Statistics Canada, 2008; Siggner & Costa, 2005). This growth in urban Indigenous populations was also largely ignored by policy makers until the late 1990s.[4] In large part, this is due to the settler conceptualization of urban centers as non-Indigenous spaces and the self-serving framing of Indigenous peoples as located in remote areas and in the historical past (Peters, 1996; Razack, 2002; Jacobs, 1996). The construction of Indigenous and urban as mutually exclusive categories has meant that "Aboriginal people are confronted again and again with explicit and implicit messages that cities are not where they belong as people with vibrant and living cultures" (Peters, 1996, p. 60). This mapping of Indigenous peoples disregards the historical geographies of cities and the contested claims to title to a large number of urban spaces in Canada. For instance, Ottawa, our research site, is on unceded Algonquin territory and currently subject to a comprehensive land claim.

There are two major caveats regarding our understanding of urban Indigeneity that need to be addressed if research is to capture the complex and dynamic nature of urban Indigenous realities. First, there is a paucity of available data. This is due to issues such as the under coverage of urban Indigenous populations in the Census, as well as relatively little academic interest in urban Indigeneity. Second, urban Indigenous populations are heterogeneous. There is great variability among Indigenous peoples within Canadian cities and across different locales, making any definitive statements about urban Indigeneity problematic (Graham & Peters, 2002; Proulx, 2006). Therefore, the term "urban Aboriginal" needs to be problematized, since it tends to suggest a clear-cut and closed category, notwithstanding the actual fluidity and variability subsumed under this label (Lobo, 2001; Proulx, 2006). Given that "urban Aboriginality" as an umbrella category is constituted by a multiplicity of structural relations, representational strategies, shifting locations, experiences, practices, and discourses, it is of limited analytical use. For this reason, we focus on one segment of this population, in a specific locale: the Inuit in Ottawa, where, as with Inuit elsewhere in Southern Canada, little research has thus far been conducted.[5]

As we will see, the mobilization of the community for culturally specific social and cultural services has resulted in a number of tensions within the larger Aboriginal category and between Northern and Southern Inuit realities. In light of the problems of categorization, we argue (1) that the experiences of urban Inuit are worth examining on their own terms, because although many urban Inuit experiences are similar to First Nations and Métis experiences, they are also distinct in some respects; and (2) that urban Inuit are part of a process of Inuit transnationalism and can be conceptualized as a transnational community.

We argue that urban Inuit experiences and identities—although similar to those of First Nations and Métis—are in important respects distinct from them and share much in common with transnational migrants. They are similar in being shaped by colonial, racialized, and gendered processes of regulation and social categorization (Lawrence, 2003, 2004) and in the fact that urban realities tend to face even greater complexities than nonurban ones (Proulx, 2003; Jackson, 2002). Nevertheless, as we will explore further in this chapter, urban Inuit experiences arguably have much in common with transnational experiences, facing similar linguistic, cultural, and other barriers as transnational migrants. Among these is that southern Inuit cannot return home often, given the extremely high travel costs to the Arctic. Not only is there geographical dislocation, exacerbated by high transportation costs, but cultural and linguistic barriers exist with respect to accessing social and other services in Southern cities. A lack of shared frames of reference, in some situations, can lead to serious conflicts with non-Inuit institutions and service providers. Several of our participants shared stories about experiences with schools, banking institutions, and the Children's Aid Society; and the disruption that cultural misunderstandings and stereotyping in these situations has caused in their lives. In short, urban Inuit experiences are not unlike non-English or non-French speaking immigrants arriving in Canadian cities.

Inuit transnationalism is a process that we conceive as qualitatively different from transregionalism (a process whereby individuals move from one region of a country to another), even though it remains distinct from trans-statal movements, those who cross nation-state boundaries (Kearney, 2004, p. 218; Hannerz, 1996). In other words, we apply notions of transnational and diasporic Indigeneity to urban Inuit who, according to our conceptualization, have crossed a national boundary in moving from the Inuit Arctic to the South, yet still remain within the Canadian nation-state. This form of transnational Indigeneity has similarities to transnational migrations among other ethnic groups who seek to make their homes and to construct community in urban centers away from their homelands. We see here similar sorts of connections that other "mobile subjects have to localities" and similar connections to the "webs of cultural, political, and economic ties" with which such subjects are involved (Inda, Xavier, & Rosaldo, 2002, p. 19).

Our recognition of Inuit as having a separate set of experiences is not only based on the specificity of Inuit historical, cultural, and geographical circumstances, it is also based on Inuit resistance to their categorization as "Aboriginal" and "urban Aboriginal," which has tended to homogenize and essentialize the myriad experiences and differences among Indigenous people living in cities. By this we mean that this process of categorization has tended to unify all Aboriginal experiences, and that the grouping in itself positions Aboriginality as having an inherent core or "essence" that defines the behaviors and identities of people within the category.

That being said, "urban Aboriginal" remains an important operational category because of its currency with respect to broader policy and funding issues, though it remains problematic, as federal funding tends to privilege First

Nations peoples living on reserve, sidelining those living off-reserve, as well as the Inuit and Métis (Inuit Tapiriit Kanatami [ITK], 2004a, 2004b; Newhouse & Peters, 2003). This has meant that the actual recognition of Aboriginal rights has differed significantly between groups and according to geographic location.[6] Urban Inuit find themselves in a particularly vulnerable position, since available funding is allotted primarily to the four Inuit homeland regions of Nunatsiavut (Labrador), the Inuvialuit Settlement Area (North West Territories), Nunavik (Quebec), and Nunavut. Although Inuit are the least urbanized among Indigenous groups in Canada, with fewer than 20 percent living outside of these homeland areas (Statistics Canada, 2008), they nevertheless constitute a growing urban Indigenous population, particularly in Ottawa.

The struggle for Inuit-specific resources within the broader Aboriginal category has created a number of difficulties for urban Inuit as it is fought on the terrain of authenticity. In mobilizing for funding, urban Inuit have had to perform their Inuit social and cultural differences in ways that relate directly to the Arctic in order to legitimate their needs for culturally appropriate programs and services. Thus, Southern Inuit need to access the Northern cultural capital associated with authentic Inuit cultural and linguistic practices in order to gain support for urban Inuit community, cultural, health, and educational facilities. This fosters a special form of transnational connectedness or rootedness in urban centers.

Despite the constant grant-writing and lobbying efforts that urban Inuit have been engaged in to obtain culturally relevant services and Inuit control over these services, Inuit are still marginalized among urban Indigenous populations. This problem is described as follows in the report of the 2005 One Voice Workshop, which sought to address urban Inuit issues:

> Inuit, a unique people with their own culture, language, and history, are often forgotten. [...] Inuit are frequently not able to obtain funds due, as well, to this pan-Aboriginal approach as funds are often distributed on a per capita basis. Since Inuit are the smallest population of Aboriginal peoples in urban settings, they are frequently given a very small portion of Aboriginal funds. This pan-Aboriginal approach in services and programs is simply not working. (TI, 2005, p. 7)

The importance of Inuit-specific funding and programming based on the distinct needs of the urban Inuit population was also stressed by the participants in our interviews and during a focus group discussion that was held to address community concerns. For instance, one community worker who we interviewed noted that

> [one thing that] is really difficult [is] when governments fund programs for Inuit, they fund them in the regions up North. [Yet] ... the biggest growth for the population ... has been for people moving to the South, and yet we are constantly fighting for dollars. ... [I]f we were up in the North, it would be easier to find dollars, I believe. So, it's getting the urban population recognized as a distinct group who needs services. ...

> People just are not aware of the urban population ... mainstream services don't work. So, that's not the answer, the answer is definitely to come up with services that are specific to the population. And the argument is harder and longer, so therefore it takes longer to get the services. It's a constant fight to get that money.[7]

This quotation illustrates, as noted earlier, that there are also tensions that arise from the privileging of Inuit in the Arctic over those who live in Southern Canadian cities, which mirrors dominant understandings of who and where Inuit are. These dominant notions can be seen, for instance, in the Indian and Northern Affairs Canada definition of Inuit as "the Aboriginal people of Arctic Canada. Inuit live primarily in Nunavut, the Northwest Territories and northern parts of Labrador and Quebec" (Indian and Northern Affairs Canada [INAC], 2004). The lack of recognition that Inuit reside outside of traditional homelands has contributed significantly to new forms of Inuit cultural production, as urban Inuit mobilize for resources and recognition in cities. These new forms of Inuitness are rooted in the Arctic North but are produced in the culturally pluralistic South. This ongoing struggle in Inuit community-building in Ottawa will be explored further in this chapter.

Inuit Community-Building in Ottawa

The community-based participatory research project that this chapter draws on grew out of a research partnership with the Ottawa Inuit Children's Centre (OICC) and a Carleton University research team. The OICC is a community-run center, which houses the Sivummut ("Going Forward") Head Start Program, the Tumiralaat ("Little Footprints") Inuit Child Care Centre, and the Inuit Family Literacy Program. The goal of our research has been to investigate the experiences of Inuit living in Ottawa and issues relating to community development. Through interviews, focus groups, and participant observation, we have explored how Inuit negotiate their transnationalism. More specifically, we have addressed questions related to the cultural and social needs of Inuit in Ottawa, including family life, children's school work, social life, culture, and language. In the spring and summer of 2007, we interviewed 20 members of the Inuit community, using a set of collaboratively developed, semistructured questions. Interviewees were selected using a snowballing method, where Inuit from the OICC and other Inuit organizations in Ottawa were approached to be interviewed. These people then suggested others who might be interested in participating in the project.

Ottawa is home to the largest Inuit community in Southern Canada. According to the 2006 census, 8,395 Inuit lived in urban centers outside of Inuit homelands. The "urban outside Inuit Nunaat"[8] category accounts for 17 percent of all Inuit. The number of urban Inuit was up about 60 percent from a decade earlier. Statistics Canada (2008) lists the urban centers outside Inuit Nunaat with the largest Inuit populations as Ottawa-Gatineau with 725, Yellowknife with 640, Edmonton with 590, Montreal with 570, and Winnipeg with 355. Yet, according to the Inuit community center in Ottawa, Tungasuvvingat Inuit (TI),[9] the actual number of Inuit living in Ottawa exceeded 1,000 in 2005, and each year this figure increases (TI, 2005). As noted in the report of the Urban Aboriginal Task Force (2007), the statistics on Ottawa's Aboriginal population tend to hide a significant and increasing need for programs targeting the growing Inuit population. Both the undercounting of Inuit as well as their subordination within the larger Aboriginal category have had a negative impact on the capacity of the Inuit community organizations to deliver services.

Similar to the diversity within First Nations and Métis urban communities, Inuit move to and take up residence in urban centers in the South for a variety of reasons related to health, employment, education, and family. As is the case with Inuit living in other cities, such as Montreal and Winnipeg, many Inuit arrive in Ottawa to receive medical treatment and some end up staying in the city once the treatment has finished. A relatively large number of Inuit come for post-secondary education, to attend programs offered by Nunavut Sivuniksavut, the Inuit Art Foundation, Algonquin College, and Carleton University, among others. Some Inuit have moved to the city for employment with national Inuit or Aboriginal organizations, or with the federal government. Others are in Ottawa for family or personal reasons, to be with parents, siblings, or members of their extended family, to seek better education opportunities for their children, or to flee abusive or otherwise difficult situations in the Arctic. In short, however, the "promise of a better future" (Hage, 2005, p. 474) unifies most of the Inuit coming to the city, similar to other migrant populations.

The dynamics of migration and diaspora are different for most Inuit in comparison with many First Nations and Métis in the city. One of the key differences lies in the ability of many members in the latter groups to return to their home communities regularly, perhaps maintaining a rootedness to their territorial homelands in more concrete terms. For Inuit in Ottawa, the prohibitive costs of Arctic travel make such connections less viable, especially for those without high-paying government jobs. Nevertheless, despite these geographical and economic constraints, "rootedness" is produced and reproduced in the maintenance of relationships to home communities—relationships that continue to be important elements that shape urban Inuit realities. New technologies facilitate this maintenance, as do visits to the South by community members and relations seeking health services or attending cultural or political functions. Even if face-to-face interaction is rare, many of the participants in our research project talked about keeping frequently in touch with family and friends in the Arctic with the help of e-mail, instant messaging, webcams, and telephone.

Inuit social networks in Ottawa are not only cultural and linguistic, but geographical as well. For instance, people with relatives from particular regions tend to be identified with particular locales. People coalesce, at certain times, around these geographical identities that often extend beyond the particular region that people are from. In fact, in addition to those who have left the Northern territories, there are also Inuit who have been raised in the South, either as a result of parents moving South or through adoption into Southern families. Over the course of our research, several participants noted that tensions can arise between Inuit who moved to Ottawa from the Arctic and Southern-born Inuit, given that the linguistic and cultural skills and knowledge of the Inuit homelands clearly mark Inuitness within the commonsensical understanding of it. As one woman explains,

> I think on occasion there are some tensions, absolutely. I think there is some tension between Inuit that live in/ which we call urban Inuit [and] those who are Inuit who've grown up North and come here. There is some tension between those that have Inuktitut and those who don't. But I think it's an underlying thing, I don't think, to me, I've never had it be obvious or blatant or/ but I do hear people talk/ speaking of it.

A number of interviewees noted that the label "urban Inuit" is usually applied more narrowly to Inuit who were raised in the South or have lived here for most of their lives. Inuit raised in the South may lack the linguistic and cultural skills, which have become desired cultural capital for those who wish to connect with family members and communities and to be part of Inuit collectivities in the Arctic. Indeed, these forms of cultural capital, including the knowledge to "perform" one's Inuitness through throat-singing, drumming, or Inuktitut language practices, are circulating in Ottawa as well. The emphasis that Inuit parents place on enrolling their children in the Sivummut Head Start program, where Inuit language and culture are transmitted, indicates how crucial this program is considered to be. Here, Inuit knowledge is reproduced. Inuit-specific institutions have played a pivotal role in valorizing new forms of Inuitness, to the extent that urban Inuit identities have been enhanced through the exploration and practice of Inuit language and culture. As one urban Inuk points out, "I grew up all across Canada and never met another Inuk until I came to Ottawa. And it was from meeting other Inuit that I learned to throat-sing and drum dance in Ottawa. So, to me, I learned more about my culture here than I have anywhere else."

The ways in which Inuitness is constructed by urban Inuit, particularly those who have been brought up in the South, are highly relevant to the process of community-building. The urban Inuit spaces that are created and used as sites in this process are of particular importance. These sites provide linkages between networks of long-term urban residents and newcomers, which include Inuit from a wide range of historical-geographical trajectories, all of who are connected, in some contemporary or ancestral way, to the territorial Arctic. Inuit organizations, such as the TI, the OICC, and Inuit Non-profit Housing, are central nodes in these urban networks.

The heterogeneity of our interviewees—based, for instance, on their years of residence in the city and differing levels of education and employment—included the fact that Inuit have taken up residence in different parts of the city.[10] Some, with relatively well-paying jobs, live in middle-class areas of the city or in more rural areas outside the Ottawa core. However, the majority of those we interviewed live in the predominantly working-class area of Vanier (just east of the downtown area) or in the adjacent neighborhood even further east. The majority of subsidized Inuit housing units are located in this area. Yet, the need for more subsidized housing units remains. Vanier is also the area where most of the local Inuit-specific service agencies are situated, such as the OICC, and, as of 2007, the Inuit Family Resource Centre.

However, even with the social networks, housing, and community activities concentrated in a specific geographical area, the city remains in stark contrast to the more sparsely populated, tightly knit Arctic communities. As one woman explains, "In the city not everybody knows you like a small community, so you feel kinda more alone. That's pretty much it. It's different, because I'm not able to see my family all the time. It's not a walk up the street to see my uncle. It's disconnected in a way." Another interviewee adds to this sense of expansive urban space by noting that "It was just mind-boggling. And yet there are a lot of conveniences, in terms of jobs and access to health care. It's a lot easier here. But the culture shock was huge ... very overwhelming." Given the sense of dislocation that many of our participants spoke about, local Inuit organizations have become centrally important. As another participant pointed out, in reference to the city and the place of the OICC in it, "This is isolation ... Ottawa is a very big city. You come from a small community to come to Ottawa, so there is a place for people to come together and make that 'small community feel' again ... it's amazing." One key finding that has emerged in our fieldwork in Ottawa is the continued importance of Inuit social networks that are local while at the same time connecting Ottawa with the Arctic.

In this sense, the Inuit community in Ottawa is constituted both locally and transnationally. It forms a new kind of Inuitness that could perhaps be characterized as a new form of cosmopolitanism, but one that is specific to Inuit who are marginalized in relation to the Canadian North and South. This is particularly prevalent in the programs and spaces offered by the TI and the OICC, among others. They function as nodal points in networks that, for many Inuit, make it possible to move to and "survive" in Ottawa. Migration and residence patterns are bound up with gendered and class-based dynamics, all of which are played out in the processes of moving to Ottawa and acquiring new forms of symbolic capital there in order to make a living. But it is important to note that, similar to other urban Indigenous populations (Wotherspoon, 2003; Peters, 2006), Inuit in Ottawa are not uniformly disadvantaged. While there may be differences in socioeconomic status and residence, and despite a noticeable tension between the Northern and Southern-born Inuit, based on their historical, social, and cultural positionings, there are nevertheless community-based processes that unify Inuit as a recognizable, important force in the Aboriginal urban landscape. This aspect of the Ottawa urban Inuit community will be discussed in the next section.

Urban Inuitness: Transnational and Local Processes

The dominant imaginary of Inuitness[11] as firmly situated in the Arctic and the notion of territorially fixed Inuit identities has been complicated by Inuit living in cities in Southern Canada. Here, Inuit identities are deterritorialized and reterritorialized in complex and, at times, contradictory ways. Transnational, diasporic, and local processes constitute and reconstitute Inuit identities in this specific urban environment. Similar to urban Indigenous experiences, more generally, Inuit who are

> born into or entering cities consciously react to, accommodate and are shaped by the historic, local, regional and, in some cases, the transnational differences of the constitutive outside. However, they do not just mimic or submissively accept the identities they find in the cities; they also consciously identify themselves in opposition to others such as non-Aboriginal city dwellers, legislated identities, other Aboriginal cultures within cities, [and to] the cultural politics that imbue relations between them and Aboriginal and non-Aboriginal discourses on authenticity. (Proulx, 2006, p. 410)

For Inuit, notions of belonging and ties to Inuit homelands serve as the basis of community and solidarity for Inuit inside, as well as outside traditional Inuit territories. That is, Inuit realities in Ottawa remain connected and demonstrate how local and transnational processes are interwoven in the construction of Inuit difference. In the diasporic context of the Inuit community in Ottawa, Inuitness is, we argue, not completely deterritorialized, but reterritorialized through spaces and processes that symbolically, if not physically, connect urban Inuit to home communities and Inuit Nunaat. These practices include throat-singing, speaking and learning to speak Inuktitut, and having country food from the Arctic at community gatherings.

Inuit-controlled organizations have become primary vehicles for constructing a community among a dispersed and heterogeneous Inuit population in

Ottawa. For Inuit who have grown up in Southern Canada, these organizations provide a connection (and for some, the only connection) to community and cultural capital circulating in the Inuit homelands. One urban Inuk explains the difference these organizations have made in his life and the life of his child "who's got his identity":

> I find that identity is a big, a big struggle. Like, it was for me, because I didn't know where I belonged. My Mom's [non-Inuk] and my Dad's Inuit. And I went to a school where I was the only Inuit in the school and my family got teased a lot. I just didn't know where I fit in until I started coming to the Head Start program and the Family Resource Centre [run by Tungasuvvingat Inuit]. It is getting easier now, but now my son is going to school where there is only two Inuit children, including himself. He's been coming to Head Start since he was small and he knows he's Inuit—he's got his identity. The Head Start program taught me a lot about my culture, our culture, and they also taught him as well. If it weren't for a place like this, I wouldn't know my culture at all.

Similar to pan-Aboriginal, First Nations, and Métis organizations in the city, Inuit organizations and service providers, such as the TI, the OICC, and so forth, offer contexts in which Inuit identities are validated (Weibel-Orlando, 1991; Jackson, 2002). In this sense, culturally relevant social services have become important sources of community (Lobo, 2001; Proulx, 2003)—and important Inuit places within urban space. They produce a sense of locality that explicitly includes the Inuit Nunaat. This is illustrated by the description of the Inuit community center's mandate: "TI offers a supportive environment that attempts to duplicate the community spirit and cultural surrounding of the Inuit homelands. Visitors at the drop-in centre can make tea and bannock; catch up on news from home by reading northern newspaper, and socialize with other Inuit" (TI, 2008).

The conceptualization of Inuit transnationalism provides a shared frame of reference for understanding the cultural, social, and economic dislocations experienced by a large portion of the Inuit population in Ottawa. But, as Hage (2005) notes, we risk overemphasizing the transnationalism of migrant collectives when the local processes are not also considered as constitutive of the experiences of groups and individuals, as "one cannot be understood separately from the other" (p. 467). Thus, the fluidity of spaces of transnationalism needs to be taken into account. As Levitt and Jaworsky (2007) point out, "more recent scholarship understands transnational migration as taking place within fluid social spaces that are constantly reworked through migrants' simultaneous embeddedness in more than one society" (p. 131). Taking this a step further, we would argue that migrants are similarly "rooted" in more than one society.

In this era of global capitalism, interest in the Arctic, including issues around ownership and control of resource extraction and the North-West passage, has intensified North/South linkages. The increased mobility and movement of Inuit, and of both material and symbolic capital, has led to new transnational, diasporic, and local processes through which Inuitness is constituted in cities. As transnational spaces evolve and communities are constructed in urban centers, new forms of Inuitness emerge. These are not disconnected from Inuit cultural and linguistic practices, and political claims to Arctic sovereignty. Indeed, the Inuit ethnoscape is changing and urban Inuit are an important part of this transformation (Appadurai, 1996).

Conclusion

In this chapter, we have examined the complexity of Inuit migration and reterritorialization as a form of transnationalism. Our research with Inuit in Ottawa has explored the ways in which Inuit difference is reproduced and reinforced in a Southern urban center—to a large extent, through the interconnectedness of people, places, and practices with Inuit homelands. As we have seen, both transnational and local processes shape Inuit realities in Ottawa. The urban Inuit community is constantly reworking itself and uniting people based on ancestral and familial links to the Arctic homelands. This is despite serious challenges to do so, given the sociocultural differences within the group. These processes and experiences are not unlike those shared with other transnational and migrant groups.

Our claim is that rigid settler paradigms are ruptured by transnational Indigenous migrants, and that the nation-state is transcended from within. Yet, the kind of mobility that is usually attributed to urban Aboriginal groups—mobility to move between one's homeland and the new "home"—does not apply to urban Inuit in the same way.[12] Inuit transnationalism has created urban Inuit subjects, who engage in regular communication and contact with friends and relatives "back home," but who actually "do not really spend that much time 'moving'" (Hage, 2005, p. 463).

Given these realities, one could argue that "rooted cosmopolitanisms" are being produced along with new forms of Indigenous cosmopolitanisms. However, as we discussed in the beginning of this chapter, it remains an open question how useful the concept is for analyzing these particular transnational contexts. More research is needed to explore the shifting and multifaceted Inuit ethnoscape that stretches beyond the Arctic and connects Inuit across Canada. Some of the issues for further investigation are the processes of migration and the political economic dynamics in which these are embedded, the role of communication technologies and media in connecting people and places, and the reworking of Inuit subjectivities and notions of Inuitness as a result of experiences of diaspora and transnationalism.

Notes

1. "Aboriginal" is used here as a category that includes First Nations, Métis, and Inuit peoples, as specified in section 35.2 of the Constitution Act, 1982. While we use "Aboriginal" as an umbrella category for indigenous peoples in Canada, we wish to problematize its trajectory as a state categorization that has not only homogenized indigenous peoples, but also obscured the hierarchization of indigenous groups within this category.
2. In this chapter, we use the term "Arctic" instead of "North" to refer to the Inuit homeland territories. This is despite the fact that some Inuit live in subarctic regions (in Nunatsiavut and in southern Nunavik (Arctic Quebec)). We use the term "Arctic" to encompass all the territorial homelands encompassed by the term "Inuit Nunaat," which has been used by Statistics Canada.
3. We would like to thank the Social Sciences and Humanities Research Council of Canada for financial support of this project and the Ottawa Inuit Children's Centre for providing us with community resources and space. In addition to our team members Karen Baker-Anderson, Carla Turner, and Sheila Grantham, we thank Heidi Langille, Lynda Brown, Maureen Flynn-Burhoe, and all Inuit participants for their help in achieving the overall goals of our project.
4. The final report of the Royal Commission on Aboriginal Peoples (RCAP) published in 1996 marks a turning point; it identified "an acute information and policy vacuum" (p. 519) with respect to urban Aboriginal peoples. Although the report has been criticized for its exclusionary privileging of land-based notions of Indigenous nationhood and self-government (Andersen & Denis, 2003), RCAP drew attention to the realities, needs, and goals of urban Aboriginal peoples, effectively putting urban Aboriginal issues on the agenda (Graham, 1999).
5. A notable exception is Kishigami's work on Inuit in Montreal (2002a, 2002b, 2004).
6. The differential treatment of indigenous people based on legal status and location is illustrated by the current funding situation: almost 90 percent of federal funding for Aboriginal-specific programming goes to members of First Nations living on reserves, who make up less than one-third of the Aboriginal population (House of Commons, 2003, p. 6). This amounts to a massive fiscal off-loading to provinces and municipalities, which has been a contested issue.
7. Following the protocols of our research methodology, names are not used in our presentation and analysis of the interview data.
8. Inuit Nunaat refers to the Inuit homelands; Nunavut, Nunavik, Nunatsiavut, and the Inuvialuit region (see Statistics Canada, 2008).
9. Established in 1987, TI operates as a community-based resource center.
10. This spread of Inuit across the city has been found in Montreal (Kishigami, 2002a, p. 57) and characterizes other First Nations and Métis urban communities (Newhouse & Peters, 2003).
11. Historically, geographically, politically, and legally, Inuit have been imagined and positioned as distinct Northern peoples inhabiting the Canadian Arctic. Inuitness in this political-geographical sense is characterized not only by localized cultural practices that have persisted over centuries in the Arctic, but through relationships and interactions with traders, missionaries, government officials, and the state. Through the land claims and political processes, Inuitness is now often exclusively defined in relation to the traditional land bases and land claims jurisdictions—Nunatsiavut (Labrador), Nunavik (Québec),

Inuvialuit (NWT), and Nunavut (NT). In these geographical imaginings, the urban Inuit often get sidelined, not only with respect to national bodies dealing with Inuit (ITK; Pauktuutit), but in the public imaginary and state practices as well.

12 One of the most striking similarities of the Inuit interviewees was their inability to travel with any frequency to Northern communities to visit family. Each of them returned only once or twice over the course of their time in the South, due to the prohibitive costs, often in the range of $4,000–5,000, to travel to the Arctic.

References

Andersen, C., & C. Denis. (2003). Urban Native and the Nation: Before and after the Royal Commission on Aboriginal Peoples. *Canadian Review of Sociology and Anthropology*, 40(4), 373–390.

Appadurai, A. (1996). *Modernity at Large: Cultural Dimensions of Globalization*. Minneapolis: University of Minnesota Press.

Appiah, K. A. (1997). Cosmopolitan Patriots. *Critical Inquiry*, 23(3), 617–639.

Graham, K. (1999). Urban Aboriginal Governance in Canada: Paradigms and Prospects. In John Hylton (Ed.), *Aboriginal Self-government in Canada: Current Trends and Issues* (pp. 377–391). Saskatoon: Purich.

Graham, K., & E. Peters. (2002). *Aboriginal Communities and Urban Sustainability* (Discussion Paper F 27). Ottawa: Canadian Policy Research Networks.

Guarnizo, L. E., & M. Smith. (1998). The Locations of Transnationalism. In M. Smith & L. E. Guarnizo (Eds.), *Transnationalism from Below* (pp. 3–34). New Brunswick, NJ, and London: Transaction Publishers.

Gupta, A., & J. Ferguson. (1997). Beyond "Culture": Space, Identity, and the Politics of Difference. In A. Gupta & J. Ferguson (Eds.), *Culture, Power, Place: Explorations in Critical Anthropology* (pp. 33–51). Durham, NC/ London: Duke University Press.

Hage, G. (2005). A Not So Multi-sited Ethnography of a Not So Imagined Community. *Anthropological Theory*, 5(4), 463–475.

Hannerz, U. (1996). *Transnational Connections: Culture, People, Places*. London: Routledge.

———. (2007). Cosmopolitanism. In D. Nugent & J. Vincent (Eds.), *A Companion to the Anthropology of Politics* (pp. 69–85). Oxford: Blackwell.

House of Commons Canada. (2003). *Building a Brighter Future for Urban Aboriginal Children* (Report of the Standing Committee on Human Resources Development and the Status of Persons with Disabilities). Ottawa: Communication Group-Publishing.

Inda, J., J. Xavier, & R. Rosaldo. (2002). Introduction: A World in Motion. In J. Inda & R. Rosaldo (Eds.), *The Anthropology of Globalization: A Reader* (pp. 1–34). Oxford: Blackwell.

Indian and Northern Affairs Canada. (2004). Words First: An Evolving Terminology Relating to Aboriginal Peoples in Canada. Retrieved January 15, 2008, from http://www.ainc-inac.gc.ca/pr/pub/wf/index_e.html

Inuit Tapiriit Kanatami. (2004a). Roundtable on Aboriginal Issues (Speaking Notes, Jose Kusguak). Retrieved January 12, 2008, from http://www.itk.ca/publications/20040417-en-jose-summit.pdf

———. (2004b). *The Case for Inuit Specific: Renewing the Relationship between the Inuit and Government of Canada*. Retrieved January 12, 2008, from http://www.itk.ca/publications/20040419-inuit-specific-final.pdf

Jackson, D. (2002). *Our Elders Lived It: American Indian Identity in the City*. DeKalb: Northern Illinois University Press.

Jacobs, J. M. (1996). *Edge of Empire: Postcolonialism and the City*. London/ New York: Routledge.

Kearney, M. (2004). *Changing Fields of Anthropology: From Local to Global*. Lanham, MD: Rowman & Littlefield.

Kishigami, N. (2002a). Urban Inuit in Canada: A Case from Montreal. *Indigenous Affairs* (IWGIA), 3-4(2), 54-59.

———. (2002b). Inuit Identities in Montreal, Canada. *Études/Inuit/Studies*, 26(1), 183-191.

———. (2004). Cultural and Ethnic Identities of Inuit in Canada. *Senri Ethnological Studies*, 66, 81-93.

Lawrence, B. (2003). Gender, Race, and the Regulation of Native Identity in Canada and the United States: An Overview. *Hypatia*, 18(2), 3-31.

———. (2004). *Real Indians and Others: Mixed-blood Urban Native Peoples and Indigenous Nationhood*. Lincoln: University of Nebraska Press.

Levitt, P., & B. N. Jaworsky. (2007). Transnational Migration Studies: Past Developments and Future Trends. *Annual Review of Sociology*, 33, 129-156.

Lobo, S. (2001). Is Urban a Person or a Place? Characteristics of Urban Indian Country. In Susan Lobo & Kurt Peters (Eds.), *American Indians and the Urban Experience* (pp. 73-85). New York: Altamira Press.

Malkki, L. (1997). National Geographic: The Rooting of Peoples and the Territorialization of National Identity among Scholars and Refugees. In A. Gupta & J. Ferguson (Eds.), *Culture, Power, Place: Explorations in Critical Anthropology* (pp. 52-74). Durham, NC/London: Duke University Press.

Nashashibi, R. (2007). Ghetto Cosmopolitanism: Making Theory at the Margins. In S. Saskia (Ed.), *Deciphering the Global: Its Scales, Spaces and Subjects* (pp. 243-264). New York: Routledge.

Newhouse, D., & E. Peters, (Eds.). (2003). *Not Strangers in These Parts: Urban Aboriginal Peoples*. Ottawa: Policy Research Initiative.

Peters, E. (1996). 'Urban' and 'Aboriginal': An Impossible Contradiction? In Jon Caulfield & Linda Peake (Eds.), *City Lives and City Forms: Critical Research and Canadian Urbanism* (pp. 47-62). Toronto, ON: University of Toronto Press.

———. (2006). First Nations and Métis People and Diversity in Canadian Cities. Montreal: Institute for Research on Public Policy. Retrieved February 29, 2008, from http://www.irpp.org/books/archive/AOTS3/peters.pdf

Pollock, S., H. K. Bhabha, C. A. Breckenridge, & D. Chakrabarty. (2002). Cosmopolitanisms. In C. A. Breckenridge et al. (Eds.), *Cosmopolitanism* (pp. 1-14). Durham, NC/London: Duke University Press.

Proulx, C. (2003). *Reclaiming Aboriginal Justice, Community and Identity*. Saskatoon: Purich.

———. (2006). Aboriginal Identification in North American Cities. *The Canadian Journal of Native Studies*, 26(2), 405-438.

Razack, S. H. (2002). Introduction: When Place Becomes Race. In S. H. Razack (Eds.), *Race, Space, and the Law: Unmapping a White Settler Society* (pp. 1-20). Toronto: Between the Lines.

Royal Commission on Aboriginal Peoples. (1996). *Report of the Royal Commission on Aboriginal Peoples*, Vol. 4, Chapter 7 (pp. 519-621). Ottawa: Canada Communication Group-Publishing.

Siggner, A., & R. Costa. (2005). *Aboriginal Conditions in Census Metropolitan Areas, 1981-2001*.

Ottawa: Statistics Canada. Retrieved January 12, 2008, from http://www.statcan.ca/english/research/89-613-MIE/89-613-MIE2005008.htm

Statistics Canada. (2008). *Aboriginal Peoples in Canada in 2006: Inuit, Métis and First Nations, 2006 Census* (Catalogue no. 97-558-XIE). Ottawa: Statistics Canada.

Tarrow, S. (2005). *The New Transnational Activism.* Cambridge, MA: Cambridge University Press.

Tungasuvvingat Inuit (2005). *National Urban Inuit One Voice Workshop, Ottawa, October 26–27, 2005* (Report). Ottawa: Tungasuvvingat Inuit.

———. (2008). Tungasuvvingat Inuit. Retrieved February 26, 2008, from http://www.ontarioinuit.ca/html/ti.htm

Urban Aboriginal Task Force. (2007). *Ottawa Final Report* (Commissioned by the Ontario Federation of Indian Friendship Centres, The Ontario Metis Aboriginal Association, and The Ontario Native Women's Association). Ottawa: The Ontario Federation of Indian Friendship Centres.

Vertovec, S. (2007). Introduction: New Directions in the Anthropology of Migration and Multiculturalism. *Ethnic and Racial Studies,* 30(6), 961–978.

Vertovec, S., & R. Cohen. (2002). Introduction: Conceiving Cosmopolitanism. In Vertovec, Steven & Robin Cohen (Eds.), *Conceiving Cosmopolitanism: Theory, Context, and Practice* (pp. 1–22). Oxford: Oxford University Press.

Weibel-Orlando, J. A. (1991). *Indian Country, L. A.: Maintaining Ethnic Community in Complex Society (revised edition).* Chicago: University of Illinois Press.

Wotherspoon, T. (2003). Prospects for a New Middle Class among Urban Aboriginal People. In David Newhouse & Evelyn Peters (Eds.), *Not Strangers in These Parts: Urban Aboriginal Peoples* (pp. 147–165). Ottawa: Policy Research Initiative.

◆ CHAPTER EIGHT ◆

"Same Cat, Different Stripes": Hemispheric Migrations, New Urban Indian Identities, and the Consolidation of a Cosmopolitan Cosmovision

Robin Maria DeLugan

Political and economic conditions motivate the migration of indigenous people from Latin America to the United States and elsewhere around the globe. Whether arriving as political refugees from genocide and civil war, as economic refugees from poverty, or as opportunity-seekers in a globalizing world, native people challenge stereotypes that their identity is inextricably rooted to a place of origin by exchanging homelands in Mexico, Central, and South America for distant destinations. In the United States, the increase in international border crossing by indigenous migrants demonstrates the limits of a system of ethno-racial classification where, upon arrival, a migrant's nation-state origin translates as a box-to-be-checked category of ethnic identity, thereby concealing indigenous difference. However, with the increase of indigenous migration, census categories are being modified in an effort to recognize distinct ethno-linguistic identity, offering alternatives to deceptive umbrella designations such as "Latino" or "Hispanic." Census innovation is one indication that closer attention is being paid to the ethnic diversity created by new population movement from Latin America.

This chapter focuses on how indigenous migration from Latin America is transforming the cultural landscape of San Francisco, California. San Francisco has one of the nation's largest urban American Indian communities—itself a product of decades of migration and relocation from around the

United States. Today it is a place where native peoples from throughout the Americas encounter one another. As government and service providers engage with increasing numbers of indigenous arrivals from Latin America, and indigenous people from throughout the hemisphere interact, the answer to the question of who is Native American is expanding. For some American Indians and others aware of the new arrivals, international migration does not motivate any rethinking of the basis for asserting Native American or American Indian identity—a federally recognized identity that is based on legal and political treaties, yet complicated by U.S. government-informed measurements such as blood quantum and proof of tribal enrollment, and besieged or problematic on many fronts.[1] For others, both migrants and local American Indians, however, recognition that native people across the continent are related through similar historical conditions and cultural affinities, if not as spiritual kin, has been considered for some time, although maintained up to now primarily through long-distance solidarity and activism, and only recently tested through everyday, face-to-face encounters. Added to the migration mix is the participation of Chicana/os and other *mestiza/os* (people of mixed indigenous and other heritage) who are entitled to the self-conscious, creative rescue, and valorization of their indigenous heritage and culture, and whose expressions of indigeneity are as much political as cultural and spiritual. It is my experience in San Francisco that *mestiza/os* are the social actors creating linguistic (Spanish-English) and other bridges between indigenous folks from North, Central, and South America when they come together for the first time.[2] In San Francisco, one of the world's most cosmopolitan cities, international migrations and new face-to-face encounters are expanding urban Indian identity and creating new opportunities for shared meaning-making that result in new expressions of indigeneity. I argue that social and cultural gatherings among a rapidly diversifying population are strengthening what some refer to as hemispheric indigenous identity, a collective identity that is based on an inclusive—and I argue cosmopolitan—view of human being and belonging in the world.

Drawing from my ethnographic research on recent indigenous migration from Latin America to San Francisco, I explore three ongoing, related collective identity processes. First, the introduction of new ethnic diversity motivates U.S. national and local government and service providers to recognize the cultural identity of new arrivals, and I discuss how this results in the expansion of the governmental designation of Native American/American Indian. Second, I refer to social practices that bring people from diverse indigenous communities together to strengthen hemispheric collective identity. Third, I use my participant-observation research of a semipublic Maya ceremony *Waqxaqi B'atz'* (the Day of Human Perfection) to explore how new practices consolidate a shared cosmovision or worldview for its diverse indigenous audience and participants. The worldview represented through the *B'atz'* ceremony acknowledges individual and group differences within a broader framework of relatedness, thereby promoting a beneficent and inclusive sociality. By offering a transcultural view of human—and not just indigenous—being and belonging in the world, I explore how the shared meanings motivate the melding of two concepts typically seen as quite far apart: indigeneity and cosmopolitanism.

Indigenous Migration from Latin America to California

Certain indigenous groups from Mexico have participated in modern migration to California at least as early as the Bracero Program (1942-1963), a bi-national program that brought millions of temporary contract workers from Mexico to the United States, primarily to work in agriculture. Others, in particular from the southern state of Oaxaca, have continued to serve as agricultural workers in California by engaging in cyclical binational migration connected to agriculture's seasonality (Nagengast et al., 1992). In recent years, economic pressures in Mexico, especially because of the deleterious effects of the North American Free Trade Agreement (NAFTA) on small farmers, have generated new flows of increasingly diverse indigenous groups from Mexico (Lopez, 2007). The new indigenous arrivals from Mexico to California are fitting into more traditional agricultural labor roles, and the state's Central San Joaquin Valley is home to an estimated 50,000 Mixtecs and large numbers of Triqui and Zapotecs from Oaxaca (Fox & Rivera-Salgado, 2004). Mexican indigenous migrants are also increasingly laboring in the service and hospitality industries in California metropolitan areas: there are an estimated 60,000 Zapotecs from Oaxaca in Los Angeles (Poole, 2004) and 15,000 Maya from Yucatán in the San Francisco Bay Area (Burke, 2004; Bazúa Morales, 2006). While the migration of solo men continues an older pattern of male migration (e.g., the new arrivals from the Yucatán are predominantly young men), the global feminization of migration now brings increasing numbers of indigenous women to California (Ramirez, 2007). The heightened difficulty in recent years of being able to cross the U.S. borders without detection combines with the untenable economic conditions back home in Mexico to encourage settlement and the formation of new indigenous families and ethnic communities in California.

Oaxacan migration that is found in other regions of California is only now arriving in the San Francisco Bay Area. Instead, the majority of indigenous migrants to San Francisco are from other regions of Mexico and from Central and South America. During the 1980s and early 1990s, the political upheaval and civil war in Guatemala motivated the migration of indigenous Maya to the United States as political refugees (Burns, 1993; Loucky & Moors, 2000), but more recently Guatemalan Maya have arrived because of economic conditions (Davenport, Castañeda, & Manz, 2002).[3] In addition to Maya from

Guatemala, Maya from Mexico are also making San Francisco their home (Burke, 2004).[4] In recent years, many Maya from Yucatan, Mexico, have begun to turn from internal migration to tourism sites such as Cancun (Castellanos, 2003) and have come to San Francisco to work in the hospitality industry.[5] Currently, an estimated 10,000 Maya from the Yucatan reside in San Francisco, the majority of who arrived within the past 10 years. As mentioned earlier, indigenous migrants join smaller numbers of diverse indigenous groups in San Francisco with origins from Mexico, Central, and South America. In my experience these include Purépecha, Yaqui, Huichol, and Otomi from Mexico; different Maya groups from Mexico and Guatemala; as well as Quechua, Quichua, and Shuar from Bolivia, Peru, and Ecuador; and likely others, who all encounter a relatively large North American Indian population.

Expanding Urban Indian Identities

In the United States today, approximately 70 percent of the North American Indian population lives off reservations or tribal lands, and the San Francisco Bay Area has one of the largest North American Indian populations in the country (Norrell, 2005).[6] In the 1950s, U.S. government policies relocated large numbers of North American Indians from reservations to urban areas with the goal of hastening their assimilation into mainstream society. However, relocation for many had a contrary effect, and urban relocations did not lessen tribal or other cultural ties. In addition, encounters among North American indigenous people resulted in new intertribal ties, where specific tribal identity was recognized while a broader urban Indian collective identity was being forged. San Francisco's urban Indian community has been supported in part through government and nonprofit service providers, and community organizations such as the Intertribal Friendship House through pan-tribal cultural and political events and ethnic media (Lobo, 2002).[7] I contend that indigenous migrants from Latin America, displaced from original homelands and arriving in San Francisco, experience diasporic conditions and realities comparable to those that, over time, have forged the city's urban Indian community and collective identity, based on intertribal social and cultural ties. Some new arrivals from Latin America are engaging with diverse indigenous ethnic groups to expand the identity of and membership in San Francisco's urban Indian community. Few scholars have addressed the impact of indigenous migrations from Latin America, how local governments and service providers address the new arrivals both as particular ethnic groups and as Native Americans, or the new alliances and solidarities being developed between indigenous people from North, Central, and South America.

Recognizing indigenous migration

Because indigenous migrants from Latin America have been relatively "invisible," that is, generally not asserting their ethnic identity until now, absolute population numbers are hard to establish. However, as local schools, health care, and other service providers encounter indigenous migrants with increasing frequency, they often seek to learn more about the new population, in order to provide culturally competent services. As the indigenous population from Mexico and elsewhere in Latin America increases, the U.S. federal government is also responding.

In 2000, the U.S. census introduced the possibility of identifying as "Hispanic" or "Latino American Indian," thereby expanding the previous census options "Latino" or "Hispanic," which have concealed indigenous identity for people from Latin America (Murillo & Cerdo, 2004). Through a series of nested questions, the census asks if the person is "Spanish/Hispanic/Latino." The second question asks the person's race (more than one option may be selected), and it also asks for the name of the enrolled or principal tribe. Through census innovation, the category "Hispanic (or Latino) American Indian" has emerged, a category that can capture data about new indigenous arrivals, including tribal or ethno-linguistic specificity, and can allow others, including *mestiza/os*, to self-identify as indigenous.

The 2000 census count of "Hispanic American Indians" produced a modest total population of 407,000, with California having the largest population of 154,362. It is assumed that the national and state totals represent an undercount. Among likely reasons for the undercount are the introduction of new census options for self-identification and the resultant confusion that unfamiliar categories can foster.[8] Census undercounts can have a profound impact on the well-being of indigenous migrants, whose access to social services can be limited when funding for services is based on known population levels (Kissam & Jacobs, 2004). How the increasing level of official awareness and the introduction of the new ethnoracial category "Hispanic or Latino American Indian" will influence government policy toward the population, and whether the new identity register will result in new social and cultural formations, remains to be seen (Winant, 2000).

In San Francisco, service providers are beginning to gather census and health status information for the new population, and new access is provided by community organizations forming to represent and advocate for their indigenous community members. *Asociación Mayab* represents the city's growing Yucatec Maya population. By hosting public social events such as *vaquerias yucatecos* (common in Yucatán), where food, dance, and *bombas* (rhyme-based humor) unite the community, as well as language training and workshops that educate others about Maya culture and history, *Asociación Mayab* raises the profile of the Maya in San Francisco and advocates for its interests and needs.

Chan Kahal, an organization in nearby San Rafael, represents that community's Yucatec Maya population. They frequently collaborate with *Asociación Mayab*. *Grupo Maya Cusamej Junan* advocates for Maya from Guatemala and also hosts public events such as solstice and *B'atz'* New Year ceremonies, which bring indigenous people together from throughout the San Francisco Bay Area. These small community-based organizations participate in public forums and are sought out by those trying to enhance "cultural competency" in the delivery of social services. The Central American Resource Center (CARECEN) is responding to the city's changing demographics. Once dedicated to an ethnically undifferentiated clientele of Central American civil war refugees and immigrants, the organization is now developing a Meso-American Indian Health Initiative with the interest of the San Francisco Department of Public Health. *Instituto Familiar de La Raza*, one of San Francisco's largest community clinics, retains on staff an indigenous traditional healer from Guatemala. The dynamics accompanying new migration present opportunities for the study of cultural and medical pluralism as well as the incorporation of new indigenous arrivals into biopolitical regimes (Ong, 2003).

Turning to the response of the local government, the City of San Francisco's Human Rights Office held a hearing in 2006 on local Native American Issues. Although the four hours of public testimony focused primarily on Native Californians and American Indians from throughout the United States who make San Francisco their home, there was also testimony from indigenous immigrants from Latin America and others who advocated on their behalf. The commission's report, issued in 2007, is attentive to the necessity to learn more about indigenous arrivals from Latin America and to address their needs (San Francisco Human Rights Commission, 2007). As the local government addresses the interests of Native Americans, new indigenous arrivals are also being taken into account. As the population gains a higher profile through community organizations and increased attention from service providers, local, and federal government, San Francisco's urban Indian community is both expanded and transformed.

In *Native Hubs: Culture, Community, and Belonging in Silicon Valley and Beyond* (2007), Renya Ramirez focuses on the urban Indian community in nearby San Jose, California, and examines struggles, networking, and efforts to foster transnational belonging. Ramirez uses "transnational" to reference the sovereignty of American Indian tribes and nations and to highlight how migration involves the traversing of their political boundaries *within* the United States, as well as international border crossings that some migrants from Latin America make *between* hemispheric nation-states. While Ramirez is primarily addressing the experiences of diasporic North American Indians who land in urban California, she does acknowledge migration from Mexico. Ramirez uses the concept "hemispheric re-membering" to acknowledge how new migrations are uniting disparate groups, which facilitates an indigenous western hemispheric consciousness and identity. By illustrating how migration introduces new ethnic diversity but also unites disparate groups and fosters collective identity and cosmovision, or worldview, Ramirez's research parallels my own.

Hemispheric Indigenous Identity and Cosmovision

Contemporary trans-American indigenous identity has been in the making for some time. While the Quincentenary of 1992 is recognized as a major catalyst, earlier efforts can be traced to the 1940 Inter-American Indigenous Congress in Patzcuaro, Mexico, or to later efforts such as the International Indian Treaty Council established in 1974 by the U.S. American Indian Movement. The flourishing of national level indigenous movements throughout the Americas also contributes to the process of hemispheric indigenous identity-making (Bengoa, 2000). By the 1990s, throughout much of Latin America, indigenous peoples and their issues gained increasing visibility in the context of increased (yet relative) national democratization (Diskin, 1993). Local movements and struggles not only serve to consolidate collective indigenous identity at the national level (e.g., in Guatemala as represented in the pan-Maya movement), but in the process promote the solidarity of indigenous peoples and other allies throughout the Americas and beyond. Collective identity at the national level articulates with regional and hemispheric efforts by producing discourse and practices that can emphasize common goals and visions of many indigenous people. At each of the registers—national, regional, hemispheric—local culture, history, and identity are affirmed, enabling difference and specificity to be incorporated into the broader concepts of shared collective identity. Over the years, hemispheric indigenous identity has been strengthened and represented through efforts of new public institutions such as the National Museum of the American Indian in Washington, D.C. (DeLugan, 2006) and through supragovernmental organizations such as the United Nations Permanent Forum on Indigenous Issues. Thus, various exchanges acting to fulfill long-held prophecies that native peoples throughout America will unite demonstrate that the basis for hemispheric identity is at once political, historical, cultural, and spiritual.

Over the past few years, I have participated in and observed efforts in the San Francisco Bay Area that bring indigenous folks together in social, political, and cultural forums. As indigenous people from throughout the Americas encounter each other, the membership and identity of the local Urban Indian community expands, although recently generally limited to people with ancestral homelands within the political boundaries of the United States (or possibly Canada). Some, though not all, American Indians in San Francisco embrace the changes that new international migrations bring, and new intercultural dynamics challenge narrow conceptions of who is an American Indian while generating shared views and expressions of indigeneity.

In studying hemispheric indigenous migration and its effect on collective identity, I note a corollary with Paul Gilroy's thinking about the African diaspora. In *The Black Atlantic* (1992), Gilroy argues that from initial slavery and ensuing forced migration, to later postcolonial interactions of African nationals with their respective metropoles, a collective African identity and consciousness formed. The African identity and consciousness that Gilroy postulates references Africa but is not restrained by Africa. Instead, it circulates alongside global movements of capital, goods, and people. He emphasizes a collective identity based on a desire to transcend the constraints of locality or ethnicity. It is also a collective identity and consciousness that function to critique European modernity and, in particular, to challenge its political product, the nation-state.

> The specificity of the modern political and cultural formation I want to call the Black Atlantic can be defined, on one level, through [a] desire to transcend both the structures of the nation-state and the constraints of ethnicity and national particularity. These desires are relevant to understanding political organizing and cultural criticism. They have always sat uneasily alongside the strategic choices forced on black movements and individuals embedded in national and political cultures and nation-states in America, the Caribbean, and Europe. (Gilroy, 1992, p. 19)

Through a blending of movement and aspiration, the subjectivities emerging within the "Black Atlantic" are distanced from ethnic and national identity, or at least serve to problematize those identity registers when recalled.

Contrary to Gilroy's depiction of the "Black Atlantic," local and ethnic group identities travel along with indigenous migration across the Americas. Complementary to his study, however, is the way that indigenous migration results in new meaning-making, identities, and subjectivities. Just as subjectivities emerging throughout the Black Atlantic criticize Western modernity, indigenous migration consolidates views about being and belonging in the world that challenge Western views and offer an alternative guide of beneficent morality and sociality. Indigenous values criticize the values of Western modernity and global capitalism, in particular individualism, materialism, and a prevalent discrepant sense of humanity, that separate humans not only from each other but also from all creation. Individual and group distinctions are recognized, yet concomitantly placed in the larger framework of relatedness. Jace Weaver describes it thus: "Indigenous societies as synedochic (part-to-whole) rather than the more Western conception that is metonymic (part-to-part). That explains why indigenous mentality declares 'I am We'" (Weaver, 2005, p. 227). Victoria Bomberry (2001) recognizes this as *western hemispheric consciousness,* noting that it not only blurs the boundaries between tribal nations and nation-states, but also encourages alliances across difference. She also explores how, in the formation of hemispheric indigenous consciousness and identity, the local circulates alongside broader identities and aspirations, accepting and respecting difference within a holistic, universalizing notion of human and other relatedness and existence in an animated world.

Same Cat, Different Stripes: Indigenous Cosmopolitanism and Cultural Citizenship

One early morning in late October 2006, about 50 men, women, and children congregated at Parque de la Raza in the Mission District in San Francisco. The occasion was the ceremony for the Maya New Year: *Waqxaqi B'atz'*. Around the sacred fire, we stood with fixed attention as Don Paz, *ajqi'j* (spiritual guide) from Guatemala, led the ceremony. The sweet smell of chocolate, sugar, copal, and honey rose from the fire, blending with the fragrance of burning sage and fresh flowers that marked four cardinal directions. Don Paz recited the Maya calendar in Kaq'chiqel. The general instructions were in Spanish and also translated into English. The voice of a Quichua woman from Ecuador, unaccustomed to being solo in ceremonial song, trembled ... nearly in lament. A dozen Aztec dancers and their drummers in full regalia marked the structured cycles of the ceremony through rhythmic movement and percussion. They alternated with the men on the North American Indian drum and the women who accompanied in song. A Shuar shaman from Ecuador offered words of guidance. Four hours quickly passed, and on Don Paz's instructions, we kneeled one last time to kiss the earth. Following the ceremony, we enjoyed a small feast of tamales and hot chocolate provided by members of the local Yucatec and Guatemala Maya community.

During the *B'atz'* ceremony, distinct indigenous nations are recognized to link those in the circle to people across distant spaces of belonging. The last names of ancestors are recalled, marking the temporality of being and connectedness. The relatedness of human beings—seeing oneself in the other—is underlined through messages about care for others, for the young, the elderly, the sick, and the needy. "Human perfection" signifies a connection to all beings, including not only humans but also plants, animals, rocks, fire, water, earth, and wind, reinforcing knowledge that we exist and belong in an animated world. Individual identity and group memberships are recognized and concomitantly placed in the larger framework of relatedness. As such, the Maya *B'atz'* ritual demonstrates a sociality, a positive orientation of self in society. It reinforces what it means to be human, an orientation that resonates with the understandings shared by members of other indigenous groups.[9] As demonstrated by the *B'atz'*, migration brings together indigenous people from throughout the hemisphere, and some are engaging in social and cultural practices that instruct about human being and belonging in the world. It is as David Escobar, *mestizo*, Lenca Indian from El Salvador, and highly respected in San Francisco for his efforts to network indigenous leaders, sums up indigenous worldview: "Same cat, different stripes." Difference and sameness are mutually recognized in the context of an animated world defined primarily by human and other relatedness.

Cosmopolitanism is a concept that emerges when analyzing the meaning-making taking place among indigenous migrants in gatherings such as the *B'atz'* ceremonies. Cosmopolitanism points to a worldly being and belonging that influence views and practices. Postcolonial critiques of Western definitions of cosmopolitanism challenge, however, the assumption of a unitary subject, the elite status of the cosmopolitan subject (i.e., those with the capacity for world travel and other experiences that transcend the local), and see subterfuge in claims of universal world citizenship that may cover up hegemonic norms and ideologies about political economy, sociality, alterity, and other cultural views. What Homi Bhabha (2001) refers to as "vernacular cosmopolitanism" emerges from the margins, not from centers of global power, and is based on a perspective that emphasizes a multiplicity of views, experiences, and cultures—in particular the knowledges, subjectivities, and practices of subaltern populations brought into contact through global migration. Anthony Appiah (2006) also encourages us to see cosmopolitanism as a universal human trait—not as something cultivated by a privileged elite. Where classic frameworks see cosmopolitanism as antithetical to any attachment to the local, Appiah advocates instead for a "rooted" cosmopolitanism and insists that "loyalties and local allegiances ... determine who we are" and that "[a] creed that disdains partialities of kinfolk and community may have a past, but it has no future" (2006, p. 38). Importantly, for Appiah, cosmopolitanism involves obligations to others "beyond those to whom we are related by ties of kith and kin." Both Bhabha and Appiah define cosmopolitanism, not through reference to political institutions that might ensure a peaceable future without war, but instead through a worldly being and belonging informed foremost through individual contact with the other. The collective meaning-making that emerges from indigenous migration and new indigenous encounters in San Francisco offers an alternative source of cosmopolitan social values that resonates with the discussion above. Indigenous cosmopolitanism is both a conceptual framework as well as a model of beneficent sociality.

Many discussions of cosmopolitanism reference citizenship, whether simply to argue that cosmopolitans ought to think and act as world citizens or merely to criticize the provinciality of lower order citizenship regimes (Fine & Cohen, 2002). Regardless of which pole, definitions of cosmopolitanism involve some understanding that a connection between culture and citizenship signifies and informs our views and practices about being and belonging in the world. In recent years, anthropology has focused on the link between culture and citizenship, developing at least three different ways of looking at the connection. Cultural citizenship has become a key anthropological concept. Often cited are the differences presented by Renato Rosaldo and Aihwa Ong. Both Rosaldo and Ong focus on citizenship in the context of the nation-state.

Renato Rosaldo (1997) introduced the concept of cultural citizenship to emphasize the right of certain minorities in the United States, in particular Chicano or Mexican-Americans, to express their cultural distinction and to gain recognition for that distinction. In this sense, cultural citizenship points to the shortcomings of narrow, legal definitions of citizenship in multiethnic or multicultural societies where minority cultural difference can equate to "second-class citizens." For Chicanos and Mexican-Americans, the implication of cultural citizenship as a feature of full citizenship can impact cultural policies such as bilingual education. However, cultural citizenship, if confined to a policy of multiculturalism that showcases cultural difference without addressing minority group's socioeconomic marginalization, does not address the structural dimensions of cultural inequality.

Aihwa Ong (1996) turns Rosaldo's definition of cultural citizenship on its head. Instead of linking the term to the demand for recognition that she agrees ethnic communities certainly merit, she utilizes the concept to highlight the process that makes citizens into subjects of nation-state administration. Her research describes how government institutions reinforce hegemonic norms that set limits that inform the experience of nation-state belonging. Focusing primarily on Cambodian migrants and refugees, newcomers to the United States whose intimate household worlds become linked to health and welfare state agencies, cultural citizenship for Ong is synonymous with state practices and the workings of biopower.

Lynn Stephen (2003; 2007) introduces another approach to the concept of cultural citizenship. She argues that the right of Oaxacan indigenous migrant workers in Oregon to organize on behalf of better working conditions constitutes cultural citizenship. She emphasizes that the issue of workers' rights constitutes a universal human right, and therefore should not be constrained at the local or national level, no matter what the immigration status be of those seeking workers' rights. Stephen encourages us to see universally accepted definitions of human rights as cultural understandings of being and belonging, and believes that these should be universally applied to influence nation-state citizenship.

A fourth exploration of the link between culture and citizenship relevant to this chapter is Roberto Rodriguez's (2005) conceptualization of "indigenous cultural citizenship." Rodriguez defines indigenous cultural citizenship as an identity of belonging in the Americas that precedes the nation-state and as such challenges the nation-state's creation of legal and illegal human populations. From a trans-American perspective, indigenous cultural citizenship is based on a demand for recognition and a rightful presence throughout this hemisphere, and for rights to one's history, language, religion, and culture; to self-identify; to freely cross borders; to reunite families; and the right to not lose citizenship, labor, human, and cultural rights upon crossing borders (Rodriguez, 2005, p. 23). Indigenous cultural citizenship is not merely a primacy argument, that is, a claim from those who assert they were here first: "We didn't cross the border; the border crossed us." It is also a claim for an indigenous worldview with roots distinct from Western modernity. The cosmovision that is today articulated and consolidated through long-distance hemispheric engagements and bolstered through new migrations is more than just an *indigenous* model of cultural citizenship: it also communicates, as explored earlier, cosmopolitan human values. As Rodriguez states, indigenous cultural citizenship is based on "human or universal values ... [that] in modern political discourses, are identified as indigenous values" (p. 9). Indigenous values emphasize respect, peace, and humankind's relatedness to each other, to the earth, and to creation. As such, it speaks to all humankind.

In Western thought, cosmopolitanism has been linked to world citizenship. Western thinkers have sought to transcend modern sociality, where localism is blamed for ethnic conflict, war, and other strife. Indigenous cosmopolitanism, however, with its simultaneous emphasis on rootedness and universality, understands that difference can co-exist in a framework of universal relatedness, and thereby offers another view. As important as the normative principles of any source of cosmopolitan ideals, however, is what Ulrich Beck and Natan Sznaider refer to as "cosmopolitanization": the process of changing values and practices that happens foremost "from within" (Beck & Sznaider, 2006, p. 9). Through regular public gatherings and ceremonies in San Francisco, indigenous participants from throughout the Americas are engaging in collective practices that promote cosmopolitan ideals among themselves and for interested non-Indian participants as well.

Conclusion

In this chapter, I have illustrated how the increasing frequency of indigenous migration from Latin America to the United States, in particular to California's San Francisco Bay Area, is increasing ethnic diversity while expanding American Indian identity. The government has responded to indigenous migration by altering census categories that allow ethno-linguistic specificity to be identified and enumerated. New census options also allow *mestiza/os* to claim their indigenous heritage and identity. In San Francisco, indigenous migrants are forming community-based organizations to offer familiar social and cultural gatherings, as well as to inform the broader public about the interests of their particular ethnic group. Service providers collaborate with community groups to gain more information about the needs of the new population and thus be culturally competent in the delivery of healthcare and related services.

Beyond organizing to represent the needs of their members, indigenous migrants are also engaging in face-to-face encounters with other indigenous migrants with origins throughout Mexico, Central, and South America, as well as with Native North Americans. Hemispheric ties of solidarity that for decades were maintained across a long distance are now tested and strengthened through new face-to-face encounters. I use the Maya New Year ceremony, *Waqxaqi B'atz'*, which now takes place routinely in San Francisco, as an example of a new social and cultural site and practice that is uniting diverse indigenous nations and ethnicities. Migration provides new opportunities for shared meanings and values about being indigenous and belonging in the world to circulate and consolidate in practices such as *Waqxaqi B'atz'*. This meaning-making motivates me to pair the concepts of indigeneity and cosmopolitanism and to argue that an alternative source for cosmopolitan values can be discerned in a worldview that recognizes individual and group difference in a framework of human relatedness in an animated world. Classic views of cosmopolitanism interrogate citizenship to promote worldliness and escape parochialism. I suggest that the cosmopolitanism revealed through indigenous migration and the new meaning-making emerging from it can also be viewed as an engagement with the discourse on citizenship. The concept of cultural citizenship, a motif in recent anthropological thought, is given another facet when linked to indigeneity and cosmopolitanism.

Edward Fischer (2007) reminds anthropologists not to exempt from our study of indigenous representations of culture the critical eye that might see construction, innovation, and invention, even in discourses that stake a claim to enduring existence. The ceremonies in San Francisco that are reconstructed and invested with old and new meanings for a widening audience is central to the development of hemispheric indigenous identity and cosmopolitanism. As I examine how indigenous migration contributes to the consolidation of hemispheric indigenous identity and is represented by what I argue is a model of cosmopolitan ideals, I hope to avoid restating the critique of essentialism. In my exploration I am more interested in affirming any source of moral and ethical philosophy that promotes human solidarity, peace, and mutual respect. It is to revisit so as to better understand the profundity of the phrase that David Escobar uses to sum up an indigenous cosmopolitan worldview of cultural citizenship: "Same cat, different stripes." This phrase exemplifies the recognition of the plurality of individual and group differences within an inclusive framework of being and belonging in an animated, interrelated, world.

Notes

1. U.S. American Indian identity in general is a problematic topic. Acceptance, recognition, and membership can depend on issues of blood quantum, whether a tribe is federally recognized or not, or on formal tribal enrollment. Discussions and debates among Native scholars challenge such identity criteria as exclusionary and inattentive to the deep effects of colonization, while some claim it as antithetical to indigenous philosophies of relatedness and belonging (Garroutte, 2003; Rodriguez, 2005).

2. Much more can be said about why *mestizas/os* have a strong role in building bridges and networks between indigenous communities in San Francisco. My ongoing research on El Salvador's postwar nation-building and the struggle there for indigenous rights and recognition also reveal the long-distance role of *mestiza/o* Salvadorans in the United States who embrace their indigenous heritage and are motivated to support the indigenous movement in El Salvador as well. The Chicano movement serves as a model of sorts for the decolonizing and peeling back of history and culture and the exultation of indigeneity that are happening with people from other origins throughout the Americas.

3. In the same way that Maya is at once an umbrella for many distinct ethno-linguistic groups, while serving as an identity and also representing collective interests and shared understandings, the arrival of indigenous migrants from Latin America to the United States and specifically to San Francisco, California is also generating a broader indigenous identity that does not cancel out ethnic and linguistic diversity, but rather contains it.

4. The Guatemala consulate estimates that 10,000 Maya from Guatemala live in the San Francisco Bay Area, with the population concentrated in Oakland. There is an absence of census data, and more research is needed on the dynamically transforming indigenous migrant population. Anecdotally, it appears that the newest stream of indigenous migrants is Tzeltal and Tzotzil Maya from Chiapas, Mexico (personal conversation with Carlos Bazúa Morales, February 16, 2007).

5. The recent ethnographic film "El Recorrido/The Journey" by Carlos Bazúa Morales (2006) offers a rare insight into the San Francisco lives of Maya from Oxkutzcab, Yucatan, and the transnational, translocal networks that link family, friends, and states.

6. The 2000 U.S. Census estimated the North American Indian population for the five San Francisco Bay Area counties at 57,262 (Alameda County: 23,177; Contra Costs County: 14,926; Marin County: 2,684; San Francisco County: 8,971; San Mateo County: 7,504). Native American advocacy organizations criticize the undercount of these figures and estimate the population at closer to 80,000 (personal communication with Native American Health Center, San Francisco, 2008).

7. For example, the Intertribal Friendship House in Oakland was founded in 1956, keeping people connected to their culture and traditions through powwow dance, drumming, and other social activities. The American Indian Film Institute relocated to San Francisco in 1979 and recently completed its 32nd annual American Indian Film Festival. The Bay Area also hosts no fewer than six intertribal powwows a year. There are also vibrant annual commemorations of Indigenous Peoples Day, including sunrise ceremonies on Alcatraz Island. The study of U.S. urban Indian experiences is a common topic of Native American Studies (Fixico, 2000; Lawrence, 2004; Lobo & Peters, 2000).

8. The causes of census undercount of Mexican and Guatemalan indigenous communities in both inner-city neighborhoods and in rural communities in California include a census that does not account for migration patterns throughout the year, "low-visibility" housing,

language ability, census forms that do not permit more than six persons per housing unit to be enumerated, and census categories that have made it difficult to recognize indigenous households (Kissam & Jacobs, 2004).

9 I am not claiming that all indigenous groups share this understanding, and I acknowledge that in the social encounters new meanings are surely being created. Neither point takes away from the positive social values promoted through practices and expressions of indigeneity I have noted through participant-observation fieldwork in San Francisco.

References

Appiah, K. A. (2006). *Cosmopolitanism: Ethics in a World of Strangers*. New York: W. W. Norton.

Bazúa Morales, C. (2006). *El Recorrido/The Journey–Oxcutzcab*. Producciones Xibalba: San Francisco, CA.

Beck, U. & N. Sznaider. (2006). Unpacking Cosmopolitanism for the Social Sciences: A Research Agenda. *The British Journal of Sociology*, 57(1), 1-23.

Bengoa, J. (2000) *La emergencia indígena en América Latina*. Mexico City: Fondo de Cultura Economica.

Bhabha, H. (2001). Unsatisfied: Notes on Vernacular Cosmopolitanism. In G. Castle (Ed.), *Postcolonial Discourses: An Anthology* (pp. 38-42). Oxford: Blackwell.

Bomberry, V. (2001). *Indigenous Memory and Imagination: Thinking beyond the Nation*. PhD Dissertation. Modern Thought and Literature, Stanford University.

Burke, G. (2004). Yucatecos and Chiapanecos in San Francisco: Mayan Immigrants Form New Communities. In J. Fox & G. Rivera-Salgado (Eds.), *Indigenous Mexican Migrants in the United States* (pp. 343-354). La Jolla, CA: Center for U.S.-Mexican Studies, University of California, San Diego/Center for Comparative Immigration Studies, University of California, San Diego.

Burns, A. F. (1993). *Maya in Exile: Guatemalans in Florida*. Philadelphia: Temple University Press.

Castellanos, M. B. (2003). *Gustos and Gender: Yucatec Migration to the Mexican Riviera*. PhD Dissertation. University of Michigan.

Davenport, A., X. Castañeda, & B. Manz. (2002). Mexicanization: Survival Strategy for Guatemalan Mayans in the San Francisco Bay Area. *Migraciones Internacionales*, 1(3), 102-123.

DeLugan, R. (2006). "South of the Border" at the National Museum of the American Indian. *American Indian Quarterly*, 30(3 & 4), 558-573.

Diskin, M. (1993). Campesinos e Indios: Nuevos Sujetos Históricos en Centroamérica. In C. Vilas (Ed.), *Democracia Emergente en Centroamérica* (pp. 65-83). Mexico City: Universidad Nacional Autonoma de México.

Fine, R. & R. Cohen. (2002). Four Cosmopolitan Moments. In S. Vertovec & R. Cohen (Eds.), *Conceiving Cosmopolitanism: Theory, Context, and Practice* (pp. 137-164). Oxford: Oxford University Press.

Fischer, E. (2007). Strategic Identities and Subversive Narratives: On Being Maya in a Globalized World. *Vanderbilt-Journal of Luso-Hispanic Studies*, 1. Retrieved May 4, 2007, from http://ejournals.library.vanderbilt.edu/lusohispanic/viewarticle.php?id=24.

Fixico, D. L. (2000). *The Urban Indian Experience in America*. Albuquerque: University of New Mexico Press.

Fox, J. & G. Rivera-Salgado, (Eds.). (2004). *Indigenous Mexican Migrants in the United States.* La Jolla, CA: Center for U.S.-Mexican Studies, University of California,San Diego/Center for Comparative Immigration Studies, University of California,San Diego.

Garroutte, E. (2003). *Real Indians: Identity and the Survival of Native America.* Berkeley: University of California Press.

Gilroy, P. (1992). *The Black Atlantic: Modernity and Double Consciousness.* Cambridge, MA: Harvard University Press.

Kissam, E. & I. Jacobs. (2004). Practical Research Strategies for Mexican Indigenous Communities in California Seeking to Assert Their Own Identity. In J. Fox and G. Rivera-Salgado (Eds.), *Indigenous Mexican Migrants in the United States* (pp. 303-340). La Jolla, CA: Center for U.S.-Mexican Studies, University of California, San Diego/Center for Comparative Immigration Studies, University of California, San Diego.

Lawrence, B. (2004). *"Real" Indians and Others: Mixed-blood Urban Native Peoples and Indigenous Nationhood.* Lincoln: University of Nebraska Press.

Lobo, S. (2002). *Urban Voices: The Bay Area American Indian community.* Tucson: University of Arizona Press.

Lobo, S. & K. Peters. (2000). *American Indians and the Urban Experience.* Walnut Creek, CA: Altamira Press.

Lopez, A. A. (2007). *The Farmworkers' Journey.* Berkeley: University of California Press.

Loucky, J. & M. M. Moors, (Eds.). (2000). *The Maya Diaspora: Guatemalan Roots, New American Lives.* Philadelphia: Temple University Press.

Murillo, J. H. & I. Cerdo. (2004). Indigenous Mexican Migrants in the 2000 U.S. Census: "Hispanic American Indians." In J. Fox & G. Rivera-Salgado (Eds.), *Indigenous Mexican Migrants in the United States* (pp. 279-302). La Jolla, CA: Center for U.S.-Mexican Studies, University of California, San Diego/Center for Comparative Immigration Studies, University of California, San Diego.

Nagengast, C., R. Stavenhagen & M. Kearney. (1992). *Human Rights and Indigenous Workers: The Mixtecs in Mexico and the United States.* La Jolla, CA: Center for U.S.-Mexican Studies, University of California, San Diego.

Norrell, B. (July 15, 2005). A New Urban Society. *Indian Country Today.* Retrieved on September 10, 2006, from http://www.indiancountry.com/content.cfm?id=1096411232.

Ong, A. (1996). Cultural Citizenship as Subject Making: Immigrants Negotiate Racial and Cultural Boundaries in the United States. *Cultural Anthropology,* 37(5), 737-762.

——. (2003). *Buddha Is Hiding: Refugees, Citizenship, the New America.* Berkeley: University of California Press.

Poole, S. (2004). The Changing Face of Mexican Migrants in California: Oaxacan Mixtecs and Zapotecs in Perspective. *Trans-Border Institute Brief,* October 15, 2004. Trans-Border Institute, CA: University of San Diego.

Ramirez, R. (2007). *Native Hubs: Culture, Community, and Belonging in Silicon Valley and Beyond.* Durham, NC: Duke University Press.

Rodriguez, R. (2005). Toward an Indigenous Citizenship and Full Human Citizenship (A Companion to the San Ce Tojuan Documentary). Unpublished Manuscript.

Rosaldo, R. (1997). Cultural Citizenship, Inequality, Multiculturalism. In W. Flores & R. Benmayor (Eds.), *Latino Cultural Citizenship: Claiming Identity, Space and Rights* (pp. 27-38). Boston, MA: Beacon Press.

San Francisco Human Rights Commission. (2007). *Discrimination by Omission: Issues of Concern for Native Americans in San Francisco.* Retrieved September 25, 2007, from http://www.sfgov.org/site/uploadedfiles/sfhumanrights/docs/NativeAmericanReport.pdf

Stephen, L. (2003). Cultural Citizenship and Labor Rights for Oregon Farmworkers: The Case of Pineros y Campesinos Unidos de Noroeste (PCUN). *Human Organization*, 62(1), 27-38.

———. (2007). *Transborder Lives: Indigenous Oaxacans in Mexico, California and Oregon*. Durham, NC: Duke University Press.

Weaver, J. (2005). Indigenousness and Indigeneity. In H. Schwartz & S. Ray (Eds.), *A Companion to Postcolonial Studies* (pp. 221-235). Malden, MA: Blackwell.

Winant, H. (2000). Race and Race Theory. *Annual Review of Sociology*, 26, 69-185.

♦ CHAPTER NINE ♦

Indigeneity in Tourism: Transnational Spaces, Pan-Indian Identity, and Cosmopolitanism

Linda Scarangella

Transnational studies originally focused on the experiences of migrants but have recently extended to include other groups of people and types of mobility, such as tourism (Roudometof, 2005, p. 113). Images of Nativeness[1] circulate globally in media and popular culture and are also constructed and performed at tourist sites internationally in response to the public's desire to gaze upon and consume Nativeness (in addition to it being an economic opportunity).[2] Some Native people have actively engaged in this global economy of cultural production as performers at tourist sites. This chapter considers Forte's question (this volume) of how indigeneity is produced, experienced, and expressed in transnational and translocal pathways through an investigation of Native performers' experiences of identity at two tourist sites that re-present the American Wild West: Buffalo Bill Days (BBD) at a heritage site in Sheridan, Wyoming, and a recreation of Buffalo Bill's Wild West Show (BBWW) at Euro Disney in France.

The question remains open whether this engagement with transnational and translocal spaces leads to greater cosmopolitanism for the performers. In part, the question of cosmopolitanism is a difficult one because scholars do not agree on what or who is cosmopolitan. Cosmopolitanism has been variously defined as a move toward a social ideal and global citizenship, or an attitude toward the world, and has been employed as an analytical concept (Skrbis, Kendall, & Woodward, 2004, p. 115). Another problem identified in the literature is the supposed opposition between indigeneity and cosmopolitanism. Based on provisional definitions of cosmopolitanism, it is presumed that indigenous people are the Others linked to locality that cosmopolitans engage with, not cosmopolitan themselves. I do not attempt to resolve the problems with the use of the term cosmopolitanism in this chapter.³ Here I use cosmopolitan in the broadest sense as consisting of certain attributes, including mobility, recognition of interconnectedness, openness toward cultural difference, and engagement with Others (see Hannerz, 1990; Skrbis et al., 2004, pp. 116–117, 122). Cosmopolitanism as an analytical concept may be useful for explaining the ways in which these mobile performers construct and imagine themselves in the world.

First, I show how transnational and translocal spaces of performance such as tourist sites engender occasions for the evaluation, negotiation, and/or contestation of indigeneity. Second, I consider the ways in which Native performers, as mobile social actors in a globalized world, imagine themselves in transnational and translocal spaces. I maintain that their participation in the tourism industry leads to the performance of various "sociabilities." That is, Native performers imagine themselves in multiple ways. My analysis is based on over one year of research; I draw on promotional materials, participant observation, and interviews with organizers, managers, and Native performers.⁴

Case 1, EuroDisney: Transnational Performances and Experiences of Indigeneity

One of the most spectacular contemporary reincarnations of the BBWW show may be seen at Euro Disney, which is approximately 32 kilometers east of Paris, near the French town of Marne-la-Vallée.⁵ Located in the Disney Village entertainment zone, the BBWW show is based on a historical program from Buffalo Bill's visit to France in 1905. That show had twenty-three acts, including a grand entry, the famous "Rough Riders of the World," military displays, and cowboy pastimes, which consisted of rodeo-like events, historical reenactments of battles, and Indian vignettes.⁶ Several acts featured Indians, in attacks on a Pony Express rider, an emigrant train, a settler's cabin, and the Deadwood stagecoach. The "Battle of Custer" was also part of the show. Although neither Annie Oakley nor Sitting Bull appeared in the 1905 show, they are featured in the Euro Disney reinvention.

The creative team at Euro Disney modified and melded many of these acts to produce a Wild West show for modern audiences. Features incorporated from the historical show include a grand entry of cowboys and Indians, Annie Oakley and sharpshooting, trick riding and roping, rodeo-type games, and a Pony Express race, as well as vignettes of a cattle drive, a buffalo hunt, and the Deadwood stagecoach. The show thus reproduces many stereotypical representations of Nativeness because it re-presents the historic BBWW show. Still, Native performers at Euro Disney, who come from different American tribes and Canadian First Nations, actively negotiate this space. I demonstrate how this transnational space of performance facilitates a process whereby Native performers and show organizers or managers reflect on and evaluate the meaning of Native identity, which is a multiple and fluid expression. The negotiations and tensions surrounding the evaluation and representation of Nativeness reflect the power relationships at play when it comes to deciding who and what represents "authentic" Nativeness.

Figure 9.1: Entrance to Euro Disney's Buffalo Bill's Wild West Show.
Photograph by the author, 2004.

Euro Disney and the spectacularization of "Indians": authenticity, power, and knowledge

Disney creates a world of simulacra that reproduces (essentialized) American ideologies and values (Castaneda, 1993; Fernandez, 1995; Kratz & Karp, 1993; see also Bell, Hass, & Sells, 1995; Budd & Kirsch, 2005). Euro Disney's recreation of BBWW is no exception. According to the press kit, the purpose of the show is to "provide a genuine old-time experience" of the "heroic conquest of the west."[7] This contemporary show of cowboys and Indians thus inscribes anew many romantic and stereotypical ideologies and values of the American Wild West. That is, it carries over much of the discourse of the original show in that it preserves the story of the conquest and heroic cowboy life on the frontier. In addition, the Deadwood stagecoach vignette highlights the relationship between cowboys and Indians as one of conflict. "The Herd" and "Buffalo Hunting" vignettes are essential for the storyline, as they are meant to encapsulate an image of Western life (i.e., America) as consisting of cowboys and Indians, and to provide a glimpse into "scenes of pioneer life" and "Indian rituals."[8] However, representations of culture and history at the show are "Disneyfied," a process that involves simplification, trivialization, and sanitization (Bryam, 2004, pp. 4-9; cf. Fernandez, 1995). The representations of Native culture, history, and identity are not contextualized. While the herd vignette consists of extensive dialogue, the buffalo hunting vignette uses only yells and chants. According to the press kit, this scene is meant to give us an idea of "Indian rituals"; however, the audience is not privy to the meaning of the buffalo dance because there is no narration. The reenactment of Westernness and Nativeness in the BBWW show is hence selective and skewed, and identities and America's history are "Disneyfied." In sum, performances at this BBWW show do not deal with complex, subtle, and inclusive representations of histories and identities.

Despite the fact that the BBWW reenactment does not represent complex and inclusive histories, Euro Disney claims that its show is authentic.[9] Authenticity is an unachievable goal for tourist sites, according to Handler and Saxton (1988, p. 253), yet tourist sites consistently employ the language of authenticity. Many scholars have considered authenticity in relation to representations of indigenous peoples in museums, cultural tourism, or heritage sites (e.g., Adams, 1997; Bruner, 2005; Gable & Handler, 1996; Handler & Saxton, 1988; Levy, 2006; MacCannell, 1976; Olsen, 2002; Taylor, 2001; Tilley, 1997). Following Bruner's examination (2005, pp. 149-154) of discourses of authenticity at a New Salem tourist site, I consider the meaning and use of authenticity at Euro Disney's BBWW show. My examination of how Euro Disney employs discourses of authenticity reveals the negotiation of power relationships that occur in terms of authority and knowledge production.

The first way in which this BBWW show evokes authenticity is in terms of realness, what Bruner calls originality (2005, p. 150). Euro Disney seeks to fulfill the desire to gaze upon, learn about, and perhaps even experience Native culture. As artistic director Christel Grevy says, "The show is a good opportunity for Europeans to see cowboys and Indians live in person." That they are *real* cowboys and Indians is implied, and part of the draw. Christel explains further that the Natives are playing themselves and therefore do not need to learn a "role," only the show. The real and authentic character of the show is emphasized in the press release and on Euro Disney Web sites promoting the show and parade.

Euro Disney also employs a "verisimilitude" definition of authenticity (Bruner, 2005, p. 149). That is, when the producers say the show is authentic, they mean that it is a credible reproduction of the BBWW show.[10] It also appears real in substance, what Bruner (2005, p. 149) calls genuineness, in that they use handcrafted regalia and paraphernalia made using "Indian methods."[11] Euro Disney prefers to use original materials and designs for the show. According to its artistic director, the success of the show is due to this attention to detail—the authenticity of its production. Past performer and current Native recruiter for Euro Disney, Carter Yellowbird, also notes the importance of "genuineness" authenticity: the Euro Disney show is different from a craft store selling beadwork or feathers made in China or Japan, he says (personal interview, January 10, 2005).

The artistic team of the BBWW show has done research, and they feel that this research gives the show credibility. Therefore, authenticity is also linked to who can authorize or certify the authenticity of the reproduction; that is, the authority to claim authenticity (Bruner, 2005, pp. 150-151). The exhibit at the BBWW show contributes to this sense of authoritative authenticity. As Gable and Handler observed at historic sites, managers evoke authenticity in order to maintain the credibility of their sites and reproductions (1996, p. 569). In 2005, Euro Disney contacted the Buffalo Bill Museum and Grave in Golden, Colorado, for research information and images to use in an exhibit they were planning to celebrate the centennial of Buffalo Bill's visit to France (personal interview, August 23, 2005). This now permanent exhibit begins at the queue for the show, with a display of historical posters. A large screen presents a video of historical footage of the original BBWW show, and panels inside the waiting/bar area discuss Buffalo Bill's visit to Paris, the show, and Native participation. The exhibit serves to give credence to Euro Disney's BBWW show reproduction and to validate its historical accuracy and authenticity through "museum authority." As one of the managers says, "It's more than just a show."

These four forms of discourses of authenticity—originality, verisimilitude, genuineness, and authoritative—serve to establish the Euro Disney team as the nexus of power and give it the authority to represent histories and identities. However, this authority to define what is or is not authentic does not necessarily go unchallenged. One day while I was there, Native performer Ferlyn Brass, from the Key First Nation in Saskatchewan, wore a checked shirt for the show, much to the disapproval of the artistic manager (see figure 9.2).[12] Christel asked him to change, saying that a Sioux wouldn't have worn a shirt like that. Ferlyn asked how she could know that for sure. She responded that she had been told by the Indians themselves, and had also learned from the research, that Indians would have worn flowered shirts. Ferlyn declared that an Indian could have owned a shirt like that; fur traders wore checked shirts, and he could have traded for it. Christel persisted, "But they are *not Indian shirts*—it is not authentic." When Ferlyn seemed unmoved by her concern, replying that the audience would not know the difference anyway, Christel seemed discouraged. She believes that these small details make the show authentic; moreover, if she let him wear this shirt, others would want to wear different shirts as well. The discussion of authenticity faded out with both of them politely laughing it off; Ferlyn wore his checked shirt that night.

Discourses of authenticity are central to the Euro Disney BBWW show. By reproducing a Wild West show with attention to authenticity, Euro Disney continues to perpetuate the stereotypes and historical discourses of Otherness, as mentioned above. While the audience no doubt understands that this is a show, Euro Disney's engagement with multiple discourses of authenticity serves to promote the spectacle as a realistic, authentic reproduction with real cowboys and Indians, giving a sense of truth value to the representations and performances. Beyond the representations reproduced at the BBWW show, discourses of authenticity are enmeshed in a web of power relationships and the negotiation of knowledge systems. The conversation between Christel and Ferlyn was about more than whether or not a shirt is authentic for the time period. It was also a discussion about the construction of history, identity, and culture, and whose authority of different knowledges and historical understandings prevails. In sum, the disagreement over the checked shirt illustrates the power relationships at play when it comes to deciding what is authentic, what is selected for performance, and who has the authoritative knowledge to decide. The next section considers how Native performers negotiate performances as meaningful experiences for themselves and how they define Nativeness within the confines of the spectacular.

Figure 9.2 Ferlyn Brass. Photograph by the author, 2004.

Figure 9.3 Some Native Performers and Author at Euro Disney.
Photograph by the author, 2005.

Indigeneity in transnational spaces: Negotiating spectacular and lived identities

Both indigenous and nonindigenous scholars have been concerned about the appropriation of Native culture and the perpetuation of stereotypes, which are inexorably linked to colonial discourses of Otherness and superiority (e.g., Crosby, 1991; Doxtator, 1992; Keeshig-Tobias, 1997; Lischke & McNab, 2005; Yellow Bird, 2004). In an article that describes his encounter with a collection of toy cowboys and Indians, Yellow Bird argues that "cowboys and Indians [are] part of the colonial canon asserting white supremacy and Indigenous inferiority" (2004, p. 33). While the re-creation of BBWW show at Euro Disney reproduces colonial discourses of conquest and Otherness, I follow other scholars who critique the simplistic view that performing in spaces of spectacle and cultural displays are nothing but an exploitative commercial enterprise (cf. Peers, 1999; Tilley, 1997; Tuttle, 2001). Moreover, the idea that these spaces construct an "Imaginary Indian" (Francis, 1992), where Native participants are performing a story created by the dominant society, does not completely explain Native performers' experiences of identity or why they participate in these spectacular spaces (Nicks & Phillips, 2007).

When I asked Native performers whether they felt that the show challenged or perpetuated stereotypes, many of them stated that the show just follows stereotypes, some made no comment at all, and others offered their own interpretations. Most of the performers tolerate claims of authenticity and representations of Nativeness perpetuated by the show as simply part of show business, and business in general. Even so, the performers I interviewed did grapple with how to reconcile spectacular and lived experiences of Nativeness. My research indicates that spectacular performance in transnational spaces thus leads performers to reflect on and evaluate Native identity (cf. Buddle, 2004; Herle, 1994). I argue that this self-reflexivity also represents Native performers' attempt to wield power to construct and represent Nativeness in this context.

Many Native performers acknowledged the complexity of managing various subjectivities—spectacular identities produced in the show versus personal understandings and experiences of self, that is, with lived experiences of Nativeness. Some performers contemplated the persistence of the "Imaginary Indian" (Francis, 1992). Ferlyn Brass, who has performed with Euro Disney for more than four years, points out that Indians at Euro Disney are still "fabricated," like those in Hollywood movies (personal interview, September 29, 2004). Real Indians, he states, "aren't like that." However, Ferlyn also commented on how people want to see the real thing, including real Indians. Having genuine Native performers is important because audience members presume that they *are* real Natives. Ernest Rangel, a Navajo from New Mexico who has been employed by Euro Disney for the past four summers, says "[Tourists] ask all kinds of questions, like, 'What tribe are you from? Are you a real Native American? [Are] you a French or German?' And we've got to explain to them" (personal interview, August 16, 2005).

Occasionally the performers engage in other cultural performances at different venues. While they still promote Disney on these occasions, they have other goals as well. Ferlyn explains the significance of these other performances and encounters:

> When we go to schools and different places, [we] show them traditional dance, we show them fancy dancing, we show them the hoop dance, we talk about our ways. ... And we get to show our culture the way it should be, without the stage. ... So for me, I feel like I am a teacher at the same time as an artist. (Personal interview, September 29, 2004)

Kave Dust, a Crow Native American who has worked with Euro Disney for more than 10 years, agrees with Ferlyn, stating that what we see in cinema, television, and books is "fabricated by [the] white man" (personal interview, August 12, 2005). However, when he speaks in other spaces, he is representing himself: "When I go out there and do give a talk, it's the truth, and I can't always speak for all of the Indians of North America." Ferlyn's and Kave's comments highlight performers' attempt to balance their performances of Nativeness as a job (spectacular identity) with expressions of Nativeness as one's self (lived identity).

The tension between spectacular and lived expressions of Nativeness is also a concern because, as many of the performers admit, European audiences are generally not educated about Native Americans. Even though this is "just a show," some of the Native performers rightly point out that it is still important to put yourself into the performance and give it your all, to represent yourself and your community in a positive way—as Kave says, "Keep the heart in the dance." Some of the performers, including Ferlyn and Kave, are featured in brochures and posters, so how they represent themselves and their community is even more important. Ferlyn states, "I'm across the world and a long way from home and I want to make sure that when I'm done over here, I can actually be proud of what I've done over here, what I've said—make sure I've projected myself properly" (personal interview, September 29, 2004).

Another important issue that arose in interviews is that the BBWW reenactment produces "Indians of the past" as representative of authentic Indians. The notion of authenticity is often linked to a perceived opposition between traditional and modern subjectivities, a dichotomy that permeates discourse of authenticity (Jolly, 1992; Raibmon, 2005, p. 7). Comments from some Native performers reflect how they have attempted to resolve the tension between spectacular representations of the past and their personal experiences, and between traditional and modern subject positions. On the one hand, their employment at Euro Disney has led some performers to reflect on their ancestors and their experiences. Ferlyn contemplated:

> It's not a circus show; it was intended for the performances of the cowboys and Indians, the way life was first like in North America—what cowboys did, what Indians did, at that time in the Plains in the 1800s. I didn't live at that time, but I know what, and how, my [ancestors] not so long ago experienced. So I take those experiences with me, I reflect back. I wonder how, why, where, you know? I'm always growing; even in my own culture, I always grow. I've come to appreciate, in my own time, the things my ancestors did. For me it was even learning from my own ancestors. I mean, I've learned more about my ancestors than I did back home. I really appreciate what they have, what they've done. (Personal interview, September 29, 2004)

Wiley Mustus, a musician and performer from Alexis First Nation in Alberta, has been with Euro Disney's BBWW show for more than four years. He states eloquently:

> In a lot of ways I'm really grateful because it is like being Indian of the old, because the buffalo is still feeding my family. Like the old warriors used to chase the buffalo and make a hunt. It's an enactment, but we get paid to chase the buffalo. So, in a way, the buffalo is feeding me. (Personal interview, September 28, 2004)

While a few Native performers have found some meaning in their performances by connecting with their ancestors' history and experiences, reenactments of the past present a conundrum for others. Kave notes that the show may reproduce "authentic representations" of the past, but they are modern now. This seemingly contradictory view of Nativeness resonates in other public spheres of cultural display and performance. Hobbyists, for example, research Native culture and reproduce Natives' material and cultural lives, but these are Indians of the past. Kave recalls: "I said [to them] it's fine if you want to live the way we had a hundred years ago ... but we're modern" (personal interview, August 12, 2005). He goes on to say that they would rather live in houses than in tepees, and they use computers and telephones, not smoke signals! What these hobbyists, and perhaps the wider public who view these reenactments, have trouble understanding is that Native people may continue to have strong connections to their traditional knowledge and still engage in traditional acts (or customs)—they can be modern at the same time. Kave feels pressured to change the stereotypes of romantic Indians from the past, as well as hobbyist and Indianist misrepresentations and misunderstandings about contemporary Native life.

In addition, interviews revealed that performers view their lived identity as a multiple expression of tribal and broader indigenous identities, as well as being based on experiential criteria such as dancing and riding skills and traditional knowledge. First, identity encompasses experiential or personal notions of Nativeness. Many of the performers state plainly, "We are real Indians." What we do "comes naturally" for us, says Ernest Rangel (personal interview, August 16, 2005). When I asked Wiley Mustus whether he felt that he was performing himself or playing some other role, he answered that it is important to be true to yourself: "It's just me—110, 115 percent me" (personal interview, September 28, 2004). Ferlyn echoes these sentiments: "The best part [of what I do] is that I get to be Ferlyn Brass every time, just the way I am without my regalia on, or with my regular clothes on. [But] when I put on my regalia, and I stand up in front of a bunch of kids, it makes me feel good" (personal interview, September 29, 2004). Ernest similarly expresses that it is important to be yourself at Euro Disney, not only for the performers but also for those back in the community:

> The best part [about working at Euro Disney] would be being who you are. And try to bring back what we do back home, [what] we get to do here. Our cultures are so long[?]. The young generation doesn't know how to speak their own language. That's pretty sad, and you know, I was always raised traditional ... so this is like to have kind

of an opportunity. ... That's the best part about it—being who you are. (Personal interview, August 16, 2005)

Thus, as Peers discovered for Native performers at living history sites, Native performers at Euro Disney feel that they are just being themselves, "playing themselves" (Peers, 1999). Even though the performances involve reproduction of stereotypes, they also draw on personal understandings of Nativeness. Significantly, Native performers also invoke originality discourses of authenticity. Therefore, besides the importance of being yourself, I suggest that Native performers' use of originality discourses represents their attempt to obtain power and claim authority to define and represent Nativeness in this context.

Second, performers identify certain skills as being representative of Nativeness, in particular, riding skills. This type of ability makes performing at Euro Disney second nature, according to those I interviewed. Ferlyn Brass saw an advertisement for Euro Disney on the news and thought, "Yeah, I can do that ... I can ride" (personal interview, September 29, 2004). Wiley Mustus saw a poster for the auditions and thought, "Hey, I can ride a horse. Why not?" (personal interview, September 28, 2004). Tim Bruised Head, who grew up on both the Peigan Nation and the Blood Nation reserves in Alberta, was also experienced with horses, which he supplied for rodeos and shows.[13] Many of the Native performers declare that working in the BBWW show is not really work but rather an extension of their skills and knowledge, of what they normally do back home. Kave Dust states concisely: "This isn't really work; it's hard play" (personal communication, September 24, 2004). Ernest Rangel also draws on his personal experiences, having worked with horses all his life, in every job he has held. But while many Native performers are experienced with horses, performing at Euro Disney requires a different approach. Ernest regards some of the differences between riding back home and riding in the show as a matter of different knowledge systems, but understands this as part of the job: "[I]f you're riding the horse wrong, they'll tell you how to ride it. I just feel like saying, 'I'm the more experienced rider,' but I just say, you know, that you're paid to do what you're hired for" (personal interview, August 16, 2005). Hence, not only do many of the performers recognize riding expertise as a valuable skill, this expertise also reflects their distinctive knowledge base, an important point I will return to later.

Other performers also emphasized that traditional knowledge and upbringing are significant experiential aspects of identity that permeate one's performances. Kave Dust cites his experiences with horses and dancing growing up, as well as the stories his mother told him, as significant experiences that made him who he is today (personal interview, September 28, 2004). Wiley Mustus also hints at the skills, background, and attitude one needs to be successful in at Euro Disney. When I asked him what he would look for if he was a recruiter for Euro Disney, he outlined the scope of skills and background that make a good and successful performer abroad.

> First of all, you have to be athletic. You definitely have to know how to ride a horse ... dancing helps. A little bit of powwow background helps. And you have to have the look for sure. [Also,] someone who is going to go the long distance, the long haul. It takes a lot of courage to do what we do. (Personal interview, September 28, 2004)

Carter Yellowbird believes that the company should also take an in-depth look at potential performers' work history to determine whether they can succeed at this challenge: "Are they capable of leaving the community? Are they capable ... of working in Europe and being ambassadors for our people?" (personal interview, January 10, 2005). According to Carter, good performers possess not only riding skills but also a strong cultural upbringing so that they can represent Native people positively.

The above comments illustrate how performers consider riding and dancing to be important skills that are markers of Nativeness, and how these skills may connect with traditional upbringing and knowledge. In addition, these aspects of Nativeness—traditional background and knowledge (of culture, dancing, singing, and riding)—are considered essential in terms of being a good performer and successful in the show. By positioning these skills and forms of knowledge as important to their successes, these Native performers privilege Native skills and knowledge as sources of authority and power in the context of performing in spectacle in this transnational space, thereby challenging Euro Disney's authority to define Nativeness through its claims of historical accuracy and its museum exhibit.

Finally, Native performers connect to both tribal and broader indigenous or pan-Indian identities in this transnational space. The performers come from different First Nations and tribes, and they maintain their local identities through both performances and personal acts. In the show, for example, Kave acknowledges his tribe and lineage as a Crow of the Greasemouth clan with the paint he wears for his performances and his dancing. He proudly declares that it is both his privilege and his right to assert his "Crowness." Ernest Rangel says about the diversity of representation: "You know, there's different tribes here, so they do their own sacred thing—dancing and singing and stuff like that" (personal interview, August 16, 2005). For the buffalo dance, he explains, they all do their own dances from the different tribes. Performers also maintain some personal spiritual practices associated with their tribal identities. Kave explains that maintaining some traditional practices gives him strength: "I pray and smudge to protect myself, and I have my background and strength behind me. I am here, I see beyond the commercial. I am proud and have tradition" (personal interview, September 28, 2004). They may be a commodity, declares Carter Yellowbird, but Euro Disney respects their culture: "We'd go about our sweetgrass or our prayer, singing and drumming, and they supplied that as much as they can. They allowed us to, you know, practice whatever. ... I felt they treated me with respect" (personal interview, January 10, 2005). Performers therefore express their local/tribal identities through performance of specific tribal dances and by maintaining their spiritual practices.

At the same time, performers also self-identify as Native North American more broadly. Traveling abroad has meant breaking a barrier, moving beyond local and tribal identity to a broader sense of being indigenous. Kave Dust affirms: "We are all Native American. I am Greasemouth clan, Crow, Native American. I have broken the barrier. [There is] a sense of global identity ... we are indigenous" (personal interview, September 28, 2004). Ferlyn Brass proclaims: "It is a melting pot over here—Natives are from all over North America" (personal interview, September 29, 2004). Kave's comments illustrate that identity is a multifarious experience and that engaging in an international economy of cultural performance facilitates simultaneous expression of multiple identities, including broader categories such as indigenous.

Summary Case 1: Transnationalism and Indigeneity, Evaluating and Expressing Identity

The global economy of the cultural production of indigeneity that occurs in (and gives rise to) transnational spaces such as tourist sites does not necessarily result in the displacement of local Native identity, as is the case at Euro Disney. Rather, indigeneity is reengaged and reimagined in these wider social fields (Forte, this volume). I have shown how the performance of Nativeness in this transnational space engenders a process of external and self-identification in which the evaluation and expression of Native identity is multiple and overlapping. As Tilley found in his study on cultural tourism in Vanuatu, "by virtue of the practice of objectifying culture in the show people are beginning to learn that they have to negotiate and transform it" (1997, p. 86). Rather than being a representation of habitus, it provides a space for "conscious choice, contextualizing practices, modes of representation, rationalization and justification"—that is, self-reflexivity (Tilley, 1997, p. 87). Beck similarly writes of cosmopolitanism: "the defining characteristic of a cosmopolitan perspective is the 'dialogic imagination,'" in which individuals "compare, reflect, criticize, understand, combine contradictory certainties" (2002, p. 18). While Skrbis et al. (2004, pp. 129-130) opine that tourism, for example, is a form of "mundane or unreflexive" cosmopolitanism, I argue that these performers are, in fact, actively reflexive. Native performers reflect on, contest, express, and perform multiple social meanings and representations of Nativeness.

How then, is indigeneity (re)imagined and expressed in transnational pathways? Native performers at Euro Disney reconcile spectacular and lived identities by finding meaning in their performance as it connects to their own personal understandings and experiences of Nativeness. Performers highlight their status as "real Indians" and their skills and traditional knowledge as important aspects of their lived identity. In emphasizing these attributes, Native performers, I suggest, are challenging the authority and power established by Euro Disney to define "authentic" Nativeness. Thus, transnational spaces may be conceptualized as transnational social fields involving power relations (Roudometof, 2005, p. 120). Both managers and performers at Euro Disney claim cultural capital—knowledge of what constitutes Nativeness. In this transnational social field, performers' cultural knowledge is in tension with the managers' and producers' expertise of the industry and their understanding of authentic Plains Nativeness acquired through research (cf. Scales, 2002).

I have also illustrated how transnational work that involves the performance of Nativeness facilitates, in this case, the simultaneous expression of multiple identities, including broader categories such as indigenous or pan-Indian. However, Native performers also maintain and express their local identities through their performances and personal acts; their emphasis on traditional knowledge also connects to their local roots. Thus, tribal (local) and indigenous (or pan-Indian) identities are not necessarily opposed in transnational spaces such as tourism; rather, they may be simultaneously expressed. Local roots are articulated in transnational spaces, and transnational spaces generate occasions for the expression of a broader indigenous identity that includes while it transcends local and tribal expressions. This supports Beck's (2002, p. 17) proposition that the local and the global are mutually implicated in transnational spaces and globalization. Rather than an opposition between cosmopolitanism and localism, he argues that cosmopolitanism is both "routed" and "rooted" (2002, p. 19).

Beck also considers the presence of characteristics of transnationalism (such as dual citizenship and mobility) as indicators of cosmopolitanism (Roudometof, 2005, p. 116). Certainly these Native performers, who work in France but are still connected to home, and who engage in transnational tourist sites that reproduce globally circulating images of Nativeness, possess several characteristics that some scholars have identified as cosmopolitan. Being indigenous or cosmopolitan, therefore, are not necessarily oppositional subjectivities. Although performers engage in transnational work and, to a certain degree, a "cosmopolitan perspective" where the evaluation and expression of Native identity is multiple and inclusive, it is difficult to argue conclusively that these Native performers are becoming more cosmopolitan. As Roudometof opines, transnationalism does not necessarily refer to feelings or attitudes, or mean that we are becoming more cosmopolitan (2005, pp. 117, 119; also

Beck, 2002, p. 29). Yet "being and becoming" indigenous today may very well mean engaging in cosmopolitanism, or at least transnational and translocal lifestyles.

Case 2, Sheridan's Buffalo Bill Days: Pan-Indian Identity in Translocal Spaces

Images of Nativeness that circulate in popular media or "media-scapes" occur in, as they have generated, transnational and translocal spaces of cultural performance. Native Spirit Productions (NSP) is a professional performance troupe that performs indigeneity in translocal pathways. I say translocal rather than transnational in this case because NSP tours mostly in North America rather than internationally; however, they nonetheless imagine and construct indigeneity in spaces "away from home" or "en route." In this second case study, I consider the currency of pan-Indian identity as a strategy for these Native performers to negotiate translocal spaces of intercultural contact and the politics of representation at the Wild West show in Sheridan, Wyoming.

Figure 9.4 The Sheridan Inn. Photograph by the author, 2005.

Pan-Indianism is a contentious concept because it is often associated with notions of a "generic" and less "authentic" Indian identity that is the result of assimilation. Howard (1955), for example, provides one of the first definitions of pan-Indianism, arguing that it is the result of the loss of tribal knowledge and leads to the development of a nontribal culture. Given that pan-Indianism emerged from studies on diffusion and acculturation, scholars such as Jackson and Levine (2002, pp. 301–302) critique the concept, stating that it assumes a homogeneous Indian cultural expression. Conversely, Ellis maintains that pan-Indian expressions, like the Gourd Dance, do not replace tribal identities;

rather, "[they] serve a particular function in a particular place" (1990, p. 26). Following Ellis, I argue that pan-Indian identity may be conceptualized as a multiple yet unifying expression of Nativeness that does not exclude tribal or local identity, and in this case, is used to negotiate tourist encounters and contest stereotypes. I maintain that the expression and use of pan-Indian identity in tourism by NSP may be viewed as an example of mobile performers engaging in a cosmopolitan-like vision of increasing cross-cultural understanding.

Performing indigeneity in translocal pathways: Contesting stereotypes of "traditional Indians"

BBD first took place in 2003 to celebrate the 110th anniversary of the Sheridan Inn, a national historic landmark. The Sheridan Heritage Center Inc. (SHC) hired the Great American Wild West Show, a traveling variety show complete with all the essential Western and Indian acts—a spectacular production. In 2005 the SHC decided to hire individual acts from all over the United States. Whether these performers knew the history of Buffalo Bill or Sheridan was not important; but the SHC did want to hire quality acts that incorporated a historical component. In fact, BBD is more than just a Wild West show; it is a complete "Western experience." The weekend events include a historical ball, a birthday celebration complete with chuckwagon barbecue and birthday cake, a Pony Express reenactment, a historical parade, and finally, the Wild West show.[14] Although Buffalo Bill performed in Sheridan with the Sells-Floto circus in 1914, Sheridan's Wild West show is not based on any specific year. Rather, it is inspired by historic shows and includes several of their features, including a grand entry, trick shooting and roping, gun spinning, roman riding and other displays of horsemanship, an attack on a Pony Express rider, and an attack on a stagecoach.

Despite the recurring appearance of Buffalo Bill, the celebrations are not about the man himself. Edre Maier, manager of the Sheridan Inn and executive director of the SHC, states that the goal of BBD is to increase interest in the inn and boost support for restoration projects (personal communication, June 24, 2005). She says that Buffalo Bill is very marketable, and that his celebrity status combined with heritage tourism will bring attention to the inn and more generally to the history of their Western town. BBD incorporates a "living history" component (reenactment) with a heritage site (the inn) as a way of marketing both Sheridan's history and the inn. BBD therefore involves a process of "heritage-making" whereby official representations and narratives of history and identity are produced and performed; the history of the inn is further linked to metanarratives of Westernness and Buffalo Bill (cf. Kirshenblatt-Gimblett, 1995). Thus, while the main goal is to raise the profile of the inn, the SHC is also commemorating Westernness. But what about representations of *Native history*? Is there any room for alternative narratives?

In the presentation of history, heritage sites and museums often commemorate the dominant group while excluding marginal groups; that is, they give primacy to dominant society and its views of history (cf. Levy, 2006), reflecting the power of the dominant society to produce narratives and social meanings. Indeed, Wild West shows, rodeos, commemorative events, and other spaces of performance are often controlled by the dominant (white) society. Furniss shows how the Williams Lake Stampede in Alberta, for example, is controlled by non-Natives, yet requires inclusion of Native people to complete the "frontier complex" script, which is based on a dichotomy of Indianness and Western identity (1999, p. 164). These narratives, however, are not totally hegemonic. As Bruner observes, performance has the capacity to suggest alternative meanings, regardless of the abundance of official narratives (2005, p. 141). Tourist sites are contested spaces where multiple representations and performances of histories and identities exist and are negotiated (cf. Bruner, 2005; Chambers, 2000). I argue that performances of contemporary pan-Indian identity at the BBD Wild West show are a form of self-representation and agency that serve to contest official narratives and stereotypes and to highlight cultural continuity.

The question of inclusion at BBD reflects the negotiation of power—the control of representations and official narratives. Because the goal of BBD is to commemorate Western history, Native history is subsequently downplayed. Although the BBD Wild West show does not incorporate performances of Native history, it does include performances by a professional Native troupe called Native Spirit Productions (NSP).[15] These Native performers contest metanarratives of Westernness by generating alternative narratives to "cowboys and Indians." Brian Hammill, of the Ho-Chunk Nation in southern Wisconsin, and Navajo Lane Jenkins are professional performers and powwow dancers who challenge stereotypes through their performances of a contemporary pan-Indian identity. Their contemporary performances provide a sharp contrast to the historical reenactments and costumed characters of Buffalo Bill, Annie Oakley, Wild Bill, and Calamity Jane. Dressed in powwow regalia rather than traditional deerskin, Brian asks the audience, "Have you heard this song before? 'Heya, heya, heya, heya.' Well, I can guarantee you that an Indian did not write that song." Brian plays his flute and talks about traditional and contemporary music; he also speaks plainly about stereotypes and the fact that Native communities live and thrive today. Lane's performance of the Fancy Dance and Brian's Hoop Dance demonstrate their Nativeness and cultural vitality (see figures 9.5 and 9.6). This insertion of contemporary performance in combination with an educational agenda brings Native culture and identity into the twenty-first century. While Native *history* is absent in these commemorative events, Native present is being celebrated.

Edre Maier notes this disjuncture between Native past and present identity constructions: "It was definitely a representation of contemporary Native culture, because that's what you see at powwows" (personal interview, June 27, 2005). She also mentions that she was disappointed at first to hear that Brian and Lane were going to wear their brightly colored powwow regalia. Commenting on their modern look, Edre states that she is sure their regalia look great at night under fluorescent lights, but it is not "true Indian dress." In other words, it's not "traditional (authentic) Indian" clothing. Thus, even though the hoop dancers are more in tune with what Edre suggests is required for an exciting Wild West show, their inclusion concerned her because she felt that they might disrupt the historical picture the SHC was attempting to create. In the end, however, she admits that NSP's presentation was exceptional and the audience loved it; they "stole the show," she says. In fact, when I asked Edre to name her favorite part of the Wild West show, she replied, "the hoop dancers!"

The disjuncture between past and present identity constructions reflects the fact that NSP is presenting alternative social meanings of Native identity. Performing Nativeness as it is experienced *today* is one of the goals of NSP. In presenting a contemporary Native identity at BBD, they also control the *meaning* of Nativeness by controlling the use of symbols representing their contemporary Native identity. As Furniss notes, power comes not in presenting the stereotypical symbols themselves, but from the "epistemological power" the groups have "to control the meaning of these symbols" (1999, p. 181). The NSP dancers' elaborate, brightly colored powwow regalia, for example, are a recognizable sign of Nativeness, but this is not the historical deerskin attire associated with traditional Indian imagery (although it is certainly influenced by Plains dress). Without question, Brian and Lane's powwow regalia are more meaningful to them than the "traditional Plains dress" found in historical Wild West shows and reenactments that is perceived as authentic by others. I asked Brian Hammill how he felt about perhaps playing a "traditional Indian" in this type of venue and possibly reenacting historic Wild West performances. He replied,

> The way we do it here [at BBD], we're not going back to the 1880s. A lot of the other stuff in the show is 1880s; we show who we are today. We are not showing what it was like in the 1800s, we are showing what we are today. So when somebody wants me to throw on a headdress and dance around a fire, I'll tell them no, that's not what they really want, that we can do it another way which would give them the same energy and give them a better effect. (Personal interview, June 25, 2005)

Brian's statements reveal how it is possible to contest representations of Nativeness associated with Wild West shows without sacrificing entertainment value or spectacular appeal. By drawing on powwow identity markers—dress, dance, and music—to represent themselves, they contest more stereotypical and romantic representations of Indians from the past, and, more important, they present meaningful representations of self. In contrast with Euro Disney, these performers are in control of the use and epistemology of symbols of Nativeness. By presenting contemporary pan-Indian identity through dance and regalia, Brian and Lane exert agency within the confines of a heritage tourist site that, in this case, restricts Native representations of history. Their participation in the BBD Wild West show, albeit limited in comparison with Euro Disney, is significant because it demonstrates how Native performers can destabilize official narratives. NSP contests official narratives at BBD by presenting an alternative vision of Nativeness. I maintain, therefore, that the participation of these Native performers in BBD reflects their desire and ability to negotiate power by controlling representations and symbols of Nativeness.

Figure 9.5 Left, Lane's Fancy Dance. Photograph by the author, 2005.

Figure 9.6 Right, Brian's Hoop Dance. Photograph by the author, 2005.

Pan-Indian Identity, Agency, and a Cosmopolitan Vision?

The significance of employing pan-Indian identity in these types of spaces requires more consideration because performances of pan-Indian identity are occasions for *self*-representation (cf. Buddle, 2004; Ellis, 1990; Herle, 1994; Lerch, 1992; Lerch & Bullers, 1996). Pan-Indian identity transcends local expressions of identity as it includes them. The NSP Web site outlines the group's intertribal approach: "the dancers represent various nations from all across the United States as well as Canada." The powwow dances that NSP draws on are social dances suitable for public display, but these intertribal dances shared by various Native communities do not replace Brian and Lane's local identity or tribal affiliation. As Ellis argues, pan-Indian expressions do not replace tribal identities; rather, "it serves a particular function in a particular place" (1990, p. 26). And as Herle observes of powwows, pan-Indian styles and regalia cut across tribal affiliations and local tribal expressions and encourage members to imagine themselves as part of a larger community (1994, pp. 76–79). In this case, pan-Indian identity is about a shared intertribal experience, expressed through powwow dancing, music, and regalia, that serves a particular function: to provide educational entertainment for the public.

I argue that presenting a pan-Indian identity is not only acceptable, but is the preferred form of self-expression in translocal spaces of cultural performance because it may be used strategically to mediate tourist representations and encounters. Central to negotiating power—to control representations and meanings of Nativeness—in translocal pathways is NSP's approach to performance. Certain elements are integral to their performance approach: performances are didactic; they are professional, highlighting performers' skills and reliability; and they emphasize cultural continuity. Their performance approach facilitates agency in this context, which is evident in the group's ability to negotiate narratives and meanings of Nativeness.

First, one of NSP's goals is to educate the public through their performances of contemporary Nativeness. Tourist sites such as BBD and other spaces of performance are productive spaces for cross-cultural exchange. Brian Hammill formed NSP in 1997 with this intention in mind: "[It is] a way to share native culture and dances with various people from all across the United States as well as overseas." Lane Jenkins echoes this sentiment: "A lot of people ... think it's a really big deal to see Native American dancing and Native American singing" (personal interview, June 25, 2005). In our interview, Brian clearly stated their didactic priority: "We offer a good dance show and we also educate. The main thing is education through dancing, through talking, whatever. We want a show where people have a better understanding of our culture." NSP provides "educational entertainment" through dances, music, artist demonstrations, videos, CDs, and lectures at a variety of venues ranging from corporate events to rodeos and fairs, special public events and celebrations, and schools and museums.

NSP's educational agenda explicitly aims to increase cross-cultural understanding, confront stereotypes, and correct misconceptions. Participating in the Wild West show at BBD is thus an opportunity for these performers to inform the public about contemporary Native music, explain the significance of the dances, and, as stated earlier, present contemporary Nativeness as opposed to the "traditional Indian," revealing their ability to assume power by gaining epistemological control over meanings of Nativeness. In other words, they use pan-Indian identity to negotiate stereotypical representations and social meanings of Nativeness. I suggest that their performances of indigeneity in this translocal space facilitate a cosmopolitan-like experience, where performers and the public engage with cultural difference, and where performers seek to increase cultural understanding. Translocal pathways, therefore, may be conceived as spaces where indigeneity and cosmopolitan visions are worked out.

Second, Brian Hammill expresses the importance of providing a "professional face" and employees who are reliable (personal interview, June 25, 2005). This meets the requirements of clients such as Edre Maier, who are looking for dependable, professional performers. Brian is an all-rounder (hoop dancer, musician, and storyteller) who works with a core group of people whom he can depend on as *ambassadors* of Nativeness, people who have "exceptional skill and dance quality" (personal interview, June 25, 2005). Putting a professional face on for Native dancing and performance in general means that the performers' skills are highlighted—their skills as dancers, musicians, storytellers, and artists—underscoring NSP's vision of how to represent Nativeness. In addition to emphasizing their skills and contemporary representation, this professional face also defies such misconceptions as that Native people simply do not work. The group's didactic and professional approach to performing Nativeness is essential to its ability to control representation and wield agency in this space.

Third, performing pan-Indian identity provides opportunities to make statements of cultural survival. The point that Native performers at BBD present contemporary pan-Indian identity rather than representations of Native history requires some qualification. I have indicated that the limited inclusion of Native participants at BBD contributes to the erasure of Native history. However, the significance of the "past" is not completely disregarded by NSP. Brian Hammill and Lane Jenkins emphasize cultural continuity in their performances, linking the past and present. Their dances have historical roots and modern influences.[19] Brian confirms that the dances we see are not only educational presentations but also representative of dances that "have survived thousands of years."[20] Native culture not only survives, it thrives. He proudly proclaims that "the Native culture is a living culture."[21]

In addition, passing on knowledge and skills to others, as well as information to the public, is a way of keeping Native culture alive.[22] It also promotes a sense of personal satisfaction and pride. As Lane Jenkins explains,

> It makes you feel better, that you're performing for people. I don't know, it's not just performing like show-wise, it's how you feel, how you feel about yourself. And if you're doing something good, you know, keep on doing it. (Personal interview, June 25, 2005)

Beyond the personal satisfaction that comes from dancing and performing cultural continuity for the public to witness, cultural knowledge may be passed down through performance. Lane hopes that his performances are an inspiration for youth:

> Well, the best part is, I would say for myself, is to see the young generation keep on going and, you know, passing it on, passing it along. And I see a lot of different kids out there that we dance with sometimes; we dance with a couple of school kids and

stuff like that. ... I work with some kids, you know. They really wanted to dance, but they get really into it. I just try to help them along and do the best that I can.

In sum, pan-Indian identity in this context is an expression of pride, contemporary Nativeness, and cultural continuity. Expressions of identity are simultaneously tribal, intertribal, and pan-Indian. Thus, as in the Euro Disney case study, this translocal pathway leads to the negotiation of multiple subjectivities; however, unlike EuroDisney, NSP is in control of the representation and performance of Nativeness. Performers at BBD draw on pan-Indian or intertribal expressions in order to offer alternative narratives of Nativeness. I suggest that performers strategically present a pan-Indian identity because it is recognizable as indigenous, although not necessarily recognizable as a local (or tribal) expression of identity. Through their performances of contemporary indigeneity, these performers create occasions for cross-cultural exchange and public education.

Conclusions

Moving beyond arguments that center exclusively on the reproduction of stereotypes and the commercialization of Nativeness in the global economy of cultural performance, attention to the various meanings and interpretations of Nativeness in this context demonstrates the multiplicity and complexity of Native identity, as well as the negotiation of power that occurs in transnational and translocal performance spaces such as tourist sites. I have argued that these spaces engender occasions for the reflection, evaluation, contestation, and expression of Native identity, which is fluid and multiple. I have also suggested that in transnational and translocal spaces of cultural performance, performers often choose to express a pan-Indian identity based on broader categories of indigeneity and on powwow culture. In particular, NSP draws on pan-Indian identity for the Wild West show at BBD because it has transnational currency and understanding, which facilitates their participation in translocal cultural economies. In turn, participation in translocal spaces facilitates opportunities for NSP to engage in cosmopolitan like encounters. They strategically employ a pan-Indian identity to contest stereotypes, negotiate cross-cultural spaces, and educate the public. These case studies demonstrate how indigeneity in transnational and translocal pathways is simultaneously local/tribal and intertribal or pan-Indian in expression, not in opposition. Native performers engage with indigenous identity and cosmopolitan visions, without losing their local roots.

Notes

1. For my dissertation, I originally wanted to use the term *Aboriginal*; however, I found that performers at Euro Disney did not recognize or associate themselves with this term. I have chosen to use *Native* as opposed to more politically correct terms such as *First Nations* or *Native American* because it is more inclusive of both First Nations from Canada and Native North Americans from the United States. I occasionally use *Indian* in reference to historical contexts and contemporary theoretical usage, as well as when employed by the people I interviewed. When known, I include tribal and nation and/or band affiliations. Because I use the term *Native*, I use *Nativeness* as opposed to *Indianness*—sometimes used in the literature—for consistency.
2. Extensive scholarship exists on the representation of indigenous peoples and the construction of social meaning in various spaces of public display and performance, such as museums (Phillips, 2004), world's fairs and exhibitions (Raibmon, 2005; Rydell, 1984), and tourism (Stanley, 1998).
3. See Skrbis et al. (2004) for a discussion.
4. This chapter is based on my dissertation research conducted in 2004 and 2005, which was made possible by funding from the Royal Anthropological Institute of Great Britain and Ireland (Emslie Horniman Anthropological Scholarship Fund, 2004-5), Social Sciences and Humanities Research Council of Canada Doctoral Fellowship (2005-6), McMaster School of Graduate Studies Fieldwork Funding (2004-5), and the Buffalo Bill Historical Center Garlow Fellowship (2005). Thanks also to my research participants and everyone at the tourist sites, archives, museums, and libraries for their time and generosity.
5. The BBWW show has been in production since Euro Disney's opening in 1992.
6. My description of the 1905 show is based on the historical program; McCracken Library at the Buffalo Bill Historical Center (Cody, Wyoming), MS6, Series VI-A, micro roll#2.
7. *Press Information*, EuroDisney Press Kit, Buffalo Bill's Wild West Show, 2004, Press Relations, Karine Moral.
8. *Press Information*.
9. It is authentic according to the creative director of the show; interview with Christel Grevy September 27, 2004, and August 23, 2005. Claims of authenticity are also made in their Press Kit, *Press Information*, p. 5 in a section called "Authenticity, the Recipe for Success."
10. Handler and Saxton found that living-history sites similarly defined authenticity in terms of historical accuracy and the exact simulation of a place or event (1988, p. 243).
11. *Press Information*.
12. Fieldnotes, October 1, 2004, Euro Disney.
13. His family (Pat Provost and Jenny Bruised Head) also had their own horse show called the Wild Horse Show and Buffalo Chase on their reserve near Brocket, Alberta.
14. My discussion on the history of establishing BBD is based on my fieldnotes and personal communication with Edre Maier, June 24, 2005.
15. Native Spirit Productions is based out of Phoenix, Arizona.

References

Adams, K. M. (1997). Ethnic Tourism and the Renegotiation of Tradition in Tana Toraja (Sulawesi, Indonesia). *Ethnology*, 36(4), 309-321.
Bell, E., L. Haas, & L. Sells. (Eds.). (1995). *From Mouse to Mermaid: The Politics of Film, Gender, and Culture*. Bloomington/Indianapolis: Indiana University Press.
Bruner, E. (2005). *Culture on Tour: Ethnographies of Travel*. Chicago: University of Chicago Press.
Bryam, A. (2004). *The Disneyization of Society*. London: Sage.
Budd, M., & M. H. Kirsch, (Eds.). (2005). *Rethinking Disney: Private Control, Public Dimensions*. Middletown, CT: Wesleyan University Press.
Buddle, K. (2004). Media, Markets and Powwows. *Cultural Dynamics*, 16(1), 29-69.
Castaneda, T. (1993). Beyond the Trocadero: Mickey's Wild West Show and More. *Public Culture*, 5, 607-613.
Chambers, E. (2000). *Native Tours: The Anthropology of Travel and Tourism*. Prospect Heights, IL: Waveland Press.
Crosby, M. (1991). Construction of the Imaginary Indian. In S. Douglas (Ed.), *Vancouver Anthology: The Institutional Politics of Art* (pp. 267-291). Vancouver: Talonbooks.
Doxtator, D. (1992). *Fluff & Feathers: An Exhibit on the Symbols of Indianness*. Brantford, ON: Woodland Cultural Center.
Ellis, C. (1990). "'Truly Dancing Their Own Way': Modern Revival and Diffusion of the Gourd Dance." *American Indian Quarterly*, 14(1), 19-33.
Fernandez, R. (1995). Pachuco Mickey. In E. Bell, L. Haas, & L. Sells (Eds.), *From Mouse to Mermaid: The Politics of Film, Gender, and Culture* (pp. 236-254). Bloomington/Indianapolis: Indiana University Press.
Francis, D. (1992). *The Imaginary Indian*. Vancouver: Arsenal Pulp Press.
Furniss, E. M. (1999). *The Burden of History: Colonialism and the Frontier Myth in a Rural Canadian Community*. Vancouver: University of British Columbia Press.
Gable, E., & R. Handler. (1996). After Authenticity at an American Heritage Site. *American Anthropologist*, 98(3), 568-578.
Handler, R., & W. Saxton. (1988). Dyssimulation: Reflexivity, Narrative, and the Quest for Authenticity in "Living History." *Cultural Anthropology*, 3(3), 242-260.
Hannerz, U. (1990). Cosmopolitans and Locals in World Culture. In Mike Featherstone (Ed.), *Global Culture: Nationalism, Globalization and Modernity* (pp. 237-251). London: Sage.
Herle, A. (1994). Dancing Community: Powwow and Pan-Indianism in North America. *Cambridge Anthropology*, 17(2), 57-83.
Howard, J. H. (1955). Pan-Indian Culture of Oklahoma. *The Scientific Monthly*, 81(5), 215-220.
Jackson, J. B., & V. L. Levine. (2002). Singing for Garfish: Music and Woodland Communities in Eastern Oklahoma. *Ethnomusicology*, 46(2), 284-305.
Jolly, M. (1992). Specters of Inauthenticity. *The Contemporary Pacific*, 4(1), 49-72.
Keeshig-Tobias, L. (1997). Stop Stealing Native Voices. In B. Ziff & P. V.Rao (Eds.), *Borrowed Power: Essays on Cultural Appropriation* (pp. 71-73). New Brunswick, NJ: Rutgers University Press.
Kirshenblatt-Gimblett, B. (1995). Theorizing Heritage. *Ethnomusicology*, 39(3), 367-379.
Kratz, C. A., & I. Karp. (1993). Wonder and Worth: Disney Museums in World Showcase. *Museum Anthropology*, 17(3), 32-42.

Lerch, P. B. (1992). Pageantry, Parade, and Indian Dancing: The Staging of Identity among the Waccamaw Sioux. *Museum Anthropology*, 16(2), 27-34.

Lerch, P. B., & S. Bullers. (1996). Powwows as Identity Markers: Traditional or Pan-Indian? *Human Organization*, 55(4), 390-395.

Levy, J. E. (2006). Prehistory, Identity, and Archaeological Representation in Nordic Museums. *American Anthropologist*, 108(1), 135-147.

Lischke, U., & D. T. McNab. (2005). "Show me the money": Representation of Aboriginal People in East-German Indian Films. In Ute Lischke & David McNab (Eds.), *Walking a Tightrope: Aboriginal People and Their Representations* (pp. 281-303). Waterloo: *Wilfrid* Laurier University Press.

MacCannell, D. (1976). *The Tourist: A New Theory of the Leisure Class*. New York: Schocken Books.

Nicks, T., & R. B. Phillips. (2007). "From Wigwam to White Lights." Princess White Deer's Indian Acts. In J. C. H. King & C. F. Feest (Eds.), *Three Centuries of Woodlands Indian Art* (pp. 144-160). Altenstadt: ZKF Publishers.

Olsen, K. (2002). Authenticity as a Concept in Tourism Research: The Social Organization of the Experience of Authenticity. *Tourist Studies*, 2(2), 159-182.

Peers, L. (1999). "Playing Ourselves": First Nations and Native American Interpreters at Living History Sites. *The Public Historian*, 21(4), 39-59.

Phillips, R. B. (2004). Disappearing Acts: Traditions of Exposure, Traditions of Enclosure and Iroquois Masks. In M. Phillips (Ed.), *Questions of Tradition*, (pp. 56-87). Toronto: University of Toronto Press.

Raibmon, P. (2005). *Authentic Indians: Episodes of Encounter from the Late-nineteenth-century Northwest Coast*. Durham, NC: Duke University Press.

Roudometof, V. (2005). Transnationalism, Cosmopolitanism and Glocalization. *Current Sociology*, 53(1), 113-135.

Rydell, R. W. (1984). *All the World's a Fair: Visions of Empire at American International Expositions, 1876-1916*. Chicago: University of Chicago Press.

Scales, C. A. (2002). The Politics and Aesthetics of Recording: A Comparative Canadian Case Study of Powwow and Contemporary Native American Music. *The World of Music*, 44(1), 41-59.

Skrbis, Z., G. Kendall, & I. Woodward. (2004). Locating Cosmopolitanism. *Theory, Culture & Society*, 21(6), 115-136.

Stanley, N. (1998). *Being Ourselves for You: The Global Display of Cultures*. London: Middlesex University Press.

Taylor, J. P. (2001). Authenticity and Sincerity in Tourism. *Annals of Tourism Research*, 28(1), 7-26.

Tilley, C. (1997). Performing Culture in the Global Village. *Critique of Anthropology*, 17(1), 67-89.

Tuttle, P. (2001). "Beyond Feathers and Beads": Interlocking Narratives in the Music and Dance of Tokeya Inajin (Kevin Locke). In C. J. Meyer & D. Royer (Eds.), *Selling the Indian: Commercializing and Appropriating American Indian Cultures* (pp. 99-156). Tucson: University of Arizona Press.

Yellow Bird, M. (2004). Cowboys and Indians: Toys of Genocide, Icons of American Colonialism. *Wicazo Sa Review*, 19(2), 33-48.

◆ CHAPTER TEN ◆

Conclusion: From Wandering Jew to Ironic Cosmopolite: A Semi-Utopian Postnationalism

Nigel Rapport

[I]t is not so much persecution that has made the Jews a nation of wanderers, but hope. Reports of the death of indigenous cultures...have been exaggerated.
—Chaim Bermant, *Genesis*

Introduction: "Jewish" Cosmopolitanism and Postnationalism

Hosts and Guests is the title of a well-known collection of articles, edited by Valene Smith, concerning tourists and the sometimes long-suffering inhabitants of the regions that they visit. Smith defines a tourist as "a temporarily leisured person who voluntarily visits a place away from home for the purpose of experiencing a change" (1989, p. 1). Perhaps, however, what has best characterized the anthropological appreciation of tourism since Smith wrote has been the central importance of this phenomenon for understanding the contemporary world as such; the "temporary" experience of "leisure" by "persons away from home" has been centralized, theoretically, so that it now compasses the experience, ordinary and out-of-the-ordinary, of us all (cf. Graburn, 1988). "Travel," moving away from or between homes (moving as home) and "experiencing change," is something practiced by many and possessing consequences for all; with the result that it becomes neither easy nor wise to attempt to demarcate or differentiate, in any absolute way, between "hosts" and "guests."

A reciprocity and a serialization of the roles of hosts and guests, moreover, moves toward a state where neither party is clearly or absolutely "at home" in a place, or where one is at home in and through being "away." In the context of contemporary global multiculturalism and movement (as in tourism, labor migration, pilgrimage, and exile) to recognize the fluidity of the notions of hosts and guests is also to recognize the way in which one might imagine mutual hospitality being the normative role played out in social space: where one is "at home" is a matter of the nature and purpose of particular exchanges rather than absolute identities.

One of the chief crimes with which "Jews" have commonly been charged by nationalist regimes (by both the Nazis and the Soviets, for instance) is cosmopolitanism—conceiving of themselves as operating in a global space—they will play host to little attachment or loyalty, it is said, to any particular local space. One hears echoes of this prejudice, of course, with regard to many immigrant groups whose centers of orientation are called into question by local chauvinists; just as Norman Tebbit, infamous member of Mrs. Thatcher's Conservative cabinet in the 1980s, cast aspersions on Asian immigrants in Britain by doubting they supported England when Pakistan, Sri Lanka, or India were their opponents in cricket (cf. Werbner, 1996), so archnationalists have seen in "Jewish cosmopolitanism" reasons for suspicion. If he is found in most countries of the world, (even though he might be at home in none) then in a sense the "Jew" is a member of most countries. Certainly he does not limit himself unnecessarily in terms of citizenship, and is it not likely, then, that his transnational attachments, networks, and relations will outweigh in significance merely national and parochial ones? As the *Oxford English Dictionary* succinctly sums up, in common usage "*cosmopolite*" is "[o]ften contrasted with *patriot*"—and, one might add, *native, local,* or *indigene*.

However, this is precisely the "Jewish" feature on which I shall elaborate here, and which I esteem. Cosmopolitanism, I shall suggest, is the habit of mind, the proclivity and the practice that are of vital importance for the inculcating of a global social order that is "postnational"—in ethos if not yet in institution. Through the notion of being guests in any particular social milieu—guests, as it were, of the social procedures that make the contracting of mutual guesthood possible—this is a social order to which all might belong, and feel they belong.

The advent of postnationalism—in the context of institutional arrangements such as the European Union, and disarrangements such as the ethnic nationalisms in the Balkans, the Caucasus, and the Middle East —is something that is at once easy to imagine and farfetched. But then, many commentators have linked the two processes of global centripetalism and regional centrifugalism as aspects of one and the same millennial shift: a globalization that renders the nationalisms of the past two centuries obsolete even though, in the medium term, these might be replaced by virulent renascent particularism and cultural fundamentalism (Wallerstein, 1984; Robertson, 1990). We are justified, then, in employing our anthropological imaginations in considering social arrangements for this global, postnational condition. Indeed, according to Ernest Gellner (1993), we have little choice in the matter. A shared global human condition is a fact of all our lives and to pretend otherwise on the basis of some spurious, culturally relativist, or postcolonial perspective is a travesty of reality and a dereliction of our professional duty. Any "adequate" anthropology must begin from the wholly "trans-cultural" nature of the contemporary world and work toward setting up a transcultural morality (Gellner, 1993, p. 54). Of course, this will not be easy—it might be impossibly difficult—but this is precisely our predicament: "to work out the social options of our affluent and disenchanted condition" (Gellner, 1995, p. 8).

What I set out to do in this chapter is to begin with the notion of the exilic "wandering Jew," admit that this is an idiom that might reveal little about the content of actual Jewish lives, but nevertheless explore what the idiom might give onto in the way of contemporary political description and prescription. Inasmuch as society is an ongoing discursive construction, what political message might the notion of universal Jewish cosmopolitanism and transnationalism hold; what social work might the idiom perform?

The project thus complements Maximilian Forte's (2005) disinterring of the term *Carib*. Paradoxical as it may sound, in the "wandering Jew" and in the "indigenous Carib" may be found alike rhetorical practices that speak similarly to "cosmopolitan" possibilities of identity being achieved and not ascribed. How might the ideal-typical notion of cosmopolitanism be used idealistically by anthropology, I ask—in the cause of "cultural critique" (Marcus & Fischer, 1986)—for the advocating of procedures of mutual guesting in a new "world system"?

The course of the chapter proceeds from an examination of the "Jew" in the discourse of modern nationalism to an ethnographic account of Jewish lives in contemporary Newfoundland, before closing with a discussion of the themes of the volume as a whole. Using "Jew," one comes to know "indigene" as a construct and an achieved identity.

Nationalism and the Mission of the Wandering Jew

The pariah-role assigned to "Jews" in the modern project of nationalism—the desire to inculcate a national-cultural homogeneity as route to social stability and economic growth (Gellner, 1983)—needs little rehearsing. Arendt describes Jews as that incongruous, ambiguous, and opaque "non-national element in a world of growing or existing nations"—where nationhood was to become the paramount basis of group self-constitution (1962, p. 22). As Bauman elaborates (1989), Jews were represented, in their ubiquity and their dispersal, as something of an "inter-national nation" or a "non-national nation," which constantly threatened with relativity and delimitation the criterion of nationhood that was intended to determine self-identity clearly, finally, and absolutely. Not fully belonging to the country in which they lived, Jews were an enemy within: "[t]hey undermined the very difference between hosts and guests, the native and the foreign" (Bauman, 1989, p. 52). Asking questions no one else did, treating the familiar as if it were exotic, they became associated with unpatriotic, nonlocalized values concerning universalism, liberal cosmopolitanism, and humanity-as-such. Their flexibility and adaptability, their national emptiness, made them despicable.

Hence, the special place accorded to Jewry by the two great nationalistic experiments of the twentieth century, German National Socialism and Soviet Republicanism, in their ideologizing (and demonizing). The "Jewish Question" troubled Lenin inordinately, for instance (as it had Marx, and was to Stalin), and he continually sought ways to normalize "Jewish national identity" and so build erstwhile cosmopolitan and rootless Jews into a socialist democracy (1974); here, in turn, nations could amalgamate, and Judaism and Yiddishkeit eventually disappear. Zionism was a reactionary manifestation of bourgeois nationalism, Lenin concluded, but if Jews were to assume national rights and freedoms within the USSR—a national homeland in Birobidzhan, Siberia, for instance (cf. Weinberg, 1998)—then this would pave the way to their membership in a union of Soviet peoples: to their properly and proudly becoming consolidated within a totalizing Soviet cultural heritage. Anti-Semitism would be stamped out, national enmities and racial particularisms would not be exacerbated, and there need be little obstruction to all workers uniting against reactionary, international orders: the capitalist, autocratic, and clerical cultures and classes.

From this trend to make national cultures into kinds of fetich, it may be possible to detect a positive aspect—the tragedies of Hitlerism and Stalinism notwithstanding. There is a positive and hopeful sentiment, for instance, in Kundera describing the modern state of Israel paradoxically as "the true heart of Europe"; it is a "peculiar heart located outside the body," he elaborates, but what might this not tell us about the possible imaginative nature of identity, about its disseverment from territory and cultural institutionalism, and about the associational bases of community belonging (1990, p. 157). From a postnationalist Europe, might there not arise the imaginary of polities built on the voluntary and multiple memberships of freefloating individual agents?

George Steiner (1998) makes the case perhaps most eloquently. What, he ponders, as a Jew, and after the end of the bloodiest century of two millennia of bloody persecution and pogrom, is he now to make of the notion of Jews as a "chosen people"? Perhaps that there is a way to construct sociopolitical order that is not based upon categorical "identity thinking." Deriving from the "peregrine, powerless condition" in which discriminative labeling placed the

Jew, his "nobility," his "true 'election,'" may be to point the way to nonnationalism: to a postnationalism where human beings aspire "not to torture other human beings, not to make them homeless as he [the Jew] so often was." Steiner concludes,

> Could our true mission be that not of a nation state, as abominable or brave, as corrupt or inventive as any other, but that of guests (be they unwelcome) among men? For only as a guest of each other, as of this small planet, will man escape destruction. (1998, p. 15)

Again, it is not the specific "Jewishness" (or particularity) of this thesis that I am interested in exploring so much as its basal (and possibly general) propositions: being at home in the world through a universal cosmopolitanism in which one belongs not by way of "blood and soil," or any kind of fundamental or fundamentalist autochthony. One belongs on the move, is at home in movement, and resides, by right (institutionalized by just procedures), voluntarily in a progression of sociocultural milieux to which one negotiates an association for a longer or shorter period of time, for more sharply or vaguely focused purposes, by way of more multiplex or simplex contracts. Even should one stay put, one's fixity is legitimated on procedural and not on essentialist bases.

Steiner's thesis of mutual guesting seems to me imbued with estimable sentiments and to offer a utopian image. But can it be more than this? In particular, can it become a viable anthropological project: the inscribing of a blueprint proceeding from transnationalism to postnationalism? After all, the world is hardly lacking in either utopian fantasies or aphoristic fancies,[1] and anthropologists have often in the past fought shy of both political commitment and critique, and with some justification. But then, along with the recent flowering of studies within anthropology concerning nationalism, there has been the "disturbing" development (as Jonathan Spencer describes it [1997, p. 392]) of anthropologists taking a less charitable line than they were wont to on the nationalistic convictions of their informants, however deeply these are held. Nationalism, Spencer suggests, occupies a location of special sensitivity, even in the professional-anthropological consciousness, because of the gravity of the crimes that have been and continue to be committed in its name, and because of the blatantly specious claims to autochthony and authenticity with which it is commonly associated. The reflexivity that has animated anthropology since its literary turn also means that anthropologists are now less willing or able to hide behind assertions of "cultural relativism" when it comes to the question of their own judgments (cf. Rapport, 1998a). Hence, my own effort in semi-utopian ethnographic accounting.[2]

The Jewish Canadian

Newfoundland (comprising the island of Newfoundland and the mainland territory of Labrador) was England's earliest colony, founded in 1497; it became part of Canada in 1949. It retains, however, a reputation for difference and separation, also as Canada's "Have-Not Province." For, with its harsh climate, distance from main markets, history of mercantile exploitation and underdevelopment, and barely viable contemporary economy (based on the collapsing cod-fishery of the Grand Banks and only supplemented by logging, mining, and offshore oil), employment opportunities in Newfoundland have remained highly erratic. The unemployment rate can rise as high as 35 percent and, with employment often being seasonal at best, dependence on investment and welfare initiatives from external sources, primarily the Federal Government in Ottawa, can seem endemic.

The Newfoundland Jewish community, while small, grew to a position of economic security; through retail and wholesale concerns such as clothing and hardware, it came to service the island from a St. John's base (Kahn, 1987).[3] Ninety-eight percent of the population of Newfoundland remain of English and Irish extraction (the native Indians were an early casualty). However, the provincial capital of St. John's, now with a population of 180,000 (out of an island total of some 515,000), has a more multicultural, as well as well-to-do, ambience and there is a sprinkling of more recently arrived ethnicities: Vietnamese, Chinese, Greeks, Eastern Europeans, Cubans, Pakistanis, Filipinos, Italians, and Jews. The first documented Jewish settlers reached Newfoundland in the 1890s, spurred by Eastern European pogroms. The Jewish community grew to its largest size following World War II; since then numbers have dropped, with grown-up children progressing along a common immigrant path and transferring to the more lucrative Canadian mainland (and their parents then retiring near them, or else to Florida or California) (cf. Gold, 1987). By the latter years of the twentieth century, there were only some 20 to 25 Jewish families, and where two synagogues had once flourished it was increasingly difficult to afford the living of a rabbi and the upkeep of one.[4]

Occasionally, nevertheless, grown-up children do stay and work on the island, among whose number is *Israel (Izzy) Horovitz*, now in his mid-twenties and employed as an engineer in the provincial government's Department of Energy, Mines and Resources. Moreover, in recent years these stay-at-homes have been joined by some young Jewish adults from the mainland (mostly unmarried), who have come to complete their education at St. John's' Memorial University, or to teach there, or to gain an apprenticeship in their profession (medicine or law, often) before returning to the more competitive mainland fray. These people may experience Newfoundland as a "third-world country" to which they offer their skills and services (cf. Rapport, 1994a).

· CONCLUSION ·

Among their number may be counted *Mirium Hagentasch* (an occupational therapist, born in Montreal and now in her early thirties), *Nathan Bloom* (a professor of computer science at the university and in his mid-thirties, born in Toronto but resident here a number of years), and *Howard Simons* (a university dropout, now in his late twenties, who has stayed on in Newfoundland, getting by on odd jobs such as house-painting); *Nigel*, the anthropologist from Britain, has also now joined their social set.

What follows is an account, as conversational exchange, of Israel, Mirium, Nathan, Howard, and Nigel considering the nature of their identities as Jews in Canada and in Newfoundland. The exchange takes place one May 8th—Israel Independence Day—in St. John's in the mid-1980s, as I annotated and recall it.[5]

This particular "Israel Night" has seen the Jewish community mostly assembled in the synagogue hall for an evening of formal dining. This was followed by a display of Israeli folk dancing (by a troupe largely composed of the young adult mainlanders), a *hora* danced by everyone, the auctioning of birthday candles and a cake to raise money for the State of Israel and celebrate its rebirth, and finally, one or two short speeches:

> PAUL JACOBS (the President of the Synagogue): Today, as we know, is Israel's thirty-seventh birthday. It is also, of course, VE Day; so there will be celebrations, accompanying ours, in all the major Canadian cities. [applause] I'd like to call on Lionel LaRusic to say a few words.

> LIONEL LARUSIC (a learned and respected member of the community, and Auschwitz survivor): We are the blessed generation; we have seen the rebirth of the State of Israel after some 64 generations of wishing. If the rabbi will excuse me, we have already been witness to part of the Coming of the Messiah! And we all feel safer knowing Israel is there.

When the evening in the synagogue closes, it is 10:15 p.m., and Izzy, Mirium, Nathan, and Nigel decide to go downtown to a bar for a short drink. They decide on the relaxed atmosphere of "Kibitzers"; and there they find their friend Howard, also out for a nightcap:

> ISRAEL: Howard Simons! Fancy you coming out drinking here and not going to the Shul [*synagogue*] for Israel night.

> HOWARD: It's one of those difficult moral decisions: go to the Shul or enjoy yourself! [They laugh]

> MIRIUM: And it's going to be the same on Canada Day when it comes, at Pleasantville: do I watch my friends in a display of Israeli dancing—with about 14 other ethnic groups!—or do I watch a fantastic fireworks display outside the hall!

ISRAEL: It's like who do you fight for if Israel and Canada are at war!?

NATHAN: [laughing] Not quite in the same category of serious moral decisions I wouldn't say, Izzy!

MIRIUM: And not exactly likely, either.

NIGEL: Do you think you could live in Israel again, Izzy?

ISRAEL: Well, I was there for those couple of years as a teenager, but getting a job there now would be the hard part for me.

NIGEL: Couldn't your parents help?

ISRAEL: Not really. I wouldn't have any contacts to go on from my dad; he's never lived there. It was my mom who did.

NATHAN: I'd find living in Israel quite difficult right now. 'Cos some of the government policies seem so abhorrent. Like on the West Bank. It must be a bit like South African apartheid; they annex the area and then call any Jew who's living there "citizen" and any Arab not.

MIRIUM: No, come on. You should see it, Nathan. The West Bank is such a tiny area: and such a big fuss is made about it! It's blown out of all proportion. It's such a small part of the country but it's all anyone ever talks about nowadays. But really, it's a small problem in a small place.

NATHAN: I've driven through it, Mirium. ... And I've also seen how many millions of dollars have been invested there. They're never gonna be able to give it back. All that building and infrastructure: it's not like the Sinai was. So, in that case, what are they gonna do with the Arabs? They can't make them citizens or else in 40 years' time Israel will be dominated by Arabs—with their birth rates. So what are they gonna do with them? At the moment they don't have citizenship rights!

MIRIUM: So what would you do?

NATHAN: I don't know. The Israelis have gotten used to using the river water from the west bank of the Jordan now too.

ISRAEL: They should have gone all the way to Damascus in 1967 when they had the chance, and not stopped. Then there wouldn't be all this trouble with Syria and the PLO today.

NATHAN: [laughs] Yes. That would also have been a solution! Seriously, though, I don't think I could live in Israel right now. I mean Canada is generally such a level-headed kind'a place, by comparison. But in Israel you sort of feel violence bubbling up all the time.

ISRAEL: I wouldn't feel it if I had a good job as a salesman in a hi-tech company, I can tell you!

NIGEL: With your own supply of music and tapes, I know.

ISRAEL: Well, they still don't make hi-fi in Israel, but there are companies making hi-tech medical machinery and computers and I could be a salesman for someone like that. I'd like selling that kind'a stuff—and speaking English would be an advantage because they sell to the English-speaking world. So maybe that would do me. ... But then would I need to do an MBA first? In Toronto, say, or even in Israel? Probably take me two years.

NIGEL: Back to university!

ISRAEL: Yes. I could probably put up with university life for that long. I was pretty fed up with university work, and talking about it all the time, when I was doing Engineering at MUN [Memorial University of Newfoundland], I must admit. But then an MBA's not like an Engineering program or normal life at university. ... But then, two years of university would cost me $100,000, what with costs and what I'd lose not doing my job.

NIGEL: That's not the way to think of it, though.

NATHAN: Did you know the Engineering program here was originally designed by a guy from the U. of T. [University of Toronto], Izzy? I knew him quite well. And it ranks not half badly; it certainly has a good cooperative program.

ISRAEL: Right. It might not be so academic but it has a good name in industry. I was at McGill [University] for a year but that seemed to be all math and physics.

NATHAN: What amazes me here, though, is the lack of feedback in lectures: there are no questions, no correcting mistakes—except for people like David Cohen who would always correct you; and that's great: it shows you that he's following and what he understands. But the rest of them ... you sometimes wonder if they're still alive!

ISRAEL: That's the local mentality: never question unless you're 100 percent sure.

MIRIUM: I blame the denominational schooling for that. They're taught just to accept everything and question nothing.

NATHAN: How long have you been living here now, Mirium, altogether?

MIRIUM: Seven years now.

NATHAN: Wow! You're quite the Newfie! A local.

MIRIUM: No. I'm still a Montrealer. Ask Izzy. And I seem to like the culture less the more I'm here and get to know it, somehow. I don't know. It seems so defensive and against what's outside; and also anti-intellectual.

NATHAN: I was wondering how a bar called "Kibitzers" comes to be here? I mean, it's a Yiddish word. ... And how they come to mispronounce it! "Kibitzers" instead of "Kibitzers."

ISRAEL: I've never really liked coming drinking here, 'cos someone was murdered here, you know [the others look surprised]. Yes [lowering his voice]; someone called Doug Skinner was stabbed. He was working behind the bar. There was a big furore about it at the time. Nobody worked out how exactly it happened—or why even. Or even if they knew each other—'cos he was dead. And there was an awfully big fuss: 'cos there's not a lot of that kind of stuff around here.

NATHAN: I almost got into a fight outside the Peppers last Friday! I was in the line-up at 5 p.m.—why there was a line-up was because it was Happy Hour. It was silly, actually, being there, because there was no line-up outside the Fishing Admiral. Anyway, there were three of us waiting: me, David Cohen, and Fred, and after about 20 minutes we had gotten to be second in line; just one guy ahead of us. Then this drunk wanders over from the other side of the street and stands right by me and starts chatting—to avoid the line. Five minutes later he's still there and I've not said a word: he hasn't gotten me talking. So I pull out my cigarettes, 'cos I know he's sure to ask for one, and he does and I say: "Absolutely not!"

MIRIUM: I like the "absolutely"!

ISRAEL: Oh my! I can see what's coming.

NATHAN: Yes, I said: "Absolutely not! 'Cos you pushed in and didn't wait in line." So he goes off and comes back about five minutes later with a package of smokes, and goes to stand right at the front of the line now, with the first guy, and offers him a cigarette and asks him if "that creep" has gone in yet who wouldn't give him one before. So I said: "No. I'm still here ... And I still don't think you should push in." So the guy says to me: "You're living on borrowed time feller! Watch it." Anyway, I'd had enough by then, so I suggested we all go on over to the Fishing Admiral, which we did!

ISRAEL: That was a narrow escape. You must be crazy, Nath!

NATHAN: But I'm annoyed with myself, now. At the time I was quite pleased. ... But I should have told the bouncer; or looked out for a police car driving past and told them about this drunk bothering me. Of course, if the police had not stopped—then you'd have had to have broken their car windows or something to get them to take you away too! 'Cos you couldn't have been left with the drunk and them gone [all laugh]. I'm gonna be in downtown Halifax for three days soon, you know Howard. What should I see there?

HOWARD: Oh, you should have a great time! The bar scene in Halifax is a bit like here. But it's bigger and more sophisticated.

NATHAN: But before that I'm going to visit a GP buddy of mine in Carbonnear.

ISRAEL: That's quite a jump: Carbonnear to downtown Halifax, my son!

NATHAN: My buddy told me there are three categories of pain he's found in Carbonnear. One: "That's some pain!"; two (worse): "That's a *hard* pain!"; and three: "Oh my son! *That's* a pain!" [they laugh].

ISRAEL: [As the barmaid comes to clear their table of empty glasses and bottles] Anybody for another?

MIRIUM: Izzy! I'm disgusted at the rate you down a beer these days! You weren't doing that a year ago.

NIGEL: It's only "Miller Lite," though. That's just bubbles and water.

ISRAEL: [Speaking in Hebrew, since the barmaid is still present] What about those legs in that dress then? They go right the way up!

MIRIUM: [In simulated shock] Izzy!

NATHAN: Just ignore him! Thanks Miss. ... Then after Halifax, my next trip, in the summer, is to the States; I have some research to do in New York and LA, interviewing employees of some large corporations and comparing their use of computers, and how they're affected by different management structures. Then, finally, back to Toronto to see my mum, and how her cancer's doing

What I should like to point up, in reflecting on this account, is the transience of local identifications to which its participants serially play host: an ambiguity that I should like to describe as cosmopolitan. The most obvious of these is the celebration of "Israel Night" many thousand miles away by a Jewish congregation in Newfoundland, a congregation made up of people born in Newfoundland itself, in mainland North America, in Europe, and in South Africa. They can all, it is announced after dinner, feel safer in Canada due to Israel's existence. At the same time, however, it is suggested that their recollection of Israel's birthday is mediated by that of celebrations they know to be taking place simultaneously all across Canada, in memory of victory against Nazism in World War II. Then again, the Jewish community that meets in a Newfoundland synagogue is one that has been significantly swelled by a number of young mainlanders who bring with them a sense that "Judaism's something you gotta work at, not just something you're born into and that's it," as Rachel Fernstein put it. While it is they, moreover, who now lend their energy to much of the public Jewish celebration in St. John's, enlivening it with Jewish theater and Israeli folkdance, even representing "Newfoundland's Israeli Canadians" in the July 1st Canada Day "Folk-Life Festival," their dance instructor and the guiding light of their troupe is a non-Jewish Folklore student from Vancouver: "So it's not just ethnicity, any more," according to Rachel Fernstein.

Moving to the downtown bar, questions of relational loyalties and moral responsibility loom large in the discussion. Should one go out by oneself to the pub on the night like this without first joining the community at the Shul? Should one watch a display of Israeli dancing by one's peers if it means missing the sumptuous Canada Day fireworks display? How, in general, should Israel and Canada rank in one's affections? These then form part of a larger array of questions concerning where in the world one should like to live, work, visit, and study. Mainland Canada, the USA, Newfoundland, and Israel—each has its pull, and all speakers can claim personal or familial histories of global travel: all maintain contacts, relations, and research contracts elsewhere. Also prominent in their deliberations is the notion of citizenship and what it should entail. In this regard, Canada seems to exemplify more equality and individual security than other places—Israel included, where violence is always just below the surface. But then, are other places so very different after all? Even Newfoundland, it seems, with its reputation for peaceableness, has its high profile murders and its everyday street fights.

Furthermore, the parochial culture of Newfoundland, at that time replete with religious schooling and cult of obedience, leaves much to be desired when contrasted with the mainland. But then Izzy can claim to be a Newfie, born and bred, at least in comparison to the others, while Nathan regards Mirium, with her seven years' residency, as quite localized herself and can boast having partaken in Newfoundland life himself for far longer than Howard or Nigel. For Mirium, notwithstanding, years of local residency do not translate into local identity; the longer she stays, in fact, the more alienated she feels, and she resents the assimilation to local mores that she sees Izzy's penchant for beer as evincing. Izzy, meanwhile, distances himself from local relations by speaking Hebrew before and about a comely waitress, while Nathan smoothes over this impoliteness only to wonder himself at the importation and mispronunciation of a Yiddish word for a local bar and to find humor in rustic idioms for expressing pain. Finally, Nathan engages all in a discussion that links together living in St. John's with experiencing the bar scene in Halifax, Nova Scotia, with researching computing culture in the United States, and with visiting family in Toronto.

The fluidities and uncertainties of the above discussion seem to reflect the more general uncertainties and fluidities of living in the "Have-Not Province" of Canada: where the relatively recent decision to join the mainland nation-state (1949) is still a matter of regular debate—the "Be-Not Province"?—and where, indeed, the continued existence of the nation-state *per se* is the most regular issue of mainland political discourse (cf. Paine, 1999). Discursively to "reflect" fluidities and uncertainties, moreover, is to recreate and realize them; through their conversational exchange, Nathan, Izzy, Mirium, Howard, and Nigel maintain their ambiguous relations with such entities as Newfoundland and Canada, and the latter's ambiguous statuses and relations with one another.

Mutual guests to one another's conversational repartee, Izzy, Mirium, Nathan, Howard, and Nigel also belong to a series of local-cum-global identities. In a Yiddish-sounding bar, on Israel Independence Day, in a provincial city, lying within the ambit of global economic, educational, and moral markets, they partake in local verbal relations (based on the routine exchange of formulaic phrases concerning clichéd topics of debate) by which global transience is mediated. Ambiguities of identity such as these discursively pave the way, I suggest, to a possible postnationalist cosmopolitanism.

Discussion: Cosmopolitanism, Postnationalism, and Indigeneity Reconsidered

There is an apparent blindspot or contradiction at the center of this chapter that needs to be addressed. I have wanted to examine what the formulaic idiom of "the wandering Jew" might expose of actual multiculturalism, transnationalism, and cosmopolitanism in the contemporary world, and also might suggest of possible prescriptions for viable postnationalism. The idiom, I claimed, might accord with little in the lives of Jews as individuals. In the course of the chapter, however, it is precisely Jews who have come to be drafted in as instantiations of a thesis concerning "Jews" as potential postnationalists. What kind of proof is this? What purchase on a broad theory of global postnationalism is afforded by exemplification that pertains to the world's archetypal cosmopolites? Furthermore, however transnational the Jewish respondents in the chapter might be said to be, they are far from postnationalist. Their talk is peppered with chauvinistic sentiments and essentialisms of nationalistic hue concerning "Canada," "Israel," "Newfies," and "Arabs"; their identities are steeped in "othering" classifications and are far from being either individual in themselves or genuinely hospitable to others. Finally, the transnationalism of these respondents, such as it is, is founded upon an affluence and a security that allows them to travel and to pontificate, to consider migrations and to weigh options, in ways in which their local Newfoundland neighbors, never mind the poor of the West Bank, cannot.

To counter this reading, I would reiterate the distinction between Jews and "the wandering Jew." Jews no longer hold a monopoly on travel or cosmopolitan instincts, if they ever did.[6] The notion of an archetypal Jewish "wanderer" and cosmopolite must now share ethnographic space with traveling Greeks (Moskos, 1989) and Palestinians (Gonzalez, 1992), not to mention ballet dancers (Wulff, 1998) and financial consultants (Amit-Talai, 1998), and with "cosmopolitan" Jamaicans (Wardle, 2000) and Pakistanis (Werbner, 1999). Second, it is not just the affluent who travel; it would be reductive to claim that transnationalism is an index of affluence when labor migrants often include the poorest sections of humanity (Lloyd, 1979), and when the Irish peasantry made such a success of it—whether or not in Newfoundland (Mannion, 1977).

Third, to focus upon the seeming archetype—the Jew as typical cosmopolite—is to reveal the distance between essentialist classifications and the actual content of social life. Discourse has its effect in constructing the formal lineaments of a social milieu—and stereotypical oppositions and exaggerations may play important roles in shoring these constructions up (Rapport, 1995)—but life is lived in that ambiguous space that lies between form and meaning (Rapport, 1994b). Within the formal class of "Jews" are individual Jews who are more different than alike. It is not with particular automaticity or regularity or necessity, I would say then, that Izzy, Mirium, Nathan, Howard, and Nigel find themselves together in one another's company in St. John's. Their Jewishness does not make them obvious or natural or especially casual talking-partners, and in their "Jewishness," in their feelings for Israel, in their experience of non-Jewishness, in all the things that formally signal their categorical likeness, their individuality surpasses their commonality (Rapport, 1994a). The experience of social life is a tense juggling with the distances between category and selfhood, between the formal discourses of social exchange and their animation by particular, personal, momentary circumstance.

This brings us to the wider themes of the volume as a whole. We were to debate the seeming antimony between "cosmopolite" and "indigene," editor Max Forte urged: was it not the case that in practice contemporary lives were "glocal" phenomena (Beck, 2002, p. 17), where the cosmopolitan and the indigenous were not polarities so much as mutually implicating and combined principles? If Jews were not intrinsically cosmopolitan, then neither were natives necessarily localized. "Actually existing cosmopolitanism" (Robbins, 1998) was varied, plural, and polythetic: actually existing indigeneity could be expected to be likewise.

This thesis has been explored—and vindicated—along four main avenues in the volume. The first avenue is the process by which *indigeneity, as an identity, is practiced by way of translocal pathways*: the routes to being and remaining "native" are often extralocal ones. Here, then, are the Caribs of Arima, Trinidad, engaging in wider Caribbean and North American networks of indigenous peoples as part of continuing work of being Carib (Forte). Here, too, are the Aboriginal populations of Canada (Proulx) whose movement between reservation and city is part of the increasing viability of being Native American. And here are Canadian Inuit who "migrate" between the "North" and urban milieu such as Ottawa as part of an ongoing process of struggle for the right to remain different (Patrick and Tomiak).

The volume's second main avenue of exploration has been how *an articulation with global and capitalist forces might be managed on a long-term basis for the continuing effecting of viable indigenous identities*. Here, then, are Alaskan Alutiiq on Kodiak Island, historically caught between Russian and American power blocs but using their global positionality to strengthen the work of communal heritage and ancestral power (Mason). Here again are Canadian Aboriginals using their urban experiences to connect their reservations to international business concerns that afford the traditions of reservation life an economic lifeline (Proulx). And here, too, is the ongoing process of Carib "transculturation" whereby being party to an international traffic in the symbols of indigeneity has long been basic to an identity on Trinidad (Forte).

A third key avenue in the volume has *been the fluidity and flexibility with which "indigeneity" becomes part of the presentation of self-identity*. Producing a pan-Indian identity for consumption at international tourist sites becomes a currency by which Native North Americans can negotiate inclusion and differentiation in a global marketplace on their own terms (Scarangella). In particular, the construction of Inuitness in urban Canada is a site for contesting representation and categorization and asserting the right to determine discursive positioning (Patrick and Tomiak). And again, "the Alto Balsas," an indigenous region in Mexico, a group, and a way of life, enjoys multiple significations depending on whether it becomes a token of exchange within the world of arts and crafts, the politics of native resistance, or the globalized labor market (Schryer).

Fourth, the volume has explored the way in which *indigeneity, while seeming to point up an ethnic particularity, might also come to encompass a form of global creolization*. Here, then, are Indian identities in San Francisco that range between California and the Western hemisphere in their territorial groundings; they are at once urban and global, and they effect a cosmopolitan Indianness that adverts to a shared humanity (DeLugan). Here, too, is the meeting of "the Indian" and "the tourist" in a reciprocal exchange: appropriating Buffalo Bill and the Wild West, Native North Americans are empowered to control an identity that is their own (Scarangella). And here is Kwagiutl artist David Neel whose personal artistic vision comes to embody a cosmopolitan sensibility: a conception of universal fraternity that transcends all particular, ethnic, national, and religious identities (Butler-Palmer).

Carolyn Butler-Palmer's work, her emphasis on the personal artistry of achieving an individual identity on a global stage that supersedes belonging in any one cultural community, brings me back to my own ethnography. What of the seeming communitarian exclusivities that bring Izzy, Mirium, Nathan, Howard, and Nigel together on "Israel Night," first in the St. John's synagogue hall and then in Kibitzers? Confident in their joint Jewish identities, they openly assert an exclusiveness and consider an essential "Jewishness" in relation to Newfoundland, Canada, Israel, and the United States without embarrassment or fear of censure. What it is important to say about this, I believe, is that in prescribing postnationalism (as I have) one need not imagine the absolute overcoming of localism or even chauvinism so much as their *ironization*. Absolute notions of identity are made contingent by their being contextualized alongside others: one of a number of identities that contest for space in the same place; one of a number of identities to which the same individuals contract a belonging. And while it might be objected that there is nothing particularly "post" in this characterization, that nationalist feeling and affiliation has always been accompanied in the everyday with skepticism, irony and self-mockery, and, outside situations of crisis and emergency, been qualified by contradictory associations at the level of region, community, family, and so on, the label "postnationalism" nonetheless privileges a new kind of possible legitimacy—a new kind of indigeneity—and formally labels a kind of accruing of identity. When moving serially (and artfully) between a number of absolute and chauvinistic identities, and between such identities and nonabsolutist ones, absolutism can but be lived ironically; for, one is at home in one's "own" place only to the extent that others are at the same time at home in theirs—and these "places" occupy the same space.[7]

Toward this end I find the above juggling of absolutisms, of Canadian and Israeli, Newfoundland and mainland community identities, by my informants a positive step. For the possibility and experience of one absolutism is never absent from the moment of entertaining another; with the result that no absolutism is absolutely itself and each is relativized by the others. *The individual who becomes ironic about his own contrastive chauvinisms may allow himself to entertain them only to the extent that he allows others to do so too.*

What is to be looked forward to, anthropologically prescribed, is a formalization of those (postnationalistic) procedures whereby an ironization of absolute identity and rights, and the mutual right to a contractualization of guesthood, is constitutionally ensured (cf. Rapport, 2006). And much in the present volume, concerning pan-Indianism or pan-Aboriginality, gives ground for hope. Here is the cosmopolitanism, the new intercultural dynamics, of "transcending while including local and tribal expressions" (Scarangella) by way of "mature reasoning" (Mason). Here are self-classified indigenous subjects who would challenge "narrow conceptions" of homeland and belonging (DeLugan), of narrow identifications with "language, occupation, or location" (Schryer), as they aspire to a global communality of "peaceful interpersonal connection" (Butler-Palmer). *Indigenous cosmopolitans* juxtapose "feelings of loyalty and commitment to particular cultures against openness toward difference and otherness" (Proulx): they move beyond their origins to "re-root global cultural elements" (Forte).

A final irony is that there is much in the ironic prescription that it might be contended (in echoes of Kundera) that it overlaps with descriptions of the State of Israel as it already exists. In his equanimous account of what he calls this "composite" nation, then, Emanuel Marx (1980) determines to put across the inequivalencies between "nation," "state," and "society" in "Israel," and the contingencies and fluidities of these terms' provenances. "Israel," Marx explains, may be portrayed as a series of partially overlapping social aggregates, widely different from one another, which function as more or less open systems whose boundaries vary as per situation. The "state" amounts to a number of contesting organizations (institutions, personnel, and aims) which make it far from monolithic. "Nation" is tantamount neither to "Israel" nor the "state" and must be conceived of as a plural entity that has no confining geographical boundaries. "Society," lastly, is a multidimensional system whose subunits, again, are far from clearly bounded in territorial terms, and which depends on a number of generally accepted premises and ideologies to persist. More poetically put by the novelist Amos Oz (1992), Israel is not *a* country or *a* nation and no "representative picture" or "typical cross-section" can be drawn from it. Rather it is a fiery collection of arguments; a screaming assembly of some five million prophets and prime ministers, all bent on surpassing categorization, overcoming institutional encompassment, and escaping (earthly) absolutist systems (cf. Rapport, 1998b, p. 81).

For some, the above description of Israel will have likely lodged this chapter firmly in the realm of utopian imaginings, of make-believe. For those with only a passing knowledge, the endemic internal questioning of how to deal with the continuing threat to their physical survival that constitutes the most routine discourse shared by community members of the State of Israel is obscured by the external impact of an efficient Israeli Defence Force. Even for those with a sympathy for the place, such as George Steiner, conceiving of the "Jewish" mission in terms of mutual guesting calls into question "the very meaning of Israel, a meaning far less universal than is that of Judaism" (1998, p. 15).

But then an idea of Israeli nationalism as oxymoronic—a nation of guests not hosts, whose ultimate mission is the perpetration of postnationalism—adds another layer of paradox to Kundera's depiction of Israel as European civilization's "true heart." As Sartre concluded (1974, p. 225), the founding of the State of Israel might be described as "one of the most important events of our times, one of the few these days which let us keep on hoping," not only or primarily as a global refuge from anti-Semitism, but as a rebuke to those who would invoke "blood and soil" to affirm identity. Israel points paradoxically toward a postnationalism where mutual guests eschew essential-mystical links to the territories they call home.

Notes

1. Gandhi, for example, prescribed ethno-religious peace in India on the basis of Hindus bringing up Moslem children to be orthodox Moslems, and vice versa.
2. Cf. Amit and Rapport (2002) for a more detailed development of the anthropological utopianism broached here.
3. The Hebrew Congregation of Newfoundland was officially founded in 1909. By 1921 the congregation totaled 14 families, and by 1934, 37. The first synagogue was built at St. John's in 1931. Following World War II, and an influx of Allied servicemen as well as European refugees, a second synagogue was opened at the second city of Corner Brook.
4. My writing on the Jewish community refers to the period of my fieldwork in the 1980s and the still-pertinent analytical insights to be drawn from this. For more data on the more recent history of the community, see McGrath, 2006.
5. My ethnography was undertaken as part of a project to trace the network of links pertaining to the ways in which individuals in different urban settings conversed about "violence" (Rapport, 1987). "Violence" was a node of communication, a catchword, around which conversation was regularly and conveniently deployed. "Talking violence"—the violence of armed robberies, say, violence around drugs, in bars, against women, of the police, between nations, and in possible nuclear war—made transient (potentially unsafe) conversational exchanges seem expectable, routine, secure.

6. Vered Amit is of the opinion that Jews have never truly fit the characterization "cosmopolitan" (personal communication, June 12, 2000). In feudal regimes they stood variously beyond the normal and normative range of statuses in that they dealt in capital and were not tied to the land in what were largely localized societies. But their dispersed family networks and their physical movements across these were maintained by strict habits of endogamy and narrow impulses toward ethnic closure. In nineteenth-century shtetl society, even their movements were restricted; while in twentieth-century, Euro-American milieux connection with the State of Israel amounts to a form of deterritorialized nationalism. What cosmopolitan openness Jews have demonstrated, Amit concludes, correlates with assimilationist tendencies that translate into an attenuation of Jewishness as such.

7. Auge makes a similar point when imaging the surpassing of placedness by the nonplace (1995). It is not that traditional notions of fixity, of certain social relations and cultural routines having absolute rights to certain places, are banished so much as the normative singularity of placedness is exploded. Henceforward the possibility and experience of nonplace is never absent from any place, so that no place is completely itself and separate and no place is completely other. Place and nonplace represent contrastive modalities, the latter always being available for the salutary ironization of the former.

References

Amit-Talai, V. (1998). Risky Hiatuses and the Limits of Social Imagination: Expatriacy in the Cayman Islands. In Nigel Rapport & Andrew Dawson (Eds.), *Migrants of Identity* (pp. 39–59). Oxford: Berg.

Amit, V. & N. Rapport. (2002). *The Trouble with Community: Anthropological Reflections on Movement, Identity and Collectivity.* London: Pluto.

Arendt, H. (1962). *Origins of Totalitarianism.* London: Allen & Unwin.

Auge, M. (1995). *Non-places.* London: Verso.

Bauman, Z. (1989). *Modernity and the Holocaust.* Ithaca, NY: Cornell University Press.

Beck, U. (2002). The Cosmopolitan Society and Its Enemies. *Theory, Culture & Society*, 19(1–2), 17–44.

Bermant, C. (1998). *Genesis.* London: Robson.

Forte, M. (2005). *Ruins of Absence, Presence of Caribs: (Post)colonial Representations of Aboriginality in Trinidad and Tobago.* Gainesville: University Press of Florida.

Gellner, E. (1983). *Nations and Nationalism.* Oxford: Blackwell.

———. (1993). *Postmodernism, Reason and Religion.* London: Routledge.

———. (1995). Anything Goes: The Carnival of Cheap Relativism which Threatens to Swamp the Coming *Fin de millenaire. Times Literary Supplement*, (4811), 6–8.

Gold, G. (1987). A Tale of Two Communities: The Growth and Decline of Small-town Jewish Communities in Northern Ontario and Southwestern Louisiana. In M. Rischin (Ed.), *The Jews of North America* (pp. 205–221). Detroit, MI: Wayne State University Press.

Gonzalez, N. (1992). *Dollar, Dove and Eagle.* Ann Arbor: University of Michigan Press.

Graburn, N. (Ed.). (1988). Anthropological Research on Contemporary Tourism, *Kroeber Anthropological Society Papers* (Special Issue), 67–68.

Kahn, A. (1987). *Listen While I Tell You.* St. John's, NL: ISER Press, Memorial University.

Kundera, M. (1990). *The Art of the Novel.* London: Faber.

Lenin, V. I. (1974). *Lenin on the Jewish Question*. New York: International.

Lloyd, P. (1979). *Slums of Hope*. Manchester, UK: Manchester University Press.

Mannion, F. (Ed.). (1977). *The Peopling of Newfoundland*. St. John's, NL: ISER Press, Memorial University.

Marcus, G. & M. Fischer. (1986). *Anthropology as Cultural Critique*. Chicago: University of Chicago Press.

Marx, E. (1980). On the Anthropological Study of Nations. In E. Marx (Ed.), *A Composite Portrait of Israel* (pp. 15-28). London: Academic.

McGrath, R. (2006). *Saltfish and Schmattehs*. St. John's, NL: Creative.

Moskos, C. (1989). *Greek Americans*. New Brunswick, NJ: Transaction.

Oz, A. (1992). Israeli Literature. "The Raymond Williams Lecture," Hay-on-Wye Festival of Literature, May 31.

Paine, R. (1999). Aboriginality, Multiculturalism, and Liberal Rights Philosophy. *Ethnos*, 64(3), 325-349.

Rapport, N. J. (1987). *Talking Violence: An Anthropological Interpretation of Conversation in the City*. St. John's, NL: ISER Press, Memorial University.

———. (1994a). Trauma and Ego-syntonic Response: The Holocaust and the "Newfoundland Young Yids," 1985. In S. Heald & A. Duluz (Eds.), *Anthropology and Psychoanalysis* (pp. 70-95). London: Routledge.

———. (1994b). "Busted for Hash": Common Catchwords and Individual Identities in a Canadian City. In V. Amit-Talai & H. Lustiger-Thaler (Eds.), *Urban Lives* (pp. 129-157). Toronto, ON: McClelland & Stewart

———. (1995). Migrant Selves and Stereotypes: Personal Context in a Postmodern world. In S. Pile & N. Thrift (Eds.), *Mapping the Subject* (pp. 267-282). London: Routledge.

———. (1998a). The Potential of Human Rights in a Post-cultural World. *Social Anthropology*, 6(3), 381-388.

———. (1998b). Coming Home to a Dream: A Study of the Immigrant Discourse of "Anglo-Saxons" in Israel. In Nigel Rapport & Andrew Dawson (Eds.), *Migrants of Identity: Perceptions of Home in a World of Movement* (pp. 61-83). Oxford: Berg.

———. (2006). Diaspora, Cosmopolis, Global Refuge: Three Voices of the Supranational City. In S. Coleman & P. Collins (Eds.), *Locating the Field* (pp. 179-191). Oxford: Berghahn.

Robertson, R. (1990). Mapping the Global Condition: Globalization as the Central Concept. *Theory, Culture & Society*, 7(2-3), 15-30.

Robbins, B. (1998). Actually Existing Cosmopolitanism. In P. Cheah & B. Robbins (Eds.). *Cosmopolitics* (pp. 1-19). Minneapolis: University of Minnesota Press.

Sartre, J-P. (1974). *The Writings of Jean-Paul Sartre*. Evanston, IL: Northwestern University Press.

Smith, V. (1989). Introduction. In Valene Smith (Ed.), *Hosts and Guests* (pp. 1-17). Philadelphia: University of Pennsylvania Press.

Spencer, J. (1997). Nationalism. In A. Barnard & J. Spencer (Eds.), *The Encyclopaedic Dictionary of Social and Cultural Anthropology* (pp. 391-3). London: Routledge.

Steiner, G. (1998). War, Terrorism and Chaos: God's Idea of Keeping a Promise. *The Observer Review*, February 22, 15.

Wallerstein, I. (1984). *The Politics of the World Economy*. Cambridge, UK: Cambridge University Press.

Wardle, H. (2000). *An Ethnography of Cosmopolitanism in Kingston, Jamaica*. Lampeter, UK: Mellen.

Weinberg, R. (1998). *Stalin's Forgotten Zion*. Berkeley: University of California Press.

Werbner, P. (1996). "Our Blood Is Green": Cricket, Identity and Social Empowerment among British Pakistanis. In J. MacClancy (Ed.), *Sport, Identity and Ethnicity* (pp. 87–111). Oxford: Berg.

——. (1999). Global Pathways: Working-class Cosmopolitans and the Creation of Transnational Ethnic Worlds. *Social Anthropology*, 7(1), 17–35.

Wulff, H. (1998). *Ballet across Borders*. Oxford: Berg.

Contributors

Carolyn Butler-Palmer currently occupies the Legacy Chair in Modern and Contemporary Arts of the Pacific Northwest in the History in Art Department at the University of Victoria, Canada. She is interested in the aesthetic relations between various Pacific Northwest people and their cross-cultural reception. Her program of research includes questions about the politics of aesthetics, modernity, mobility, identity, and humanitarianism with respect to the arts and material cultures of Alaska, British Columbia, Washington, and Oregon. She is currently working on a book *Cosmographic Cosmopolitanism: The Life and Aesthetics of David Neel* that locates Neel's aesthetic praxis within debates about mobility, identity, and the ethics of cross-cultural relations. Professor Butler-Palmer has recently held fellowships at The Georgia O'Keeffe Museum Research Center and a University of Pittsburgh Mellon Fellowship.

Robin Maria DeLugan is Assistant Professor of Anthropology at the new University of California, Merced. Among her research interests is the historical and contemporary relations between Indigenous peoples and the nation-state with particular attention to the Americas. In El Salvador she is examining how post-civil war representations of national culture and identity bring the issue of indigeneity to the forefront to challenge ideologies of mestizaje and efforts to erase contemporary Indigenous peoples from national society. Other ongoing research examines how the increased migration of Indigenous people from Latin America to the United States motivates states to forge transnational ties with faraway Indigenous citizens. In Northern California, she is examining how new migrations increase hemispheric connections between Indigenous people of the Americas, build new ethnic communities, and transform collective identity.

Maximilian C. Forte is an associate professor and anthropologist in the Department of Sociology and Anthropology at Concordia University in Montreal, Canada. His primary area of ethnographic research has focused on the contemporary indigenous peoples of the Caribbean, and specifically the Carib Community in Arima, Trinidad and Tobago. In relation to these areas,

Maximilian published *Ruins of Absence, Presence of Caribs: (Post)Colonial Constructions of Aboriginality in Trinidad and Tobago* (University Press of Florida, 2005), and he edited the volume *Indigenous Resurgence in the Contemporary Caribbean: Amerindian Survival and Revival* (Peter Lang, 2006). Maximilian has also published his research in *Indigenous World, Indigenous Affairs,* and *Cultural Survival Quarterly*. For 10 years he served as the managing editor for an open access, peer-reviewed journal that he founded, *KACIKE: The Journal of Caribbean Amerindian History & Anthropology,* as well as a Web editor for the online database he constructed, the *Caribbean Amerindian Centrelink*. His involvement in supporting indigenous Caribbean transnationalism extended to the creation of the online Indigenous Caribbean Network. Maximilian's research for this chapter and related projects was supported by a Standard Research Grant from the Social Sciences and Humanities Research Council of Canada (SSHRC), from 2006 to 2009.

Arthur Mason is an anthropologist and assistant professor at Arizona State University and was the 2006-2007 Canada-U.S. Fulbright Scholar at the University of Calgary. Between 2001 and 2003, he served as Associate Director of Energy in the Office of the Alaska Governor. From 1992 to 1993, he served as curator of the Alutiiq Native Cultural Center on Kodiak Island. Arthur's research is concerned with Alaska's political and indigenous elite who possess the administrative positions, personal qualities, and utopian vision required for modernizing Alaskan society. In particular, he is interested in the practical aspects of how Alaska leaders aim to translate Alaskan society into the object of their image of the modern, including their increased reliance on the specialized knowledge of non-Alaskan expertise.

Donna Patrick is an associate professor in the School of Canadian Studies and the Department of Sociology and Anthropology at Carleton University in Ottawa, Canada, where she is the Graduate Supervisor in Canadian Studies. Her current research focuses on urban Aboriginal communities, particularly Inuit; indigeneity and language endangerment; the political, social, and cultural aspects of language use, mainly Inuit and Aboriginal. Her research in Northern Quebec is published in a book titled *Politics and Social Interaction in an Inuit Community* (2003) and *Language Rights and Language Survival* (2004) (coedited with Jane Freeland), as well as a number of papers on language endangerment and language rights in indigenous communities. Donna teaches courses in Aboriginal and Northern Issues with an interdisciplinary focus on historical, geographical, and social processes concerning language, culture, and nationhood; minority languages and multilingualism; language rights and policy; language, identity, and political economy and other areas in the sociology of language and sociolinguistics.

Craig Proulx is an associate professor in anthropology at St. Thomas University in Fredericton, Canada, where he is also the Chair of the Department. Craig is interested in Aboriginal experiences in cities along a variety of lines from restorative justice to community building to constructions of identity and processes of cultural production within North American cities. The anthropology of sport is a new area that he is exploring. He has published *Reclaiming Aboriginal Justice Community and Identity* (2003) and, along with coeditor Heather Howard Bobiwash, he edited *Aboriginal Experiences in Canadian Cities*, published in 2007. Craig is also an active member on the executive committee of the Canadian Anthropology Society (CASCA).

Nigel Rapport is a social anthropologist at the University of St. Andrews, Scotland, where he directs the program on cosmopolitanism and was appointed Professor of Anthropological and Philosophical Studies in 1996. He previously held the Canada Research Chair in Globalization, Citizenship and Justice at Concordia University, Montreal, where he was the founding director of the Centre for Cosmopolitan Studies. Nigel has been elected a Fellow of the Royal Society of Edinburgh. He has undertaken four pieces of participant-observation fieldwork: among farmers and tourists in a rural English village (1980-1981); among the transient population of a Newfoundland city and suburb (1984-1985); among new immigrants in an Israeli development-town (1988-1989); and among health-care professionals and patients in a Scottish hospital (2000-2001). His research interests include social theory, phenomenology, identity and individuality, community, conversation analysis, and links between anthropology and literature and philosophy. His recent books include *The Trouble with Community: Anthropological Reflections on Movement, Identity and Collectivity* (Pluto, 2002); *"I Am Dynamite": An Alternative Anthropology of Power* (Routledge, 2003); and (as editor) *Democracy, Science and the Open Society: A European Legacy?* (Transaction, 2006).

Linda Scarangella is an anthropologist and Postdoctoral Fellow at Carleton University's Institute for the Comparative Study of Language, Art and Culture (ICSLAC), in Ottawa, Canada. Linda Scarangella earned her PhD in Anthropology from McMaster University in June 2008. Her dissertation, "Spectacular Native Performances: From the Wild West to the Tourist Site, Nineteenth c. to the Present," focuses on Native North American perspectives and experiences in both historic and contemporary Wild West shows and exhibitions. A short article in *Anthropology News* (May, 2005) considers the challenges of multisited fieldwork in conducting this research. She also published an article in the 2004 issue of *Nexus* that considers the ethical issues surrounding research on Indigenous knowledge. Based on ethnographic work conducted in 2001, her article in *Anthropology in Action* (2004) examines how Salish performers create a space in tourism for the witnessing of First Nation claims of history, culture, and identity by reclaiming discourses of "the Native" through performances of place, ancestry, and cultural continuity. Dr. Scarangella's research and teaching interests include First Nations of Canada, identity and indigeneity, representation, performance and visual culture, anthropology of tourism, globalization and popular culture, narrative and oral history, ethnohistory and ethnographic research methods, and ethics.

Frans J. Schryer was Chair of the Department of Sociology and Anthropology of the University Of Guelph, Canada, at the time of writing. He has taught at Guelph since 1974, and he has held part-time teaching posts at Atkinson College (York University) and at the Centre for Rural Development Studies of the Colegio de Postgraduados at Chapingo (Mexico). He also spent four months in 1988 as a visiting researcher at the Centre for Research and Documentation on Latin America (CEDLA) in Amsterdam, the Netherlands, and was a postdoctoral fellow at the Centre for Agrarian Studies at Yale University in 1994-1995. Frans has done most of his ethnographic and historical research in Mexico, but has also carried out a study of postwar Dutch immigrants in Ontario. He is currently examining the impact of globalization on the Nahuas of the Alto Balsas region (Mexico), a group best known for its craft production (especially paintings on bark paper known as amates) and a successful struggle to stop the construction of a hydroelectric dam (in the 1990s). His recent publications include *Farming in a Global Economy* (Brill, 2006) and "Multiple Hierarchies and the Duplex Nature of Groups" (JRAI, 2001).

Julie-Ann Tomiak is a doctoral student in Canadian Studies with a specialization in Political Economy, at Carleton University in Ottawa, Canada. Her research interests include the political economy of urban Aboriginal service organizations, transnational First Nations, Métis, and Inuit positionalities, identities, and communities, and the application of intersectionality as an analytical framework.

Index

• A •

Adonis, Cristo, 9, 20, 31-33
agency, 4, 8, 179, 181-184
Alaska Native Claims Settlement Act, 1971 (ANCSA), 79, 83, 91
Alexis First Nation (Alberta), 171
Algonquin (Canada), 131
Alutiiq (Kodiak Island, Alaska), 10, 77-80, 83-92, 94n1
amate, 108, 111, 111fig.6.2, 112-113, 117, 123n16, 123nn18-19
  The Amate Tradition: Innovation and Dissent in Mexican Art (Amith), 113
amateros, 113, 121
anthropology, xiv, 1-7, 12-13, 18-19, 21, 27, 31, 33-34, 34n3, 35n5, 58, 65-66, 77, 90, 92-94, 98, 100-102, 107-109, 113-114, 119, 121, 123n17, 127, 155, 157, 191, 193, 195, 205, 206n2
Appadurai, Arjun 21, 140
Appiah, Kwame Anthony, 8, 9, 12, 31, 41, 57, 64-65, 67, 128-130, 154
  Cosmopolitanism: Ethics in a World of Strangers, 64
appropriation of native culture, 169-170
Asociación Mayab, 149
Assembly of First Nations (Canada), 28fig 2.1, 29
Assembly of Manitoba Chiefs, 29
assimilation into mainstream society, 148, 177, 201, 207n6
Australia, 9, 44-45, 47
authenticity, 9, 40, 42-43, 93, 133, 138, 165-168, 170-171, 173, 186n9, 193

Aztec, 11

• B •

banal or everyday cosmopolitanisms, 6, 7, 33, 128-129, 175
banal nationalism, 129
Barthes, Roland (1912-1980), 67-68
Beatboard, 57
beatboxer, 41
Beck, Ulrich, 3-4.7,13,41,47,156,175-177, 203
beneficient morality and sociality, 147, 152, 157
Bhabha, Homi, 6, 129, 154
Bharath, Ricardo, 9, 20, 27, 28fig2.1, 31, 34
Black Atlantic, The (Gilroy), 152
Blood Nation (Alberta), 173
Bloom, Nathan, 195-201
Boas, Franz (1858-1942), 65
bombas, 149
Bomberry, Victoria, 152-153
Brass, Ferlyn, 167-173, 175
breaking, 11
Bresson, Henri Cartier (1908-2004), 66-68, 72. *See also* concerned photography
Bruised Head, Tim, 173
Buddhism, 63, 70-73
  Four Sacred Directions (Buddhism), 63-64, 71-73
Buffalo Bill, 178
Buffalo Bill Days (BBD), 163, 178-181, 183-185
Buffalo Bill's Wild West Show (BBWW), 163-169, 171
burghers, 80, 85-89, 94n2, 94n4

Alutiiq burgher, 86
Creole families
Creole burgher, 86-88
Russian-Native Creole families, 10, 80-81, 83

• C •

California, 1, 31-32, 116, 145, 147, 14-150, 156, 158n3, 158n8, 194, 204
Campo, Suzan, 28fig2.1
Canada, 3
    Alberta, 66-67, 171, 173, 179, 186n13
    British Columbia, 28, 66, 68-69
        Vancouver, 46-49, 57, 65-66, 200
        Victoria, 57
    hip hop, 9, 39-61
    indigenous groups, 22, 27, 43, 121, 151, 164
    Inuit (Ottawa), 11, 127-144, 203
    Jews (Newfoundland), 14, 189-209
    Manitoba, 29
    Neel, David, 63-76
    Newfoundland, 14, 189-209
    Ottawa, 29, 194
        Inuit, 11, 127-140, 203
    Pacific Northwest, 43, 65, 69, 72
    Saskatchewan
        Federation of Saskatchewan Indian Nations, 27
        First Nations Universtiy, 28
        Key First Nation, 167
    Toronto, xiv, 30-31, 195, 197, 199, 201
Canadian Floor Masters, 54-55
Capa, Robert (1913-1954), 64, 67-68, 72
    see also concerned photography
Carib (Caribbean), 9, 11, 20-22, 25, 28-30, 33
Caribbean Organization of Indigenous Peoples (COIP), 22, 27
Carib, 9, 11, 17, 19-23, 28-34, 191, 203
Caribbean, 1, 9-10, 17-34, 152, 203
    Dominica, 19, 25, 29-30
    Dominican Republic, 18
    Guyana, 28-29
    Puerto Rico, 18
    St. Lucia, 19
    St. Vincent, 19, 28
    Tortola, 29
    Trinidad and Tobago, 9, 19-23, 25, 27-34, 34nn3-4, 203
Central American Resource Center (CARECEN), 150
Clifford, James, 3, 6, 10, 65, 69, 77-79, 85, 92-93
    Routes: Travel and Translation in the Late Twentieth Century, 1997, 65
concerned photography, 64, 66-69, 73
    Capa, Robert (1913-1954), 64, 67-68, 72
    Cartier-Bresson, Henri (1908-2004), 66-68, 72
    The Family of Man Exhibition (1955), 67-68
    Smith, W. Eugene (1919-1978), 67-68, 71-72
cosmopolitan cosmovision, 145, 185
cosmopolitan patriots, 6, 8, 31
cosmopolitanism
    aboriginal hip hoppers, 39-61
    Alutiiq (Kodiak Island, Alaska), 77-96
    banal or everyday cosmopolitanisms, 6, 7, 33, 128-129, 175
    Carib, 17-37
    cosmopolitan cosmovision, 145, 185
    cosmopolitan patriots, 6, 8, 31
    Cynics, 64-65
    discrepant cosmopolitanisms, 6, 65
    elite cosmopolitanism, 27, 33, 128
    Latin American indigenous migrants (San Francisco, Calif.), 143-161
    inverse cosmopolitanism, 11
    Inuit (urban), 127-144
    Jews, 189-209
    Kant, Immanuel, 4-5, 12-13, 14n1, 64, 86, 94n4
    latent cosmopolitanisms, 7
    liberal cosmopolitanism, 192
    Nahuas, Alto Balsas, 97-125
    Neel, David, 63-76
    new cosmopolitans, 8-9
    passive cosmopolitanisms, 7
    postcolonial and precolonial cosmopolitanisms, 7
    pre-modern and modern cosmopolitans, 6, 42-43

rooted cosmopolitans, 8-9, 12, 31, 40-44, 48, 59, 129, 140, 154
technological cosmopolitanism, 129
non-traditional communication and other technologies, 22, 48-54, 58-59, 84, 129, 136, 140
tourism, 163-188
unconscious cosmopolitanisms, 7
universal cosmopolitanism, 193
vernacular cosmopolitanisms, 6, 12, 154
    Bhabha, Homi, 6, 129, 154
working class cosmopolitans, 6
See also hosts and guests, postnationalism, travel
Cosmopolitanism: Ethics in a World of Strangers (Appiah), 64
Council for the Development of the Carib Community (CDCC), 28
Cree, 40, 53
Creole, 19, 80-81, 85-88, 94n5
    Alaska Creole, 80
    Creole burgher, 86-88
    Kodiak Creole, 80, 86
    Russian-Native Creole families, 10, 80-81, 83
creolization, 19
Crow (Greasemouth Clan), 170
cultural citizenship, 153-157
    Ong, Aihwa, 150, 155
    Rodriguez, Roberto, 155-156
    Rosaldo, Renato, 132, 155
    Stephen, Lynn, 155
cultural survival, 46
Cynics, 64-65

• D •

Desjarlais, Shawn, 44
deterritorialized nationalism, 207n6
diaspora and indigeneity, 17, 26, 30, 48, 132, 135, 138, 140, 148, 150
Dick-Read, Aragorn, 29
discrepant cosmopolitanisms, 6, 65
Dominica, 19, 25, 29-30
Dominican Republic, 18
Dust, Kave, 170-175

• E •

eco-tourism, 21, 31-32
elite cosmopolitanism, 27, 33, 128
Escobar, David, 154, 157
ethnic nationalisms, 190
Euro Disney (France), 163-170, 172-174
    Brass, Ferlyn, 167-173, 175
    Bruised Head, Tim, 173
    Buffalo Bill's Wild West Show (BBWW), 163-169, 171
    Dust, Kave, 170-175
    Rangel, Ernest, 170, 172-174
    Mustus, Wiley, 171-173
    Yellowbird, Carter, 167, 169, 174
exploitative commercial enterprise, 12, 169-170

• F •

Fancy Dance, 179, 181fig.9.5
Federation of Saskatchewan Indian Nations (FSIN), 27
Fischer, Edward, 155
flow, 41
flowing, 41
Fox, Desrey, 28
Four Sacred Directions (Buddhism), 63-64, 71-73
France (Marne-la-Vallée and Paris), 2, 12, 105, 113, 163-164, 167, 176, 186n6
Frederick, Hillary, Chief, 29
Frederick, Jacob, 29
freestylin', 41

• G •

Garifuna (Caribbean), 19
Geertz, Clifford, 2, 18
Gilroy, Paul, 152
    The Black Atlantic, 152
Gli-gli Carib Canoers, 20, 29-30
globalization, 2-4, 18, 21, 33-34, 35n5, 46, 48-49, 59, 64, 93, 106, 109, 118, 121, 145, 164, 176, 190, 204
Gourd Dance, 177
Grupo Maya Cusamej Junan, 150

Guanaguanare, 9-10, 14, 20, 23-26
Gumbaynggirr, 44
Guyana, 28-29
Guyanese Organization of Indigenous Peoples (GOIP), 28

• H •

Haggentasch, Mirium, 195-201
Halpin, Marjorie, 65-67
Hammill, Brian, 179-182fig. 9.6, 183-184
heritage
    heritage epistemes, 92-93
    heritage work (Kodiak Island, Alaska), 77-84, 88-93
    museum's role, 11, 81-82, 84, 91 See also museums
hip hop, 39-59
    Cree, 40-53
    definition, 40-41
    gangsta, 49, 56
    in-reach and out-reach, 48, 51, 54,58
    Inuit, 49-50, 54-56
    Metis, 57
    performers
        Canadian Floor Masters, 54-55
        Desjarlais, Shawn (Canada), 44
        Manik 1derful (Canada), 44, 48-49
        MC Wire (Australia), 44, 47
        Munki Mark (Australia), 45
        Northerners with Attitude (Canada), 48-51
        OS12 (Canada), 44, 47
        Smallboy, Rex (Canada), 40, 44-45, 54
        Team Rez Official (Canada), 52-53
        Tribal Wizdom (Canada), 46
        Tru Rez Crew (Canada), 52
        War Party (Canada), 40
    rap, definition of, 40-41
    YouTube videos, 48-54
Ho-Chunk Nation (Wisc.), 179
Hoop Dance, 179, 180, 182fig.9.6
Horovitz, Israel, 194-201
hosts and guests, 189-190, 205-206
Huichol (Mexico), 148
human rights, 4, 14n1, 67, 150, 155

hybridity, 58, 64

• I •

identity and land, 11, 24-25, 42-43, 146, 148-149, 151, 205
    Inuit, 128, 132-136, 138-140, 141n4, 141n11
    Jews, 207n6
Ignatieff, Michael, 67
Magnum Degrees, 2003, 67
indigenous peoples
    Alexis First Nation (Alberta), 171
    Algonquin (Canada), 131
    Alutiiq (Kodiak Island, Alaska), 10, 77-80, 83-92, 94n1
    Aztec, 11
    Blood Nation (Alberta), 173
    Carib (Caribbean), 9, 11, 20-22, 25, 28-30, 33
    Cree, 40, 53
    Crow (Greasemouth Clan), 170
    Garifuna (Caribbean), 19
    Gumbaynggirr (Australia), 44
    Ho-Chunk Nation (Wisc.), 179
    Huichol (Mexico), 148
    Inuit, 11, 49-50, 54-56, 127-148
        definition of, 134
        urban Inuit, 127-148
    Key First Nation (Sask.), 167
    Kwagiutl, 9-10, 63, 65, 69-70, 72-73
    Lenca (El Salvador), 154
    Maya (Guatemala and Mexico), 146-149, 151
    Meti, 57
    Mixtec (Mexico), 147
    Mohawk, 30, 71-72
    N'laka'pmx First Nation, 43
    Nahua, Alto Balsas (Mexico), 11, 97-125
    Navajo, 179
    Navajo (New Mexico), 170
    Otomi (Mexico), 148
    Peigan Nation (Alberta), 173
    Purépecha (Mexico), 148
    Quecha (Andean), 148
    Quicha (Andean), 148
    Shuar (Andean), 148
    Sioux, 167

Sun Bear Tribe, 32
Taíno (Caribbean), 18-27
Triqui, 147
Yaqui (Mexico), 148
Zapotec, 147
Inter-American Indigenous Congress (Patzcuaro, Mexico, 1940), 151
International Indian Treaty Council (1974), 151
Intertribal Friendship House, 148, 158n
Inuit, 11, 49-50, 54-56, 127-148
    definition of, 134
    urban Inuit, 127-148
Inuit Family Resource Centre, 137
Inuit transnationalism, 127, 130-132, 134, 139-140
inverse cosmopolitanism, 11

• J •

Jarecki, Eugene, 29
Jenkins, Lane, 179-181fig.9.5, 183-184
Jewish transnationalism, 191, 201-202
Jews
    cosmopolitanism, 190-191, 207n6
    Israel, 192, 195-197, 200-202, 204-207
    Israel Independence Day, 195, 201
    Jewish Canadian, 194-201
    Jews (Newfoundland), 194-201
    nationalism, 191-193
        German National Socialism, 192
        incorporation into nation, 192
        Jewish question, 192
        Soviet Republicanism, 192
    Newfoundland Jewish Community, 194
    wandering Jew, 189, 191-193, 201-202

• K •

Kant, Immanuel, 4-5, 12-13, 14n1, 64, 86, 94n4
Key First Nation (Sask.), 167
Kodiak Island, Alaska, 10, 77-96
Kuwaiti Smoke Creature (Neel), 63

Kwagiutl, 9-10, 63, 65, 69-70, 72-73

• L •

land
    identity and land, 11, 24-25, 42-43, 146, 148-149, 151, 205
    Inuit, 128, 132-136, 138-140, 141n4, 141n11
    Jews, 207n6
land claims
    Alaska Native Claims Settlement Act, 1971 (ANCSA), 79, 83, 91
    Algonquin, 131
    Alutiiq, 10, 78-79, 83, 90-91
    Inuit, 141n11
    land rights
        British Columbia, 69
        Nahuas, 99, 101
language survival, 120
latent cosmopolitanisms, 7
Lenca (El Salvador), 154
liberal cosmopolitanism, 192
Life On The 18th Hole (Neel), 71-72
Linduff, Katheryn M., 70

• M •

Manik 1derful, 44, 48-49
Manuel, George, Chief, 28
Maier, Edre, 180-184
Maya (Guatemala and Mexico), 146-149, 151
Maya New Year Ceremony. *See Waqxaqi B'atz'*
MC, 41
MC Wire, 44, 47
Mercredi, Ovide, Grand Chief, 28-29
meshchane (burgher families). *See* burghers
meshchanstvo. *See* burghers
Meti, 57
metropolitanism, 19
Mexico, 1,3,11,66, 204
    Alto Balsas Nahuas, 97-125
    migrants from, 143, 147-151, 157, 158n4, 161
Miami, Fl, 20, 30

migrants. *See* migration
migration, 1, 6, 10-11, 19, 42, 58, 65, 127, 190
    Caribbean, 17-18, 23
    Inuit, 11, 127-144
    Jews, 194, 202
    Kodiak Island, Alaska, 10
    Nahuas, 98, 1010, 112, 114-120
    non-aboriginal migrant rappers, 45
    Latin American indigenous, 11, 145-161
    migrants. *See* migration
Mixtec (Mexico), 147
Mohawk, 30, 71-72
Munki Mark, 45
museum art, 111, 113-114
museum authority, 167-168
museum's role, 11, 81-82, 84, 91
museums, 11, 78, 81-82, 84, 91, 166-167, 174, 179, 183, 186n2
    Buffalo Bill Museum and Grave (Golden, Colo,), 168
    Canadian Museum of Civilization (Hull, Quebec), 66
    Mexican Fine Arts Museum (Chicago, Ill.), 113
    National Museum of the American Indian (Washington, D.C.), 151
Mustus, Wiley, 171-173

• N •

N'laka'pmx First Nation, 43
Nahua, Alto Balsas (Mexico), 11, 97-125
nation-state, 14n1, 35n5, 152, 155
    Aboriginal youth and the, 58
    Canada, 72, 127-128, 130, 132, 140, 141n11, 210
    Caribbean, 18
    Greek city-state, xiv
    hemispheric nation-states, 150
    Israel, 192-193, 195, 205-207
    Mexico, 102-105, 120
    non-state political actors, 3
    Russia, 84-85, 88
    USA, 10, 78-79, 81-83, 88-89, 92, 155
nationalism, 3, 14n1, 24, 64, 92, 190-193, 206

banal nationalism, 129
deterritorialized nationalism, 207n6
    ethnic nationalisms, 190
nonnationalism 193
postnationalism, 13-14, 190-193, 201-202, 204-206
transnationalism, xiv, 2-5, 11-13, 20-22, 26-27, 29-31, 33-34, 34n3, 34n5, 42-43, 115, 117, 119, 120-121, 127-128, 130-134, 138-140, 150, 158n5, 163-165, 169-170, 174-177, 185, 190-191, 193, 201-202
Native Hubs: Culture, Community, and Belonging in Silicon Valley and Beyond (2007), 150
Native Spirit Productions (Phoeniz, Arizona) 177, 179-183, 185
    Fancy Dance, 179, 181fig.9.5
    Gourd Dance, 177
    Hammill, Brian, 179-181-182fig.9.6, 183-184
    Hoop Dance, 179, 180, 182fig.9.6
    Jenkins, Lane, 179-181fig.9.5, 183-184
Native Youth Movement (NYM), 46-47
nativeness, 163-186n1
Navajo, 179
Navajo (New Mexico), 170
Neel, David, 9, 10, 63-75
    Buddhism, 63, 70-73
    Four Sacred Directions, 63-64, 71-73
    photojournalism, 63, 66
    travels
        Bangkok, Thailand, 70-73
        Calgary, Alberta, 66-67
        Dallas, Texas, 67
        Vancouver, British Columbia, 66, 68-69
    See also concerned photography
Neel, David, works of:
    Kuwaiti Smoke Creature, 63
    Life On The 18th Hole, 71-72
    Number One Hero – Sitting Bull, 71
    Our Chiefs and Elders: Words and Photographs of Native Leaders, 65, 68
    Portrait of Lily-Bee and Mertel Holloway, 67-69, 72

Self Portrait with Chief Charlie James Swanson, 68-69, 70
What One Man Can Do, 63
Young Chief – Waxwaxam, The, 63-64, 68-73
Neel, Ellen, 72
new cosmopolitans, 8-9
New Mexico, 170
New World Movement, 19
Newfoundland Jewish Community, 194
nonnationalism 193
Northerners with Attitude, 48-51
Number One Hero – Sitting Bull (Neel), 71

• O •

Ong, Aihwa, 150, 155
OS12, 44, 47
Otomi (Mexico), 148
Ottawa Inuit Children's Center (OICC), 134
Our Chiefs and Elders: Words and Photographs of Native Leaders (Neel), 65, 6

• P •

pan-Aboriginal. See pan-Indianism
pan-Indianism, 1, 13, 21, 46-48, 119, 133, 139, 148, 151, 163, 174-175, 177, 182-185, 203, 205
pan-indigenism. See pan-Indianism
passive cosmopolitanisms, 7
Peigan Nation (Alberta), 173
People's National Movement (Trinidad & Tobago), 20
photojournalism, 63, 66
physical survival, 206
Podlasley, M., 42-43
Portrait of Lily-Bee and Mertel Holloway (Neel), 67-69, 72
postcolonial and precolonial cosmopolitanisms, 7
postnationalism, 13-14, 190-191, 193, 201-202, 204-206. See also nonnationalism, transnationalism

power relationships, 168
Puerto Rico, 18
Purépecha (Mexico), 148

• Q •

Quecha (Andean), 148
Quicha (Andean), 148

• R •

Ramirez, Catherine, 20, 30
Ramirez, Renya, 150-151
  Native Hubs: Culture, Community, and Belonging in Silicon Valley and Beyond (2007)
Rangel, Ernest, 170, 172-174
rap, definition of, 40-41
Rapport, Nigel, 195-201
re-presentation, 9, 33, 45, 47, 51, 55, 163-164
represent, to, 41
representation, 164-166, 168, 170-172, 174-175, 177-186n2
Rodriguez, Roberto, 155-156
rooted cosmopolitans, 8-9, 12, 31, 40-44, 48, 59, 129, 140, 154
Rosaldo, Renato, 132, 155
Routes: Travel and Translation in the Late Twentieth Century (Clifford), 1997, 65
Russian American Company, 84-86
Russia, 10, 79-88, 90-91, 94nn4-5, 203

• S •

sampling, 41
Saskatchewan Indian Federated College,
Self Portrait with Chief Charlie James Swanson (Neel), 68-69, 70
Sheridan Heritage Center (Sheridan, Wyoming), 178-180
  Buffalo Bill Days (BBD), 163, 178-181, 183-185
Shuar (Andean), 148
Simons, Howard, 195-201
Sioux, 167

Smallboy, Rex, 40, 44-45, 54
Smith, W. Eugene (1919-1978), 67-68, 71-7 *see also* concerned photography
South Africa, 6, 47, 196, 200
spectacular vs. lived experiences, 163, 165. 169-171
St. Lucia, 19
St. Vincent, 19, 28
Steiner, George, 192-193
Stephen, Lynn, 155
stereotypes, 2, 11, 34n3, 49-53, 57, 114,119,132, 145, 164-165, 168-170, 172-173, 178-181, 183, 185, 202
    reserve-centric foci, 9, 39-40, 43
Sun Bear Tribe, 32
survival, 23-24, 46
    cultural survival, 46
    language survival, 120
    physical survival, 206
synedochic vs. metonymic, 152
Sznaider, Natan, 156

• T •

Taíno (Caribbean), 18-27
Team Rez Official, 52-53
technological cosmopolitanism, 129
    non-traditional communication and other technologies, 22, 48-54, 58-59, 84, 129, 136, 140
Thailand, 10, 68, 70-73
Tilley, Virginia Q. 26-27, 166, 169, 175
Tortola, 29
tourism, 10, 12, 21, 31-32, 35n4, 99, 148, 164-185, 189-190, 214
    authenticity, 166-168, 171
    Buffalo Bill, 178
    eco-tourism, 21,31-32
    Euro Disney (France), 163-170, 172-174
    exploitative commercial enterprise, 12, 169-170
    Maier, Edre, 180-184
    museum authority, 167-168
    Native Spirit Productions (Phoenix, Arizon), 177, 179-183, 185
    nativeness, 163-186n1
    pan-Indian identities, 174-175, 177, 182-185
    power relationships, 168
    representation, 164-166, 168, 170-172, 174-175, 177-186n2
    Sheridan Heritage Center (Sheridan, Wyoming), 178-180
    Buffalo Bill Days (BBD), 163, 178-181, 183-185
    spectacular vs. lived experiences, 163, 165,169-171
    stereotypes in tourism, 164-165, 168-170, 172-173
    tourist sites, 164, 175
    Williams Lake Stampede (Alberta), 179
tourist sites, 164, 175
tradition, 3, 8-9, 30, 32, 35n5, 39-40, 43-48, 54-59, 66, 77-78, 90-92
Transnational Indigeneity beyond Stereotypes of the Local or the Hype of the Global, Canadian Anthropological Society and American Ethnological Society, University of Toronto, May 8-12, 2007, ix
Transnational Indigenous Peoples' Movement (TIPM), 26-27
transnationalism, xiv, 2-5, 11-13, 20-22, 26-27, 29-31, 33-34, 34n3, 34n5, 42-43, 115, 117, 119, 120-121, 127-128, 130-134, 138-140, 150, 158n5, 163-165, 169-170, 174-177, 185, 190-191, 193, 201-202
    Inuit transnationalism, 127, 130-132, 134, 139-140
    Jewish transnationalism, 191, 201-202
travel, 6, 9 12-13, 20-22, 24, 27, 30, 31-34, 65-66, 70, 84-85, 97, 99, 100, 102, 105, 115, 118, 120, 152, 154, 175, 178, 189, 200, 202
Tribal Wizdom, 46
Trinidad and Tobago, 9, 19-23, 25, 27-34, 34nn3-4, 203
Triqui, 147
Tru Rez Crew, 52

• U •

unconscious cosmopolitanisms, 7

United Nations Permanent Forum on Indigenous Issues, 151
United States of America, 1,3,10, 18, 29, 80, 82, 84, 97, 100-101, 114-121, 123n24, 145-148, 150-151, 155-156, 158nn2-3. 178, 182-183, 186n1, 201, 204,
    California, 1, 31-32, 116, 145, 147, 14-150, 156, 158n3, 158n8, 194, 204
    Kodiak Island, Alaska, 10, 77-96
    Miami, Fl, 20, 30
    New Mexico, 170
    Puerto Rico, 18
    Wyoming, 163, 176, 186n6
universal cosmopolitanism, 193
Urban Aboriginal Task Force, 135
U.S. American Indian Movement, 151

• V •

vaquerias yucateros, 149
vernacular cosmopolitanisms, 6, 12, 154
    Bhabha, Homi, 6, 129, 154

• W •

Walcott, Derek, 17-18

Waqxaqi B'atz' (Day of Human Perfection), 150, 153-154, 157
War Party, 40
western hemispheric consciousness, 151-153
    synedochic vs. metonymic, 152
What One Man Can Do (Neel), 63
Williams Lake Stampede (Alberta), 179
working class cosmopolitans, 6
World Council of Indigenous Peoples (WCIP), 28
Wyoming, 163, 176, 186n6

• Y •

Yaqui (Mexico), 148
Yellowbird, Carter, 167, 169, 174
Young Chief – Waxwaxam, The (Neel), 63-64, 68-73

• Z •

Zapotec, 147

Lightning Source UK Ltd.
Milton Keynes UK
UKHW011557241121
394521UK00011B/201